DUE DILIGENCE AND THE BUSINESS TRANSACTION

GETTING A DEAL DONE

Jeffrey W. Berkman

Due Diligence and the Business Transaction: Getting a Deal Done

ISBN-13 (pbk): 978-1-4302-5086-9

ISBN-13 (electronic): 978-1-4302-5087-6

Trademarked names, logos, and images may appear in this book. Rather than use a trademark symbol with every occurrence of a trademarked name, logo, or image we use the names, logos, and images only in an editorial fashion and to the benefit of the trademark owner, with no intention of infringement of the trademark.

The use in this publication of trade names, trademarks, service marks, and similar terms, even if they are not identified as such, is not to be taken as an expression of opinion as to whether or not they are subject to proprietary rights.

While the advice and information in this book are believed to be true and accurate at the date of publication, neither the authors nor the editors nor the publisher can accept any legal responsibility for any errors or omissions that may be made. The publisher makes no warranty, express or implied, with respect to the material contained herein.

President and Publisher: Paul Manning
Acquisitions Editor: Jeff Olson
Developmental Editors: Robert Hutchinson, Ralph Moore
Editorial Board: Steve Anglin, Mark Beckner, Ewan Buckingham, Gary Cornell, Louise Corrigan,
     James DeWolf, Jonathan Gennick, Jonathan Hassell, Robert Hutchinson, Michelle Lowman,
     James Markham, Matthew Moodie, Jeff Olson, Jeffrey Pepper, Douglas Pundick,
     Ben Renow-Clarke, Dominic Shakeshaft, Gwenan Spearing, Matt Wade, Steve Weiss,
     Tom Welsh
Coordinating Editor: Rita Fernando
Copy Editor: Cat Ohala
Compositor: SPi Global
Indexer: SPi Global
Cover Designer: Anna Ishchenko

Distributed to the book trade worldwide by Springer Science+Business Media New York, 233 Spring Street, 6th Floor, New York, NY 10013. Phone 1-800-SPRINGER, fax (201) 348-4505, e-mail orders-ny@springer-sbm.com, or visit www.springeronline.com. Apress Media, LLC is a California LLC and the sole member (owner) is Springer Science + Business Media Finance Inc (SSBM Finance Inc). SSBM Finance Inc is a Delaware corporation.

For information on translations, please e-mail rights@apress.com, or visit www.apress.com.

Apress and friends of ED books may be purchased in bulk for academic, corporate, or promotional use. eBook versions and licenses are also available for most titles. For more information, reference our Special Bulk Sales–eBook Licensing web page at www.apress.com/bulk-sales.

Any source code or other supplementary materials referenced by the author in this text is available to readers at www.apress.com. For detailed information about how to locate your book's source code, go to www.apress.com/source-code/.

Apress Business: The Unbiased Source of Business Information

Apress business books provide essential information and practical advice, each written for practitioners by recognized experts. Busy managers and professionals in all areas of the business world—and at all levels of technical sophistication—look to our books for the actionable ideas and tools they need to solve problems, update and enhance their professional skills, make their work lives easier, and capitalize on opportunity.

Whatever the topic on the business spectrum—entrepreneurship, finance, sales, marketing, management, regulation, information technology, among others—Apress has been praised for providing the objective information and unbiased advice you need to excel in your daily work life. Our authors have no axes to grind; they understand they have one job only—to deliver up-to-date, accurate information simply, concisely, and with deep insight that addresses the real needs of our readers.

It is increasingly hard to find information—whether in the news media, on the Internet, and now all too often in books—that is even-handed and has your best interests at heart. We therefore hope that you enjoy this book, which has been carefully crafted to meet our standards of quality and unbiased coverage.

We are always interested in your feedback or ideas for new titles. Perhaps you'd even like to write a book yourself. Whatever the case, reach out to us at editorial@apress.com and an editor will respond swiftly. Incidentally, at the back of this book, you will find a list of useful related titles. Please visit us at www.apress.com to sign up for newsletters and discounts on future purchases.

The Apress Business Team

I dedicate this work to my amazing wife Dana for her unwavering love and support, to my father, Jordan W. Berkman, whose insightful advice regarding difficult legal issues, for an old-time country lawyer, never ceases to amaze me, to my mother Arlyne B. Berkman, whose intellect and spirit I miss every day, and to Bernice Kornfield, whose faith in me has no boundaries.

Contents

About the Author

 **Jeffrey W. Berkman**, principal at the Berkman Law Firm, PLLC, has represented entrepreneurs, companies, and investors in connection with domestic and cross-border transactions, M&A, venture capital, private equity, secured financing, joint venture agreements, and other business transactions in the US, Asia, and Europe. He also provides corporate advice in a number of areas, including business formation and start-up issues, advising small, emerging and established businesses as an outside general counsel, partnership matters, licensing, distribution, franchise, employment and other commercial contracts, commercial real estate transactions and providing advice on numerous other business law matters. Berkman is a member of the Board of Directors of Carmike Cinemas, Inc. (NASDAQ: CKEC). The Berkman Law Firm was chosen as a 2012 finalist by the *New York Enterprise Report's* Best Accountants and Attorneys for Privately Held Companies. Berkman writes about business law issues relating to small and emerging businesses on his blog www.mybizlawyerblog.com, has been a lecturer for continuing legal education classes and a presenter at a variety of seminars and business workshops. The Berkman Law Firm (www.berkmanlawfirm.com) is a corporate/business law firm advising startups, emerging and established companies, investors, entrepreneurs, inventors and business ventures in a variety of industries, including IT, Internet-based retailers and services, software and hardware development, e-learning, entertainment and new media, retailers, food/restaurant outsourcing, management consulting, healthcare, and real estate.

Preface

The genesis of *Due Diligence and the Business Transaction: Getting a Deal Done* is a blog post I wrote about the importance of companies conducting due diligence on their own business before going to market to sell the company or raise financing. Although this book focuses primarily on the due diligence investigation from the perspective of an entrepreneur or company purchasing or investing in a closely-held business, it eventually comes full circle in the final chapter to the benefits to the target company of conducting internal due diligence. The due diligence investigation is not the exclusive tool of purchasers of, or investors in, a business but should be conducted by the parties on both sides of any of a variety of proposed business transactions.

Although even the most seasoned entrepreneur or professional advisor will benefit from this book, my main goal is to explain the fundamental concepts of due diligence to entrepreneurs and investors who are less experienced in the process, to provide them a road map for conducting a due diligence investigation, and to show them how to organize and assess the information gathered in an investigation to make prudent determinations on how and whether to proceed with the proposed transaction at hand.

I illustrate and develop these lessons through eight hypothetical case studies constructed to demonstrate the different ways of conducting due diligence in various types of business deals. All the case studies and associated due diligence questionnaires that recur throughout this book are distilled from my many years of professional experience as a venture capital lawyer and business lawyer and are devised for pedagogic purposes only. Any resemblance to identifiable entities or situations is unintended and purely coincidental. The legal, financial, and business concepts and issues that inform the hypothetical transactions and questionnaires in this book should nonetheless be fully understood so that you can adapt them with suitable modifications to the specific business proposals you will have occasion to investigate. Because each deal involves its own financial and legal issues, complexities, and risks, you are strongly advised to consult legal counsel and other professional advisors with experience in handling corporate matters before entering any transaction. When considering entering into a business deal, you will benefit from a strong grasp of the fundamentals of due diligence presented in this book, which will enable you to engage with your professional advisors as a knowledgeable participant in the due diligence process.

This book examines the following topics regarding due diligence of a non-public company:

- The fundamental goals of the due diligence process and how a well-prepared due diligence plan will define the strategy for the investigation.

- The components of the due diligence questionnaire, including the standard, transaction-type, and deal-specific questions that generally comprise the questionnaire.

- The necessity of tailoring the due diligence questionnaire to the actual facts underpinning the transaction.

- A review of circumstances in which material, legal, financial, technological, operational, or other business issues will result in termination of the transaction.

- Determining when the results of the due diligence investigation do not require termination of the deal and can instead create an opportunity to renegotiate transaction terms more favorably.

- The application of the due diligence concepts discussed in the book to real-world transactions, such as purchasing an interest in a fast-food franchisee.

- Factors affecting the timing of the due diligence investigation, deal exclusivity, drafting the due diligence clause, and utilizing pre-closing conditions, post-closing covenants and related post-closing enforcement mechanisms (adjustments, escrow and indemnification) to address issues discovered during the due diligence investigation.

- Practical considerations affecting the due diligence investigation, including the possible role of a non-binding letter of intent; factors influencing the scope of the review; forming the due diligence team; the necessity of expanding the investigation beyond the due diligence questionnaire; and the importance of self-imposed due diligence before a company seeks to sell its business or bring on investors.

Introduction

A Client Walks into a Lawyer's Office to Discuss the Results of a Due Diligence Investigation . . .

No, this is not the beginning of another lawyer joke, but rather the start of a dramatized discussion of a typical problem often revealed during a *due diligence investigation* in the context of the sale of a business. The conversation between the lawyer and his client, Jack, unfolds as follows:

Date: October 22
Place: Office of Jack's Attorney

Lawyer: Hi, Jack. Thanks for coming to the office. I know you wanted to complete the purchase of the business of ABB Internet Retailer Company to take advantage of the holiday season, so let me fill you in on the status of the transaction.

Jack: Actually, I'm glad you asked me to stop by. Leah, the seller, has been calling me every day, wondering whether we're going forward with the purchase of the company. She's complaining that we negotiated and executed the letter of intent some time ago, and she's put a lot of time into preparing her employees and clients for the transition to my company. She's wondering why the transaction has been dragging on for so long. She even said the other day: "This isn't some multimillion-dollar Wall Street transaction. Do you have other motives, such as backing away from the deal or looking to reduce the purchase price?" I assured her that we aren't trying to renegotiate the deal and that I'm as anxious as she is to complete the purchase.

Frankly, I'm concerned as well. I need to close the deal and turn my focus to integrating ABB's web site and business into my business so we're ready for the holiday season. However, I can't do this until I'm sure if, and when, the deal will close.

Lawyer: I understand your concerns completely. I realize the holidays are approaching and you'll lose holiday revenue if the transaction doesn't close soon. I've been trying to push this transaction forward, but the seller's attorney has been slow in responding to my due diligence requests. Unfortunately, I had to wait several weeks for the seller's attorney to return the due diligence questionnaire and provide copies of the documents I requested.

When you and I reviewed the LOI, remember that I said I don't advise proceeding with the purchase until I'm satisfied with the results of the due diligence investigation. In fact, in general I prefer not to spend too much time reviewing a draft of an asset purchase agreement until completing the due diligence for two reasons.

First, the information that's disclosed by the seller or uncovered by me during the due diligence process affects how I approach the draft of the purchase agreement. For instance, I might demand that the purchase agreement include certain additional warranties, postclosing indemnifications, and holdback of a portion of the purchase price to cover material due diligence issues.

Second, the due diligence investigation can uncover issues that are so significant that my recommendations could be (1) to renegotiate the purchase price or other terms, (2) to walk from the deal, or (3) to agree to proceed with the transaction only if the issue or issues can be addressed before closing or through post-closing assurances from the seller.

The last scenario is the situation we have here. I've discovered a major issue and I don't recommend moving forward until the seller resolves the matter.

Jack: That doesn't sound good at all. I also don't understand what issues there could be. My review of the web site and the seller's unique order processing software—the key asset I'm really after in this deal—looked great. So what's the problem?

Lawyer: If you recall, due diligence involves several different aspects, depending on the nature of the transaction. In this case, the key areas were financial review, due diligence relating to the customer list, review of the technology, and due diligence regarding various legal matters. Although you're satisfied with the functionalities of the web site and the ABB order processing software, there are legal issues relating to it. It seems that Leah had a partner, Dana, who developed the ABB proprietary software that is at the heart of business assets you are purchasing.

Jack: *That doesn't seem like a big deal. Dana is no longer part of the business; Leah bought her out for a hefty sum last year.*

Lawyer: *Well, that's the issue. Dana never assigned her rights in the ABB software over to ABB Internet Retailer Co.*

Jack: *Leah told me months ago that, even though Dana developed the software before she entered into the business with Leah, at the time ABB was formed, Dana contributed the software to the company.*

Lawyer: *That may have been the intention and, in fact, the understanding between Leah and Dana, but the problem is that there are no documents showing that the ABB software was assigned to the company. Because Dana created the software, under copyright law she is the author and thus the owner. Although Leah may have a claim that it was contributed to the company, and the partners understood the software was owned by ABB, none of this is sufficient to give me comfort that Dana cannot claim, at some point, that she owns the software, not ABB. You want to buy the assets of ABB, not a potential lawsuit. Even if you ultimately won the suit, it would cost you a lot of money to litigate. If you lost, it would require purchasing or licensing the software from Dana at a substantial cost.*

Jack: *[silence] That shouldn't be a problem. Dana and Leah are still friends, so Dana will sign whatever is needed.*

Lawyer: *It may not be that easy. We don't know how Dana will respond until Leah discusses the issue with her. However, I can tell you from experience that when there is money on the table, ex-partners are not always happy to say yes without some compensation.*

Jack: *Regardless, you come well recommended so I'm sure you can resolve this without additional cost or delay, right?*

Lawyer: *I'll certainly look for ways to resolve this as quickly as possible without substantial cost, but the ball is very much in Dana's court. However, I can't recommend moving forward until the matter regarding the ABB software is resolved.*

Jack: *This isn't what I expected to hear today. I need to call Leah and find out why she didn't take care of this huge issue before Dana left ABB.*

Lawyer: *OK. Also, I have a couple other issues we need to discuss that were uncovered during the due diligence, but they're smaller issues that can be addressed through the terms of the asset purchase agreement, and require the seller to agree to a reasonable holdback in escrow of part of the purchase price.*

Jack: *I need to run to another meeting—ironically, with another retailer who I was hoping to convince to enter into a joint venture after I integrate the ABB software into my business. I can't stomach any more bad news right now, so let's talk about the other issues you found after my meeting.*

Lawyer: *I'll contact Leah's attorney about the software issue and my other concerns. In particular, I'll advise him that the seller needs to get an assignment of the software from Dana before we can proceed. I'll circle back with you on this and the other issues after I speak to the seller's attorney.*

However, if you don't want to hear any other bad news, I suggest avoiding a call from your computer consultant as he found some bugs in the software.

Due Diligence: Critical in a Business Transaction

Although the foregoing dialogue between Jack and his lawyer about Jack's intended purchase of Leah's company is fictional, it faithfully represents a type of conversation that commonly results from due diligence investigations undertaken before the purchases of businesses. It is an unsettling conversation for anyone buying or selling a business, because it calls into the question the ability of the parties to close a transaction into which each party has invested substantial time and money and which has been a major distraction from the operation of his or her own business. Yet due diligence is a critical part of the process.

This book will periodically tune into the ongoing conversations between Jack and his attorney—comprising "Case Study 1: The ABB Transaction"—because they will illustrate due diligence themes that are important to you as a party or agent to a business transaction, including the following:

- How to conduct due diligence when contemplating buying a business, investing in a company, providing a business loan, becoming a member of partnership, licensing intellectual property, or buying into a franchise

- How to calibrate the correct scope and breadth of the due diligence investigation depending on the nature of the transaction and your tolerance for cost and delay, especially in smaller or apparently simple deals

- How the results of due diligence may and often will change the elements of the final deal

- How to draft the due diligence questionnaire and information requests so they protect your interests
- How the results of the due diligence affect the scope, terms, and conditions of the definitive transactional document.

When you are buying a business, it is essential that you conduct due diligence. The nature of the transaction, the type of products and services offered by the company, and the scope of the target company's business operations dictate the breadth of the investigation. Financial and legal advisors are obvious participants during the process, but transactions often also require assistance from other professionals in a wide variety of fields to investigate and advise on such issues as: environmental matters; patent or other intellectual property review; foreign tax, accounting, or legal questions; privacy, the Health Insurance Portablility and Accountability Act, data management, and security matters; and new or evolving technologies.

If you do not conduct proper due diligence, you may later stumble into serious or even devastating problems, or you may pay an inflated price for the business. This book shows you how to conduct a due diligence examination, what to look for, how to spot red flags, and how to uncover hidden issues that sellers might not want you to know. It also explains how information learned through due diligence can lead to termination of the deal or a substantial alteration of the material terms.

Due diligence is not just for business buyers and investors; it is often no less essential for business sellers and companies that are seeking to raise financing. Sellers and companies raising capital will learn from this book how to conduct due diligence on your own firm, how to uncover issues that might scare off buyers or investors, and how to solve lingering problems before commencing a significant business transaction.

My goal in this book is to provide you the due diligence road map that I developed through stewarding investigations in transactions running the gamut from the acquisition of mom-and-pop businesses to multimillion-dollar private companies, private equity transactions, and commercial real estate projects. The due diligence principles, case studies, and sample plan and questionnaires set forth in this book offer a practical guide to due diligence for anybody who is buying a business, selling a business, investing in a startup or emerging company, or entering into a major agreement with another company.

The next chapter returns to the pending transaction between Jack and Leah by flashing back to the conversation Jack had with his lawyer when he initially engaged him on the deal.

What Is Due Diligence?

The Importance and Parameters of Due Diligence

Let's back up in time and listen to the first face-to-face conversation Jack had with his lawyer about due diligence in connection with Jack's intended purchase of Leah's gift card company.

Date: August 24
Place: Office of Jack's Lawyer

Jack: Thanks for meeting with me. As I told you on the phone, I have an Internet greeting card company and I recently made an offer to purchase ABB, an Internet gift card company that offers customized gift cards from a variety of apparel, jewelry, electronics, appliance, and other large retailers. What makes ABB an interesting company for my business is (1) its relationship with its retailers, (2) ABB's customer list, and, most important, (3) the company's web site and ABB order processing software. I don't want all of ABB's business—only certain assets: the web site, the ABB software, certain trademarks/trade names they use for the gift card business, the customer list, and the agreements with the stores. I don't want the ABB employees, except one whom I'll need post closing to help with the transfer of the retailer relationships to my company and the integration of the ABB software onto my current platform.

> **Lawyer:** As I mentioned in our previous phone conversation, the deal should be structured as an asset purchase, because you don't want the entire business of ABB and you certainly don't want to be liable for any obligations of ABB. It's typical for the seller's attorney to prepare the initial draft of the asset purchase agreement, so I'll look at that carefully when it comes in. But for now, we need to focus on the due diligence investigation.
>
> **Jack:** I think I understand generally why a due diligence investigation is important, and I already mentioned to ABB that I want someone to look at the software and the back end of the web site. Leah, the sole owner of ABB, commented to me that I should tell my lawyer not to waste time or increase the costs of the deal with unnecessary due diligence. She said, "It's a straightforward deal, after all."
>
> **Lawyer:** I certainly have no intention to running up the costs of either party, but I need to protect your interests, and that includes a due diligence investigation, which is appropriate based on the nature of the transaction. It's not something you want to forgo. So, let me review with you, in general, what is involved in a due diligence investigation, and then we can talk about specific financial, legal, and other matters that should be examined given the nature of the transaction.

The lawyer has tried to explain to his client that due diligence is an important component of a business transaction. Reasonable anxieties about cost, delay, or the seller's walking from the transaction must be weighed against the harm that could result from blindly entering into a deal. What the lawyer also makes clear is that due diligence is not the same for each transaction and that the appropriate strategy depends on a number of factors. Preliminary to considering the variable factors that enter into the design of a due diligence strategy appropriate to a specific situation, the next section answers the general question, what is *due diligence?*

Due Diligence Defined

Dictionary definitions of *due diligence* are descriptive, alluding to the research and analysis of a company or organization done in preparation for a business transaction. However, as with any simple definition, reducing an understanding of due diligence to a few words of description paints a woefully incomplete picture of its significance in a business transaction. The true significance of due diligence is as much *prescriptive* as descriptive, as distilled in the following admonition:

▨ **Caution**   Do not engage in any important business transaction until a due diligence investigation tailored to the nature, scope, and terms of the transaction has been completed.

Most of us base our day-to-day consumer decisions about purchasing goods or engaging services—trying a new restaurant, downloading a smartphone app, buying the latest high-definition television, hiring a lawyer, and so on (Table 2-1)—on informal processes of due diligence. Though we rarely think of it in this way, we routinely perform various types of due diligence—legal, financial, technology, personal, and environmental—depending on the products and services we are considering buying for ourselves.

Table 2-1. Examples of Due Diligence in Our Daily Lives as Consumers

Transaction	Possible Investigation	Type of Due Diligence
Purchasing a television	Read online reviews; compare pricing	Due diligence on the products; valuation
Hiring a lawyer	Ask the Bar Association	Due diligence on the services
Trying a new restaurant	Ask a friend who ate there	Product due diligence
Hiring a lawn service	Check licensing and insurance coverage	Legal due diligence
Buying a publicly listed stock	Read financial statements	Financial due diligence; business valuation
Downloading the latest smartphone app	Read customer reviews	Technology due diligence
Purchasing a house	Get title insurance	Legal due diligence
Purchasing a new appliance	Read energy-efficiency labels	Environmental due diligence
Dating someone new	Ask for a friend's opinion of your potential date	Personal due diligence

These examples of due diligence in our everyday lives suggest that the essence of due diligence is educating ourselves adequately before buying a product or engaging the services of a third party. The legwork required of average consumers to be well-informed buyers and to ensure they are getting the right product or service at the right price is simply a less structured and detailed form of the due diligence that an entrepreneur or investor should perform before entering into a business transaction.

Before purchasing products or engaging services, diligent consumers research company/service provider profiles and reputations, assess the quality of products or services, compare the value of products or services, and sometimes conduct background checks or investigations of potential hires. Entrepreneurs apply due diligence criteria to business transactions similar to those criteria consumers apply before buying products or hiring professional services: investigate the company and its business operations, research the products or services offered by the company, determine the appropriate valuation of the target company, and examine management capabilities and perform background checks and investigations of founders and key personnel (Table 2-2).

Table 2-2. Commonalities between Consumer and Business Due Diligence

Consumer Action before a Business-to-Consumer Transaction	Analogous Investor/Partner/ Purchaser Action before a Business-to-Business Transaction	Areas of Due Diligence
Research the company or service provider	Research the company of interest or the seller	The company and the seller
Research the product being purchased or service being hired	Research the products or services of the company of interest	The products, services, and assets (in other words, the business operations)
Conduct price comparisons	Research the valuation of the company, its goods and services, and/or the transaction to determine reasonable value	The valuation
Conduct a background check and investigation before hiring someone	Conduct background checks and investigations of the founders, majority owners, and key employees; examine management capabilities	The personnel

Due diligence in a commercial business transaction involves examining and becoming educated in the four key areas of a business before entering into any type of transaction with it: (1) the company and the seller, (2) the products, services and assets, (3) the valuation, and (4) the personnel (Table 2-2). And although the focus given to each of these areas varies depending on the nature of the transaction and the goals of the parties—variables explored in this chapter and Chapter 3, respectively—these four aspects of any business are the four *business cornerstones* of any due diligence investigation. I incorporate these business cornerstones into an operational definition of due diligence as follows:

▒ **Definitions** *Due diligence* involves the processes of examining and developing the necessary level of understanding of four factors—the company and its business operations (in other words, its products, assets, and/or services and how the company functions); determining an appropriate valuation of the business, assets, and transactions; and vetting management capabilities, key personnel and employment matters—before entering into a business transaction with, investing in, licensing assets or services of, or purchasing all or part of a business or its assets. The four *business cornerstones* to be investigated carefully in a due diligence examination are the *company*, its *business operations*, the *value* of the business and/or its assets, and its *people*.

From the perspective of this definition of *due diligence* in terms of the four business cornerstones, the next section considers the question of when a due diligence review should be conducted.

Due Diligence: A Fundamental Aspect of Most Business Transactions

Most entrepreneurs and investors recognize the importance of conducting due diligence in preparation for the purchase of securities or the merger of companies. The types of business deals for which it is routine that at least one of the parties conduct due diligence include the following:

- A loan transaction
- The purchase of a business or its assets
- Purchase of a company (whether a merger or business buyout)
- Purchase of stock or interests in a company, such as with a private placement
- The purchase of real estate

Other business transactions in which the need to conduct due diligence is equally important yet may be overlooked include the following:

- Purchasing a right to operate a franchise from the franchisor
- Starting a company with a partner or partners
- Licensing a product, services, technology, or intellectual property from a third party

- Licensing a product, services, technology, or intellectual property to a third party

- Entering into a joint venture

- Engaging a third party to design and/or develop a product, service, or technology

- Engaging a third party to manufacture or provide a product, service, or technology

- Entering into various types of contracts that are crucial to your business

These lists demonstrate that due diligence investigations are not restricted solely to decisions about whether to buy or invest in a business or purchase real estate; rather, they apply to a broad array of prospective business transactions. Moreover, the process is not confined to assuring the interested party of the legal and financial soundness of the transaction; rather, it extends to providing the interested party a sufficient level of comfort regarding the cornerstones of the business being investigated—the company; its products, services, assets and operations; the appropriate value of the company and/or its assets and the potential transaction; and the personnel who are essential to the success of the potential business relationship.

The Goal of Due Diligence: Understanding the Business Cornerstones

If the ultimate goal of the due diligence process is to achieve an appropriate understanding and comfort level with respect to the four business cornerstones of the transaction you are contemplating, what precisely should you learn from your examination of each the cornerstones? The goals of a due diligence examination corresponding to each of the four business cornerstones are shown in Table 2-3.

Table 2-3. Due Diligence Goals

The Business Cornerstone	The Due Diligence Goal
Company	To understand the legal and financial structure of the company and identify potential organizational or structural risks
Business Operations	To understand the nature of the business and its products, assets, and services, assess the operational aspects of the business, and identify and measure legal, financial, and business risks
Valuation	To determine an appropriate valuation of the company and/or the transaction and identify and measure financial risks
Personnel	To identify the key personnel and ascertain whether they are capable of operating the business, executing business plans, and/or fulfilling postclosing obligations

The common denominator of these four goals is that the due diligence process imparts to you a level of understanding sufficient to enable you to decide whether to engage in the contemplated transaction. To achieve this understanding, the due diligence investigation necessitates not only examining materials and data provided by the company but also information obtained from various sources outside the target business, including public and private information and the advice of professional consultants. Although the entrepreneur or investor will rely on a number of outside sources for information, the most important source of information is the target company itself. To this end, arguably the most important component of the investigation is a *due diligence questionnaire* tailored to the transaction.

Definition The *due diligence questionnaire* asks the target company to provide answers and documents in response to a series of questions tailored to the contemplated transaction.

Preparing the due diligence questionnaire requires you to consider a number of fundamental legal, financial, operational, and personnel-related questions corresponding to each cornerstone (Table 2-4). Before providing the questionnaire to the target company and anyone else participating in the due diligence, you need to select and fashion questions based on the nature of the transaction. A properly developed due diligence questionnaire, composed of general and transaction-specific questions, is essential to elicit the information required to make an informed decision regarding the proposed transaction.

Table 2-4. Fundamental Questions to Address in a Due Diligence Questionnaire

Cornerstone	Goal	Fundamental question	Nature of question
The company	To understand the legal and financial structure of the company and identify potential organizational or structural risks	• How is it organized?	Legal
		• Who are the owners?	Legal
		• What are its key types of property and assets?	Assets
		• Are there legal issues rendering the deal too risky?	Legal
The business operations	To understand the nature of the business operations and the company's products, assets, and services; and to identify potential legal, financial, and business risks	• What is the nature of the business?	Products, services, and assets
		• What products and/or services does it offer?	Products, services, and assets
		• What and where are its markets for the products and services?	Legal; financial; products, services, and assets
		• What are the potential business risks?	Legal, financial
Valuation	To determine an appropriate valuation of the company and/ or the transaction and identify potential financial risks	• What are the revenues, if any, and how are they derived?	Financial
		• What is the value of the assets?	Financial
		• What are the liabilities and expenses?	Financial
		• What is the market for the goods or services?	Products and services, financial, legal
		• Is there an opportunity for growth?	Products and services, financial
		• What are the financial risks?	Financial
Personnel	To identify the key personnel and ascertain whether they are capable of operating the business, executing business plans, and/or fulfilling postclosing obligations	• Who are the key personnel and how well have they managed the business operations?	Personnel
		• What is the experience of the key personnel?	Personnel
		• What is the background of the personnel?	Personnel
		• What are the significant personnel risks?	Personnel, legal, financial
		• Are there retention concerns?	Personnel, legal, financial

Think of due diligence as a process of first hearing the company's business story—as it may have been provided in an investment presentation or business plan—and then conducting an investigation to see if the story could be corroborated. A proper due diligence examination includes not only broad-based legal and financial questions but requires that you identify the critical areas of the business and gear your inquiries to the specific business and the nature of the transaction involved. As Chapter 3 will discuss in detail, tailoring the due diligence questionnaire to the nature of the transaction and the target company's business operations is essential to conducting a productive due diligence examination. First, however, it is important to create a due diligence plan as it will define the goals and the strategy of the due diligence.

Creating the Due Diligence Plan

A written due diligence plan serves as a road map for preparing the due diligence questionnaire and for examining a company's business operations. Legal or financial professionals and seasoned entrepreneurs who have conducted or been involved in due diligence may tell you they have never prepared a due diligence plan. They might take the position the questionnaire can be prepared after the terms of the transaction have been agreed on. This approach is analogous to those of authors who write novels without developing a written story outline and do-it-yourselfers who assemble items without reading instructions. Professional advisors and serial entrepreneurs may not actually prepare a written due diligence plan, but they have devised an unwritten approach based on their understanding of the transaction and what their professional experience has taught them about how to conduct the examination to verify the presumptions that underlie the terms of the deal.

A due diligence plan essentially (1) sets out the story as told by the company about the business deal, perhaps during an investment presentation or during conversations with company founders, and (2) identifies the claims that need to be verified by you and your professional advisors before proceeding with the business deal.

A good plan is extremely helpful in identifying both the general areas to be included in the due diligence review as well as any particular issues that are necessitated by the structure and terms of the deal. Devised before and as the basis for preparing the due diligence questionnaire, the plan establishes the goals of the due diligence review or—stated another way—asks what the reasons are for conducting the examination in the context of the particular transaction.

■ **Tip** Think of the due diligence plan as your attempt to write a story about someone you don't know very well. First, you need to get the facts about that person, and then you need to verify those facts.

Armed with your understanding of the purpose of a due diligence plan, the next issue is to draft it. Again, the framework of the plan should be built on the four business cornerstones mentioned earlier. Homing in on these four aspects helps you address the following:

- What is the nature of the transaction?

- What must be understood and verified about the company or potential partner in light of the proposed transaction?

- How are the products, services, and assets of the company essential to the success of the transaction, and what issues need to be verified about these elements of the company's business?

- What needs to be understood and verified about the business operations?

- Is the valuation appropriate in light of the transaction?

- Are the key personnel capable of meeting the terms of the proposed deal?

It is not possible to address these questions unless the key components of the business deal are identified. By way of example, consider the proposed purchase of ABB by Jack to see how these questions narrow the focus of the plan.

- *Question: What is the nature of the transaction?* **Answer:** Asset purchase.

- *Question: Because it is an asset purchase deal, what are the key assets being purchased?* **Answer:** Software, customers, contracts with chain stores.

- *Question: Does purchasing software/intellectual property raise issues in addition to the purchase of assets in general?* **Answer:** Yes, there can be specific issues that arise regarding ownership of intellectual property that differ from general business assets.

- *Question: Does the purchase of customers raise additional issues?* **Answer:** Yes, there are legal questions regarding transfer of customers, and there are practical considerations.

- *Question: Do the chain store contracts raise additional issues?* **Answer:** Yes, there can be issues regarding assignability as well as value in light of the specific terms of each agreement.

- *Question: What is the consideration/price to be paid?* **Answer:** All cash at closing.

- *Question: Will any of the seller's employees be hired by the purchaser?* **Answer:** No, but the assistance of one or more employees may be needed for a brief time to help with the post-closing transition.

Jack needs to focus on the particular issues that arise in the ABB transaction relating to software, customers, and chain store contracts, which are the essential assets he wants to acquire. Having determined the aspects of the deal that require special attention in the due diligence process, Jack is in a better position to prepare a plan for conducting the investigation.

Based on the question-and-answer scheme just outlined, the Overview portion of the ABB Due Diligence Plan might look as follows:

ABB DUE DILIGENCE PLAN: OVERVIEW

1. Nature of the transaction is an asset purchase of ABB, a gift card seller for multiple chain stores

2. Key assets being acquired

   A. ABB proprietary ordering software

   B. Customers

   C. Contracts with chain stores

3. Are there specific issues raised by the assets to be acquired?

   A. ABB software: ownership rights

   B. Customers: transferability and practical issues

   C. Chain store contracts: assignability

4. Consideration/purchase price

   A. Purchase price in cash at closing

   B. Value of the assets

5. Personnel

   A. No personnel to be transferred

   B. Reconsider requiring assistance of the seller with the transition?

The Overview portion of the ABB Due Diligence Plan identifies the key aspects of the ABB transaction in terms of the four business cornerstones:

1. *company:* ABB, a gift card retailer for multiple chain stores

2. *products, services, assets, and nature of the operations:* ABB software, customers, chain store contracts

3. *valuation:* to be determined

4. *personnel:* currently not part of the deal but transition assistance may be needed as more is learned about the business operations

The subsequent portions of the plan will identify potential issues raised by the transaction that are known at this early stage of the due diligence. One of the issues that deserves close attention is the ABB software. Recall the conversations between the lawyer and Jack about the potential purchase of ABB. During the conversation that led off this chapter, Jack told his lawyer that he wants to purchase certain assets of ABB, especially the ABB order processing software, because it is great software and will complement Jack's current business quite well.

The following is part of a discussion Jack has with Leah, the seller, after the initial meeting with his lawyer.

Date: August 31
Place: Offices of ABB

Jack: Well, Leah, I think it's time we move forward with discussing possible deal terms. As I've mentioned, I think my business could benefit and grow substantially by integrating it with key components of your operation. I have, of course, spent substantial time on your web site to test your services by ordering various merchant gift cards. I remain very impressed with the ease of use of the web site and the order process.

Leah: Thanks Jack. I'm pleased you see the value in the assets we've developed at ABB.

Jack: From my tour of your operations, and a conversation we had with your technology guy, Phil, it's clear the order processing software is top-notch. Now, from what I understand, you developed this software in-house and it is not just some off-the-shelf program anyone can purchase, right?

Leah: Yes. We created the software. No one else has it or offers it as a licensable product. ABB owns it. I have to say that I don't know as

much about the technology behind the order processing system. I'm more of a creative, idea, marketing person with the connections to the major retailers, which is why I hired Phil when Dana, my old partner, left the business. She originally created the software and brought it to me because she knew my connections to the big chain stores was crucial to making her software into a viable business. But, no worries. She contributed the technology to the company. I bought Dana's shares when she left the company, so ABB owns the software.

Jack: That's good to hear, because I am not interested in the transaction if Dana owns the software.

Leah: I bought all her shares, so that should put you at ease. Here's a copy of the agreement that indicates she sold me the shares. Take it and have your lawyer look at it.

Jack: Great, great. That seems settled. Now let's talk about your contracts with the major retail chains.

To summarize this conversation: Leah tells Jack that ABB owns the software because Leah bought Dana's shares in the company. This is Leah's version of the story as it relates to ownership of the technology that is key to the transaction moving forward. Leah believes ABB owns the software because Dana purportedly contributed the software to ABB when she became a shareholder in ABB. Furthermore, Leah has an agreement that shows she bought Dana's shares in ABB.

As we learned in Chapter 1, there is an open issue regarding whether Dana still owns the software, because she never assigned it to ABB. The due diligence conducted by the lawyer after the above August 31 conversation uncovered a significant difference between Leah's story—one she truly believes—and the true state of facts regarding the ownership of the ABB software. This example demonstrates how due diligence is necessary to verify a story someone tells you about his or her business and operations.

Because owning the software free and clear is critical to Jack's transaction, the next portion of his due diligence plan needs to be laid out to clarify who really owns the software, as shown in the "Software Ownership and Viability" portion of the plan:

ABB DUE DILIGENCE PLAN: SOFTWARE OWNERSHIP AND VIABILITY

---

6. ABB order processing software

    A. Background: Essential aspect of the transaction. The ABB software was developed by a former founder of the company and is now purportedly proprietary software owned by ABB. The software is the basis for the order processing system that the client wants to integrate into his existing business.

    B. Main issues

        1. Verify ownership of the software by ABB

        2. Confirm the technology works

    C. Questions

        1. Did the former partner develop the software? (Legal)

        2. Was the software ever assigned to ABB or contributed to the company by the former partner? (Legal)

        3. Does ABB now have all rights, title, and interest in and to the software? (Legal)

        4. Who, if anyone, should be engaged to test the software?

Now let's listen in again as Jack and Leah continue their August 31 conversation.

Date: August 31
Place: Offices of ABB

Jack: Ok, we discussed the software, can we now turn to the contracts ABB has with the big chain stores as they need to be included in the transaction. Not only are they a significant part of the business I will be purchasing, but I want to try to capitalize on the relationships with the big retailers for my current business.

Leah: You can have these contracts. As part of the deal, I will just notify the retailers that your company bought the business. That shouldn't be any issue.

Now, what does Jack's lawyer think of all this?

Date: October 24
Place: Jack's office, where he takes a call from his lawyer

Lawyer: Hi Jack. I realize that the October 22 conversation was probably a bit unsettling given my concerns about the ABB Software, and you probably don't want to hear about more issues, but we may have a problem regarding the contracts between ABB and its retailers. After reviewing them, it is clear that each contract requires consent from the owner before it can be assigned to your company. We need to contact every retailer and get their consent.

Jack: What a hassle! There are a lot of contracts, and Leah assured me that the contracts are assignable during our August 31 meeting.

Lawyer: It gets worse. The retailers are not obligated to consent to the assignment. You would have to execute a brand new agreement with any retailer that will not give its consent to your assumption of their agreement with ABB. Plus, the retailer may not agree to the same terms. If I were you, I'd tell Leah that if she wants to move forward with this sale, she needs to get the consents from her retailers.

Jack: I'll give her a call now and tell her she needs to be responsible for the getting the retailers onboard. I won't go any further with the deal if she doesn't agree to make this happen.

It's becoming quite clear to Jack that due diligence is extremely important to his potential transaction. He's encountered yet another possible barrier to acquiring what he wants. This problem area is addressed in the "Assignment of Chain Store/Retailer Agreements" portion of the due diligence plan:

ABB DUE DILIGENCE PLAN: ASSIGNMENT OF CHAIN STORE/RETAILER AGREEMENTS

7. ABB retailer contracts

    A. Background: Essential aspect of the transaction. ABB has a series of contracts with major retail chains that must be assigned as part of the transaction.

    B. Main issues

        1. Confirm contracts are assignable

        2. Confirm the terms of the agreements are acceptable

    C. Questions

        1. Are the contracts assignable or are new agreements required? (Legal)

        2. If the agreements are assignable, what are the financial and business terms? (Financial/legal)

Last, Jack's lawyer has discovered there could be legal issues relating to the contemplated transfer of ABB's customers to Jack's business. This concern is addressed in the "Customer" portion of the due diligence plan:

ABB DUE DILIGENCE PLAN: CUSTOMER TRANSFER

8. ABB customers

   A. Background: Client wants to purchase all current customers of the seller, ABB.

   B. Main issues:

      1. Verify transferability of customers

      2. Verify value of customers

   C. Questions:

      1. Can the customers be transferred to the purchaser? (Legal/practical)

      2. Are there privacy issues? (Legal)

      3. How can credit card and personal data be transferred? (Legal/practical)

      4. Will the customers transfer to the purchaser willingly? (Practical)

      5. What is the value of these customers? (Financial)

Items 1–8 comprise the ABB Due Diligence Plan for Jack and his lawyer. They identify the key aspects of the transaction and the issues known at this point that might affect Jack's ability or desire to proceed with the transaction.

Two lessons to take away from the construction of the ABB Due Diligence Plan: First, due diligence is not a set process in which one size fits all. It must be tailored to the specific terms of the proposed business event. Second, a due diligence plan assists in identifying significant components of the transaction and the issues arising from them that affect the scope and focus of the due diligence examination.

Based on the issues raised thus far, Jack and his lawyer can now create a series of detailed questions that will be gathered in their due diligence questionnaire. Although in some cases it might not be practical to prepare a full-blown due diligence plan that details every aspect of the transaction to be reviewed and verified, the benefit of preparing even a brief version of a plan is that will focus the strategy for the due diligence examination based on information known at the early stages of the deal.

Tip No matter how small the transaction, create some version of a due diligence plan. Even an outline that contains key issues can help you draw out the initial issues and keep you on track as you prepare the due diligence questionnaire and consider what other avenues of due diligence to pursue. Before finalizing the plan and moving on to the preparation of the due diligence questionnaire, revise it iteratively to make sure you are addressing the nature of the business, the proposed terms of the business transaction, and any information that may be learned during the initial phases of the investigation.

The Due Diligence Questionnaire

The *due diligence questionnaire* is the actual application of the due diligence plan. The questionnaire is created by compiling a series of questions regarding the business cornerstones, topics, and issues identified in the plan. The information and documents provided in response to the questionnaire are used to elaborate and corroborate the financial, legal and business operations picture that the subject company has given a potential purchaser or investor concerning its business, valuation, and personnel. The questions are designed to elicit the information that provides the requisite level of comfort to proceed with the transaction, exposes issues that counsel against proceeding, or suggests the need to revise the terms of the deal.

Typically the questionnaire is used in private transactions by purchasers buying a company or all or some of the assets of a company, or by a person buying shares in a closely held (private) company.[1]

---

[1]Due diligence is a major component of any transactions involving a public company, but this area is beyond the scope of this book.

▨ **Tip** Due diligence is applicable to more than mergers and acquisitions or investment transactions. Do not overlook the importance of conducting a due diligence examination in a variety of other business deals as well.

The issues to be addressed in the due diligence questionnaire are far more dependent on the nature of the transaction and business operations than the size of the deal or the company. One caveat is that the examining party may decide, or the target company may insist, on limiting the scope of the due diligence based on costs, the disruptive effect on the business, or other concerns associated with extensive due diligence (Chapter 9).

▨ **Note** The due diligence investigation can be a lengthy process that affects the costs of the transaction and time necessary to complete the deal. Although the party conducting the investigation wants to be thorough to ensure the deal is appropriate, practical considerations of expense and timing may necessitate limiting the scope of the due diligence review.

Leaving the cost–benefit analysis aside, consider why the nature of the transaction—as opposed to the size of the deal or company—is usually the focus of the due diligence questionnaire by looking at two hypothetical proposed transactions:

> *Transaction 1:* A private lender proposes to make a secured loan in the amount of $5,000,000 to ABC Co., which has annual net profit of $100,000. The loan will be secured by equipment and machinery at ABC Co.'s factory.

> *Transaction 2:* A private lender proposes to make a loan of $500,000 to XYZ Co., which has an annual net loss of $10,000. The loan will be secured by equipment and machinery at XYZ's factory.

The due diligence for each transaction is the same and involves a series of questions seeking to establish whether

- The borrower is a duly formed company, in good standing, and has the authority to enter into the transaction.

- The borrower has the financial ability to meet the loan obligations.

- There are no loans or other obligations that would be superior to the new loan.

- The borrower owns the collateral without any claims of third parties.

- The collateral is unencumbered.

- There are no existing or potential tax claims.

- There are no pending or threatened claims, no lawsuits or judgments, or no bankruptcy proceedings against the company or its assets.

- The value of the machinery and equipment is sufficient to satisfy the loan in the event foreclosure is necessary.

Even though the amounts of the loans differ and the companies are in substantially different financial situations, the due diligence still focuses on the same concerns: the borrower's ability to meet the loan terms and the ability of the lender to foreclose on the collateral and recover at least the principal amount of the loan (and hopefully the interest) in the event of default.

Just for fun, let's change one fact in both deals: the collateral is no longer equipment but is royalties received from license of the borrower's patent portfolio. Now we have additional issues to consider:

- The borrower owns the patents, as demonstrated by filings in the Patent and Trademark Office.

- All rights, title, and interests of the named inventors of the patent have been assigned to the borrower.

- The license agreements are valid and enforceable.

- A bankruptcy of the borrower/licensor does not affect the right to enforce the license agreements.

- The terms of the license agreements support the value of these licenses as collateral for the loan.

The lesson here is that the due diligence questionnaire is not one-size-fits-all. Rather, the questions need to be drafted to elicit information relevant to the nature and the specific terms of the transaction at issue.

The questionnaire generally consists of a number of standard or common questions relevant to almost all business due diligence. These are the *standard questions*. It also contains questions that are common to specific types of deals (such as an asset purchase transaction vs. an investment in a company). These are the common questions based on deal type. Last, the questionnaire contains questions that arise as a result of specific or unique aspects of the deal as well as from financial or business terms of a transaction (such as an asset purchase deal involving equipment vs. one involving the purchase of intellectual property (IP)). These are deal-specific questions. The following section discusses the standard due diligence questions. The *deal-type* and *deal-specific* questions are addressed in Chapters 4.

Due Diligence Questions: Standard Questions

The party conducting the due diligence generally poses a series of core questions regardless of the nature of the transaction. These standard questions are designed to elicit and confirm basic legal, financial and operational information about the four business cornerstones. To see the commonality of these cornerstone questions, compare the basic information sought by the parties in the following eight case studies of different types of business deals.

▓ **Case Study 1** *The Loan Transaction*: Overlook, Inc., a computer networking company, wants to expand its computer networking and repair business. It has negotiated with the landlord to lease the additional space next door. It intends to purchase additional equipment, including computers and servers, and hire two new employees. Although the business is apparently profitable, it does not have sufficient funds for the expansion and therefore has negotiated with Lucy, a private lender, for a loan in the amount of $100,000. The loan will have a five-year term and an annual interest rate of 9% payable monthly. It will be secured by all the assets, including the receivables, of Overlook, Inc.

▓ **Case Study 2** *Purchase of the Assets of ABB*: You've read about the proposed transaction between Jack and ABB, which sells gift cards offered by a variety of major chain stores. Jack has offered to purchase certain assets of ABB, including its software, customers, and contracts with the retail chains.

▓ **Case Study 3** *Purchase of SamGar Technology, LLC*: SamGar Technology, LLC, wishes to sell its business to Kobe Zander, a software developer. Zander has offered to purchase all the membership interests in SamGar for $175,000. SamGar wants to structure the transaction as a sale of the equity, rather than the assets, because its accountant has determined that sale of the membership interests is preferable from a tax standpoint. Zander is willing to purchase the equity in the company because he believes the value of the enterprise is closer to $300,000, less an outstanding loan that is, according to SamGar, $65,000.

▓ **Case Study 4** *Purchase of Series A Stock in Karly Medical Device Co.*: Hannah Nicole is the majority shareholder and managing director of Venture Medical, LLC, a fund investing in new medical technologies and health care businesses. Venture Medical has signed a nonbinding letter of intent to purchase Series A Preferred Shares in Karly Medical Device Co., a developer of a potentially groundbreaking medical device for conducting colonoscopies. Venture Medical will invest $500,000 for a 33% share of Karly Medical, reflecting a posttransaction valuation of the company of $1.5 million.

▓ **Case Study 5** *Purchase of a Strip Mall*: Debra Lynne has signed a nonbinding letter of intent to purchase a strip mall consisting of five stores from Mr. G Development Corp. Of the five stores, four are occupied. The vacant store was leased previously by a dry cleaner. Lynne wants to expand the strip mall by adding four more stores on a portion of the undeveloped property. The neighbor, KornPrem Enterprises apparently has a right of first refusal to purchase the strip mall, which the property owner argues was terminated. Lynne also wants to put in a fast-food franchise with a drive-thru. The purchase price is $1.2 million.

▓ **Case Study 6** *Exclusive License of Patents from Jordan Creatives, Ltd.*: Kilbourn Pet Toys wishes to enter into an exclusive license of three patents covering designs for indestructible doggy chew toys and teeth cleaners. The licensor, Jordan Creatives, Ltd., owns the patents but has not actually developed any pet toys. Furthermore, the licensor has its offices in Hong Kong but the actual company is a British Virgin Islands entity.

▓ **Case Study 7** *Purchase of 50% of a Music Store Owned by a Friend*: Adrian has negotiated to purchase 50% of the membership interests of a music store now owned by his friend, Rowland. Rowland, who has been operating the store successfully for 10 years and is an expert at repairing stringed instruments, especially electric guitars, recently invested in a restaurant/bar. He wants to spend about half his time growing the restaurant business, including promoting it as a venue for bands. One of the employees also has been building an excellent reputation for repairing stringed instruments. Adrian is well known for repairing electric and traditional pianos, but knows nothing about repairing guitars and has never operated a retail store. Rowland has offered to sell 50% of the company to Adrian for $35,000, plus an agreement to replace Rowland as the personal guarantor on a $50,000 business credit line, of which $20,000 is outstanding.

▓ **Case Study 8** *Purchase of a Fast-Food Franchise from a Franchisee*: Ellen Kay has entered a memorandum of understanding for the purchase of 33% of the LLC membership interests in KMF Franchisee, LLC—a franchisee that owns four franchises of Rocky Robbins Ice Cream Bar, Inc.—for $225,000. KMF Franchisee owes $100,000 to Mishy Enterprises, representing the purchase price for an earlier buyout of its equity interest in KMF. Mishy has complained that it was underpaid for its 33% interest and is considering opening a competing franchise across the street. KMF has many full- and part-time employees. The four stores are managed by Lara Melanie, who is in the last year of her four-year contract.

If you believe these deals are markedly different and therefore require substantially different approaches to the due diligence review, you are both right and wrong. Although these proposed transactions raise questions that are particular to each transaction, they also share of a number of common issues that require verification through the due diligence investigation. However, before homing in on specific issues raised by the particular facts of a transaction, the due diligence questions should first focus on confirming basic information relating to each of the business cornerstones. These standard questions are designed to confirm basic information about the target business or potential business partner before the potential purchaser, lender, investor, or partner begins to consider whether the actual deal terms are justified in light of the results of the due diligence review. Put simply, the particular transaction terms are of little import if the target company's responses to the standard due diligence questions do not provide the requisite level of comfort to proceed with the transaction.

These standard questions cover the following topics: (1) company/entity basic information; (2) ownership of the key assets; (3) financial and tax-related matters; (4) significant agreements, contracts, and undertakings; (5) legal questions common to most transactions; and (6) information about key personnel and employees. In the remainder of this chapter, I describe several key issues under each of these topics, followed by a statement regarding how the information obtained from the target business should be used by the examining party, and then an explanation of the legal, financial, or other important matters as they relate to the various case studies. This organizational structure is intended to illustrate the almost-universal importance of the standard questions regardless of the type of business transaction.

Topic 1: Basic Company Information

The typical due diligence questionnaire starts with a series of questions that seek basic background information about the company, its corporate structure, and ownership.

Issue: The proper name of the entity (including any d/b/a names), the address of the business operation and assets, and the jurisdiction of incorporation

This information is needed to do the following:

1. To draft the deal documents. (The same principle applies to all the case studies.)

2. To conduct Uniform Commercial Code (UCC), lien, judgment, tax, litigation, bankruptcy, and other searches regarding the company and its assets (see Chapter 9).

   a. *Secured Loan Transaction* (Case Study 1). The lender needs to be sure the assets the borrower is pledging are, in fact, unencumbered and there are no third parties who may have superior claims to the assets in the event the lender needs to foreclose on the loan as a result of a default. The lender also needs the information to determine where to file a Financing Statement (Form UCC-1) to obtain a security interest in the pledged collateral.

   b. *Sale of Business: Asset Sale* (Case Study 2), The purchaser wants to purchase the assets free and clear of any liens or potential claims.

    c. *Sale of Business: Stock Purchase* (Case Study 3). In the sale of a business through a stock transfer, the buyer is concerned not only that the assets are unencumbered but also that there are no judgments, tax liens, or other liabilities with respect to the company, because those liabilities remain after the transaction.[2]

    d. *Purchase of Series A Preferred Stock* (Case Study 4). The purchaser wants to consider the risks of investing in a company in which the key assets are pledged as collateral and to determine whether there are judgments or liens against the company or its assets.

    e. *Purchase of Strip Mall* (Case Study 5). Through title, lien, judgment and litigation searches, any undisclosed mortgages, liens, judgments or causes of action on the property will be uncovered.

    f. *Exclusive License Agreement* (Case Study 6). The licensee wants to make sure the IP is not encumbered and that there aren't any liens, judgments or causes of action against the licensor that could result in a termination of the license.

    g. *Purchase of 50% of Music Store* (Case Study 7). As with the sale of a business, the purchaser of an interest in a business wants to be sure there aren't any liens, encumbrances, claims or judgments that could lead the business to lose some or all of its key assets.

3. To determine whether there are legal issues under the laws of each jurisdiction (in the United States and internationally) where the business and assets are located (applies to all case studies).

4. To determine tax obligations for each location where the company does business.

5. To determine if the target business has assets or business operations located outside the United States, requiring the purchaser to determine the status of the assets under foreign law and further, as discussed in Chapter 9, whether to engage the assistance of foreign counsel.

---

[2]Similarly, in a stock buyout, the purchaser needs to verify that title to the shares can be transferred to the purchaser free and clear of any claims or encumbrances.

It is logical that a party entering into a transaction needs to have the proper name and address of the other party to the deal; but, as demonstrated by the previous list, there are a number of other reasons this very basic information is important. Consider, for example, if you are the purchaser of the business in Case Study 3 and learn after the closing that there is a state tax lien for $250,000 against the company that you failed to discover because you did not know the company operated under an assumed name (d/b/a or "doing business as") in that state. The takeaway here is that the failure to obtain the most basic information relating to a business can render your investment valueless.

Issue: Information about the company and the rights of equity owners as contained in the formation and governing documents and corporate minutes

Obtaining all the documents relating to the formation of the entity, including the articles of incorporation, resolutions, shareholder agreements, voting agreements, investor rights, rights of first refusal, options, or any other agreements relating to the rights and obligations of shareholders, is very important to understand basic formation information about the company and the rights and obligations of the owners of the business. To get the answers you need to address these topics, you might ask the following questions.

1. *Can the company provide documentation confirming the legal existence of the entity?*

2. *Is the entity in good standing and does it have the legal authority to enter into the transaction?*

3. *Do the formation documents (and any amendments thereto)—such as the articles of formation, bylaws, or operating agreement (for a limited liability company)—contain restrictions, need certain member or shareholder approvals, or even require amendments to the governing documents to meet the terms of the transaction?* Consider just a few examples how the governing corporate documents affect the rights and obligations of the company and its owners:

   a. By the terms of a company's governing documents, certain transactions may require the approval a class, or a supermajority, of the shareholders. A shareholder (in a company) or a member (in an LLC) could have the right to approve certain major transactions, including the sale or license of the assets, sale of the business (Case Studies 2, 3, and 5), loans over a certain amount (Case Study 1), or issuance of new stock (Case Study 4).

b. The company charter or articles of incorporation may require an amendment as a condition to the issuance of preferred shares (Case Study 4).

c. Additional concerns regarding applicability of the law of a foreign country are raised by the fact that in the license agreement transaction (Case Study 6) the entity is a Ltd., which is not a U.S. entity. Thus, the transaction may raise questions regarding the formation and validity of the entity, and the enforceability of the transaction against a non-U.S. licensor.

4. *Can the target company demonstrate that no other person or entity has any rights to the assets or equity that may be the object of the particular transaction or the right to approve the transaction?* Consider just a few examples:

a. A right of first refusal regarding the assets of the company would be an impediment to any transaction involving the sale of the assets (Case Study 2), of the business (Case Study 3), of the property (in the case of the strip mall, Case Study 5), or possibly of a license agreement (Case Study 6).

b. A right of first refusal on the equity in a company could be an impediment to the preferred share transaction (Case Study 4) or the sale of the membership interests in the music store (Case Study 7).

5. *Is there a shareholder agreement, any voting rights agreements, an investor rights agreement, or any other undertakings between the owners and the company affecting the rights of a purchaser, the capitalization of the entity, or even the ability to legally complete the transaction?*

6. *Do the minutes of meetings of the board of directors, shareholder meetings, and resolutions of the managing body of the entity include decisions that may affect materially the right or ability of an entity to enter into a transaction—things not in the company's formation or governance documents?*

Issue: The ownership structure of the business

The party conducting the due diligence needs a clear picture regarding the ownership and structure of the company. To get the answers you need to resolve this issue, you might ask the following questions:

1. *What is the capital structure of the business?* Buyers should ask for a capitalization table with current and historical ownership information, the stock or membership register or for a list detailing the number of shares (and different classes of shares, if they exist) owned by each shareholder or the percentage of ownership (in the case of an LLC), and the right of any person or entity to acquire shares or interests in the company (whether pursuant to options, warrants, convertible rights or other agreements) in order to obtain an understanding of the ownership of the company, including the controlling shareholders, members, and partners.

2. *What are the rights of the shareholders, members, or partners in a business?* Any membership/share purchase agreements not only shows who owns interests in the company, but also reveals special terms and rights a stockholder, member, or partner may have received.

3. *Who has any rights to acquire or an interest in the company?* Buyers should ask for documents relating to the issuance, grants, and cancelation of options, warrants, profit interests, or other rights to own or acquire ownership interests in the company to determine, for example, whether anyone has rights to acquire interests, which would result in *dilution* of current owners.[3]

---

[3]*Dilution* means a reduction of the ownership interest of an owner. It can occur, for example, as a result of the issuance of new shares, the exercise of any right to purchase additional shares, or the conversion of a loan into equity. An existing owner may have been granted a form of antidilution, which is important information for a new investor since it will affect the capitalization of the entity. New investors often demand anti-dilution rights as a condition of the investment to reduce the dilutive effect from the issuance of new shares.

4. *Are there approval or similar rights vested in any person or entity holding an interest in the company?* Agreements regarding rights or obligations of stockholders, members, or partners—including shareholder agreements, investor rights agreements, voting agreements, and partnership agreements—are significant because they can include obligations the company may have to certain members, shareholders may have to the company, or shareholders may have to each other.

The formation documents, shareholder agreements, and investor rights agreements may include a variety of requirements that must be met before any transaction can occur, may disclose impediments affecting the ability of the parties to enter into a deal, or may impose obligations on anyone becoming a shareholder or interest holder in a company. Consider how this plays out in the context of a lender who provides a loan (Case Study 1) only to discover later, after the borrower is in default, that a shareholder agreement required the approval of a particular class of shareholder for the transaction. Or what about a transaction in which a company issues new shares or sells its assets but fails to honor a right of first refusal? Binding conditions such as these are usually simple to discover when proper due diligence is conducted, including a review of the corporate formation and governance documents and agreements.

Topic 2: Ownership of Assets

When people buy a car, they check the title to make sure the seller is in fact the owner of the vehicle. Similarly, when purchasing the assets or stock in a company, buying real property, investing in a business, or licensing products or IP rights, the ownership or rights to the assets must be verified.

Issue: Ownership of key assets

The standard due diligence questions should include questions confirming ownership of the tangible and intangible assets and real property of the business or of those assets or stock membership interests that are relevant to the transaction. To get the answers you need to resolve this issue, you might ask the following questions:

1. *Can the target company demonstrate it owns all right, title, and interest to the business assets or the particular assets or stock being sold or IP rights to be licensed free and clear and without claims of any third party?*

2. *If any of the assets were acquired from a third party, can the seller provide a purchase agreement, bill of sale or similar document evidencing the transfer of the assets to the company?*

3. *If any of the assets were contributed to the business by a founding member or shareholder, is there a contribution agreement or a written acknowledgment demonstrating such contributions (as in the ABB Transaction in Case Study 2)?* Absent a contribution agreement or other form of acknowledgment (for example, the operating agreement of an LLC), the company may not even own the key assets.

4. *Can the individual sellers of shares of a company or membership interests of a limited liability company prove their right, title and interest in the shares free and clear of any third party claims?*

5. *Is there a deed (and any related title documents) showing the ownership, or a lease granting occupancy, establishing the rights to, and any restrictions on, ownership and use of business locations?* In a real estate deal (such as the strip mall in Case Study 5), the title insurance company seeks to obtain proof of the seller's ownership in the real property free and clear of any liens or other encumbrances or restrictions.

Issue: Ownership of intellectual property

Many businesses use some form of IP during their operations. In some circumstances, the IP is owned by the business whereas in others it is used pursuant to a license. Regardless, IP is often the key asset, or at least is important to the operation of a business, and ownership or a proper license to use it must be established. So, *how are IP rights confirmed?*

To get the answers you need to resolve this issue, you might ask the following questions:

1. *If the IP was acquired from a third party, is there adequate documentation of the transfer of the ownership rights to the target company?* The purchaser should be able to confirm the transfer (through a database search) with the United States Patent and Trademark Office (USPTO) and/or any equivalent foreign governmental body where IP rights are registered.

2. *Did the founding members/shareholders execute technology contribution agreements to transfer the technology to the company?* If not, serious questions will exist as to whether the company (as opposed to a shareholder) in fact owns the IP.

3. *Did the corporate entity obtain invention assignment agreements from employees and consultants to preclude conflicting claims regarding the rights to the IP?* Without these agreements, an employee or consultant may later claim the company does not own the IP.

4. *Did the company outsource development of its IP? If so, were all rights obtained from the developer in the development agreement?*[4]

5. *Does the company have license agreements for third-party software, or any other products or IP necessary to the operation of the business?*

6. *Are the key domain names registered in the name of the corporation/business entity rather than a third party (who is often one of the founding members)?*

In many transactions, it is quite obvious why the standard questions seek to verify a company's ownership and rights to IP. For example, an entrepreneur who has decided to purchase a business in which software or technology is the crown jewel (as in Case Study 2, the sale of ABB to Jack) certainly wants to make sure that the company owns the IP that underlies the major asset in the transaction. Anyone contemplating the purchase of preferred shares in a technology-based company, taking patents or other IP as collateral for a secured loan, or entering into a license agreement likewise needs to ensure ownership of the IP.

However, less obvious is a transaction in which technology is not the central focus of the potential transaction but still requires due diligence regarding the company's IP rights. Consider the transaction involving Adrian's interest in becoming a 50% owner of Rowland's music business (Case Study 7). At first blush, Rowland's music store does not seem to be a business in which technology rights are a concern for Adrian joining as a business partner. Yet, what if Rowland relies on third-party software to schedule music lessons for the store's students or relies on software to track inventory? The need to confirm a proper license and the terms of these software licenses and applications becomes apparent. Let's add a wrinkle: Rowland has developed a proprietary pedagogical tool for guitar teachers. What seemed like a transaction that would not require IP-related due diligence is now a deal in which the failure to verify these rights is a fundamental due diligence mistake.

---

[4]A related issue arises where open source code has been incorporated into the software, as the use of open source code can impose royalty-free licensing obligations on the owner of the software.

Topic 3: Financial/Tax Matters

A review of a company's financial information ultimately seeks to confirm the financial stability or instability of the company, the valuation assigned to the business or particular assets for the purposes of the transaction, and compliance with appropriate accounting and tax methodologies and rules.

Often, investors engage a financial professional, such as an accountant, investment banker, a business broker, a business valuation expert, or an appraiser, to assist with the valuation of the business or its assets. Other expertise may be required to conduct a financial due diligence review, depending on the nature of the company and the transaction, and may include international tax experts and accountants in foreign jurisdictions where the company has offices or does business.

In general, financial due diligence examines whether the actual financial and valuation data points support the information provided by the company in presentations, investment documents, financial statements, and projected financial statements.

Issue: Financial status of the company as documented by company financial records

The party conducting the due diligence needs to confirm the financial status of the business and/or the value of its assets. In almost all transactions, the standard due diligence questions include requests for basic financial information, such as financial statements, in order for the purchaser or investor to obtain a clear understanding of the company's financial situation in light of the particular transaction. The party conducting the due diligence will request information from the target company with the goal of answering the following basic financial questions:

1. *What do the financial statements demonstrate about the company's revenues, expenses, tax liabilities and other key financial indicators?*

2. *Are there positive or troublesome trends relating to the revenues and expenses of the company?*

3. *Does the company have the ability to repay its loans and meet all of its other obligations?* The ability of a company to meet its financial obligations is obviously important in the loan transaction (Case Study 1), but it also important in each of the other case studies.

4. *Is the financial information accurate and properly recorded by the company?*

5. *Are there any red flags calling into question the purported financial status of the company?*

6. *Are there outstanding tax liabilities or unresolved tax issues, including assessments and audits?*

7. *Is the valuation that underlies the purchase price for the assets of or the stock or an interest in the target company supported by the financial information?* If the valuation is not borne out by the financials of the company, then the purchase price for the assets or ownership interest needs to be renegotiated or the transaction terminated.

The eventual scope of the financial review and the actual documents and information requested vary depending on the deal type and transaction terms. Through common deal-type questions and the specific-transaction questions (Chapter 4), the due diligence questionnaire focuses on financial issues based on the nature and terms of the transaction.

Topic 4: Significant Agreements, Contracts, and Undertakings

The standard questions generally include requests for information regarding significant agreements or undertakings by the company under examination.

Issue: The company's material agreements or undertakings

The company may have entered into a number of types of agreements that you need to review because one or more contracts could materially effect your decision to proceed with the transaction. To get the answers you need to resolve this issue, you might ask the following questions:

1. *Are there any loan, guarantee, surety, and indemnification agreements or other financial undertakings?* Any of these agreements can create material financial obligations for the company.

2. *Are there agreements granting rights to assets or stock of the company, which may include a pledge of assets, an option to purchase, a right of first refusal, a license, and a lease?* Encumbrances on the assets or rights granted to purchase or use the assets affect the ultimate financial value of the business.

3. *Has the company entered into agreements creating business relationships with a third party, including a partnership agreement, joint venture agreement, letter of intent, memorandum of understanding, or similar agreement?* These agreements may include significant obligations restricting the rights of a company to enter into or to perform any of the terms of a transaction.

Issue: The financial and business terms of key customer agreements

The terms of major customer agreements are significant to financial and legal due diligence and must be reviewed to determine what are the rights and obligations created by any customer agreements. To get the answers you need to resolve this issue, you might ask the following questions:

1. *Is a lucrative customer agreement due to expire or is a significant customer facing financial troubles?* This event would raise concerns regarding projected revenues and would undermine valuation of a business.

2. *Are a majority of the customers of the business subscription-based and how do these subscriptions work?* For example, consider the effect on the financials if you discovered that the majority of the subscriptions are due to expire three months after the transaction is supposed to close, a significant piece of information that was not included in the seller's offering materials. Your initial understanding of the revenues of the company would dramatically change—along, of course, with the valuation of the company.

3. *Do the client service agreements impose unreasonable financial or other business obligations on the target business?* The customer agreements could include unfavorable pricing terms, long-term unfavorable contractual commitments, or an unrestricted return or cancelation policy.

4. *Has the company granted a lease or licensing agreement that does not reflect the fair market value of the real property or asset?* In the strip mall transaction (Case Study 5), a finding that a long-term lease for the largest store is below market rates negatively impacts the company's financials.

Obtaining a clear picture regarding customers and clients is obviously important when buying or investing in a business that relies on these revenues (Case Studies 3, 4, and 5) and is significant in other transactions as well. For instance, confirming the company's current and projected revenues is important to determining the ability of a borrower to repay a loan (Case Study 1) or to determining whether the assets, business, real estate, or IP to be purchased or licensed can generate the revenues necessary to justify the purchase price (Case Studies 2, 5, and 7).

Issue: Supplier/vendor agreements

If a company relies on specific suppliers or manufacturers for the lion's share of its goods and products, or in support of its services, these supplier agreements and the suppliers themselves must be vetted. Financial instability of a significant manufacturer or agreements with near-term expiration may affect the ability of the company to operate. Therefore, an important topic in the due diligence review is obtaining a clear understanding of the company's most important suppliers. To get the answers you need to address this topic, you might ask the following questions:

1. *What are the material terms of the contracts between the company and its major suppliers?* For example, in ABB Transaction (Case Study 2), if the major retail chains require a significant step-up in fees paid to these stores, then Jack needs to consider these costs in his financial modeling of the ABB transaction.

2. *Are the costs of obtaining the products or services rising?* If a supplier of the musical instruments for Rowland's music store is raising its prices, then Rowland's margin will be reduced (Case Study 7).

3. *What is the financial status of the manufacturer (or distributor) of the company's products?* If the only manufacturer of the company's products is in financial trouble, the business risks may be too great for a purchaser or potential investor (Karly Medical, Case Study 4).

Issue: Lease agreements

If a business leases rather than owns its locations, the lease agreements need to be reviewed to determine the status of the leases. To get the answers you need to address this topic, you might ask the following questions:

1. *Is the lease assignable?* If not, it would require consent of the landlord prior to assignment in the case of a sale of the business or its assets, which could be a major impediment or substantially raise the cost of operating the business for the purchaser.

2. *Does the lease contain onerous financial terms or severe restrictions on use of the premises?* For example, consider the impact on a company's business plans if it was prohibited from a planned renovation of one of its store location because the landlord exercised its absolute right to reject any changes to the premises (KMF Franchisee, Case Study 8).

3. *Does the lease include an option to renew? If yes, on what terms?* The answer to the question has a different effect depending on whether the target company is the lessee or the lessor in a particular transaction. If the company is the lessor (as in the strip mall transaction, Case Study 5), the absence of a renewal option in its leases creates an opportunity for the company to raise its rents and thereby increase revenues. If the target company is the lessee (as in the KMF Franchisee deal, Case Study 8), the absence of a lease renewal option creates uncertainty about the future use of the location and the cost of retaining the lease.

4. *Does the lease justify the purchase price?* This is a major financial question for the buyer of the strip mall (Case Study 5).

Issue: Product, technology, or service license agreements

Product, technology, and service licenses are a significant aspect of more and more businesses. Some businesses generate all or a portion of their revenues from licensing, while others rely on the licensing of products, technology, or services to operate their business. Any issues with these licenses could have a significant impact on one or more aspects of the operations of the business. The status of product, technology, and license agreements is a fundamental question for the diligence review. To get the answers you need to resolve this issue, you might ask the following questions:

1. *Are the product, technology, and service licenses assignable?* For example, as in Case Study 2, are software license necessary to operate the ABB assets assignable to the purchaser?

2. *Are the financial and business terms of the license reasonable?* Unfavorable license terms can raise questions about the ability to operate, or materially impact cost of operating, a business.

3. *Is there any concern about the financial stability of the licensor?* For example, a licensee of a patent should be concerned about the financial status of the patent owner (see Case Study 6).

4. *Are the third-party software, networking, and other technology agreements important to business operations aligned with reputable vendors and do they include adequate customer support, up-time guarantees, technology updates, and remediation obligations?* Consider, for example, the harm to a company that utilizes third parties to provide computer networking or other technology services from frequent or extended down times with respect to the services.

Topic 5: Common Legal Questions

The topics highlighted thus far raise common legal issues that should be addressed regardless of the nature of the transaction. For example:

- When examining general information about the target company, confirming proper formation of the entity under state or foreign law is a significant legal issue that the due diligence questions should address.

- In a transaction involving the purchase of assets or a business, investment in a business, the licensing of IP, or providing a loan, many standard questions should focus on proving that the business legally owns the assets.

- A shareholders agreement, investor rights agreement, operating agreement, bylaws, voting agreements and other agreements between shareholders and the company can impose obligations on the company, including rights of first refusal, voting obligations, restrictions on transfer, buy–sell obligations, tag-along rights and antidilution obligations. A purchaser of the company or investor would certainly want to know what rights and obligations are vested in the company or its shareholders by virtue of these agreements.

- Joint venture and partnership agreements can create business arrangements with significant legal implications.

- Contracts, such as customer agreements, leases, and IP licenses, raise several legal issues, including assignability in the event of a change of ownership.

Other standard legal topics that should be addressed when conducting due diligence for most types of transactions include the following issues.

Issue: Necessary licenses to conduct business

Businesses may require a variety of approvals, permits, or licenses to oper-ate under federal, state, and local laws. Although a company manufacturing or selling hazardous substances clearly requires certain government approvals, there are a slew of other regulated businesses under state, federal, and local laws that are less obvious (such as modeling agencies, spas and salons, health clubs, and document destruction contractors). The due diligence examination needs to verify that the company and certain employees have all regulatory approvals, licenses, and permits.

Issue: Compliance with applicable laws

Aside from laws that clearly apply to the operation of a business—such as adher-ence to health and safety regulations for a manufacturing business or environ-mental regulations in the case of a auto repair shop—the buyer must ensure it is in compliance with the less obvious laws, rules, or regulations that also apply to the conduct of the company's business. Some examples include the following:

1. *Local zoning laws and municipal ordinances can prohibit or restrict severely the operation of a business.* For example, cities have famously used such laws to limit where adult bookstores can be located. But even noncontroversial businesses can find they are subject to a variety of restric-tions, such as those that may affect their ability to erect a store sign, add a drive-thru, or even put tables outside a coffee shop during the summer.

2. *Privacy laws, which are applicable to any company that receives, has access to, collects, or maintains information sub-ject to privacy regulations, affect many operations.* These include retailers who have customer credit card data, social media companies that receive personal customer information, website-based businesses, software applica-tions that collect data, and just about any other company that collects personal data.

3. *The Health Insurance Portability and Accountability Act (HIPPA) applies not only to health care providers, but also to a variety of companies that collect personal medical data.* The regulations are quite stringent, and if they affect a proposed transaction in any way, potential buyers should know them.

4. *Environmental, health and safety laws include rules and regulations that affect a wide swath of businesses, and a company's need to demonstrate compliance is a major concern in the standard due diligence questions.* The standard due diligence questionnaire will therefore contain such questions as the following:

   a. *Does the company operate a business involving hazardous or toxic chemicals, or involve activities otherwise subject to environmental rules and regulations?* This is an obvious if a transaction involves a gas station or purchase of a chemical company, but it can apply just as easily to a restaurant, a dry cleaner, an auto body shop, or a manufacturer of technology that includes lithium batteries.

   b. *Have there been any investigations or notices of any investigations, or have there been any orders, fines, or judgments against the business under any environmental or health and safety laws?* A purchaser or investor needs to be aware of the existence of environmental claims by state or federal agencies because of the potential liability created by these claims (Strip Mall, Case Study 5).

   c. *Has a Phase I environmental assessment been conducted or should it be conducted, as is standard practice for the purchase of a commercial property?* A Phase I is necessary where the transaction involves the purchase of real estate (Strip Mall, Case Study 5).

   d. *Have fines been repeatedly imposed against the company by the Occupational Safety and Health Administration (OSHA)?* These fines are not only an issue because of the cost but also because of what they may indicate about any protocols and procedures the company has in place to meet workplace health and safety standards.

   e. *Are there numerous citations of health code violations?* Consider whether you would want to invest in a restaurant if it had numerous health code violations (KMF Franchisee, Case Study 8).

Issue: Compliance with the company's governing documents

A company's governing documents—such as the certificate of incorporation, corporate charter, bylaws (for a corporation), the articles of association and operating agreement (for a limited liability company), or the partnership agreement—set forth obligations, restrictions, and terms affecting governance of that particular business entity. These *corporate governance documents* must be reviewed before entering into any transaction, because they may contain restrictive provisions such as the following:

- Preclude the specific transaction because it violates the company's corporate charter

- Require supermajority or unanimous shareholder/member approval, or the consent or a particular class of shareholder or member

- Mandate that the company provide certain members or shareholders right of first refusal before engaging in a transaction with a third party

- Require that the company take specific action as a result of the transaction, such as issuing more shares to prevent the dilution of shareholders

In addition to the corporate governance documents, the managing members or board of directors, by a resolution or consent, may have adopted financial, operational, or governance policies or rules that affect the business materially.

Issue: Legal claims and proceedings

A common concern is to ensure that the company, its personnel, and assets are not subject to any judgment, pending or threatened lawsuits, or civil or criminal governmental investigations. To get the answers you need to resolve this issue, you might ask the following questions:

1. *Have any monetary judgments or awards been entered against the company?* This question is significant because a monetary judgment could be enforced against the company or its assets. Some of the risks include the following:

    a. In a transaction involving the purchase of a company, any existing judgment creditor has a monetary claim that it can then seek to enforce against the company, regardless of the fact that ownership has changed hands.

    b. If a creditor has obtained a judgment against certain assets, an asset purchaser could lose those assets in a foreclosure or must pay off the creditor to avoid a foreclosure.

c. The sale of a commercial building for which the bank has obtained a judgment for failure to pay the mortgage may result in the bank's right to foreclose on the property.

d. In a loan transaction (Case Study 1), a lien that is deemed to be superior to the lender's security interest could wipe out or reduce substantially the ability of the lender to recover its loan on the borrower's default.

e. In a transaction involving the purchase of commercial property, there is a major concern if the purchaser learns there is a judgment imposing substantial fines and ordering costly environmental remediation (consider the strip mall in Case Study 5)

2. *Have any judgments in equity (as opposed to monetary judgments) required or forbidden the company or its personnel to take certain actions?* Consider the following examples:

a. If, in the ABB transaction (Case Study 2), Dana sues and obtains a judgment stating that she is the rightful owner of the ABB software, ABB cannot sell it to Jack.

b. In the licensing transaction (Case Study 6), a court order finding that a third party is a rightful owner of the patent or is its exclusive licensee would render invalid the license that the buyer thought it was obtaining.

c. A court order prohibiting a company from offering its products or services in certain markets, or even from making certain marketing statements about its products or services, would severely undermine the valuation of the business.

3. *Are the company, its founders, or key personnel the subject of any civil, criminal, or administrative action, proceeding, or investigation by any government or regulatory authority?* These actions can alter materially the ability to proceed with a transaction. Consider the following examples:

a. A pending action by the Environmental Protection Agency or state environmental regulators involving real property that is part of a commercial real estate transaction.

  b. An investigation by environmental regulators regarding proper disposal of oil by an auto body shop that is being sold.

  c. An audit by state tax authorities regarding the collection and payment of sales tax, which could result in tax liabilities for the successor to a business or the assets of a business.[5]

  d. Investors want to make sure a company and its controlling shareholders have not been the subject of an investigation by the Securities Exchange Commission before it purchases shares in the company (as in the preferred Series A transaction, Case Study 4).

  e. Investors or potential partners in a business (for example the Music Store, Case Study 7) should be concerned whether the business is subject to a number of complaints or investigations under employment laws that could result in substantial fines or damage awards against the company. If the business owner, founder, director, or key officer has a substantial judgment against him or her, or has been investigated or is the subject of a pending lawsuit, criminal, civil, or administrative proceeding, the ability or the desire to move forward with a transaction could become a major issue.

 4. Are there any settlements involving a civil or criminal matter or the settlement of any investigation by any governmental or regulatory authority? A settlement can impose obligations or restrictions on a company, its assets, and its personnel, which can undermine a proposed transaction.

A judgment, award, settlement, pending claim, investigation, or proceeding involving a business or its assets—depending on the nature of such judgment, settlement, or proceeding—can, among other things, affect the financial condition of the company or its assets, raise serious issues regarding the ownership

---

[5]This is a major issue in states such as New York that still require compliance with bulk sales rules on the sale of the assets of a business. In New York, the bulk sales law requires the purchaser to file a notice with state tax authorities in connection with the sale of all or part of the assets of a business required to collect sales tax. The notice must be filed prior to taking possession of the assets or paying for them, whichever comes first. The purchaser is liable for any sales taxes owed by the seller if it fails to file the notice and await clearance from the tax authorities before releasing the purchase price to the seller.

rights with respect to the company's assets, undermine the ability or authority to operate the business or complete the proposed transaction, and raise doubts in the mind of a potential investor or partner concerning the founders or key officers of a company.

Topic 6: Employees/Key Personnel

The standard due diligence examination should, for most transactions, include questions relating to general employment matters designed to secure the following information:

- Ensure compliance with employment and labor laws

- Obtain a clear picture regarding the terms under which the key employees and the labor force are employed

- Confirm the company's ownership of employees' work product as well as proper protection of company proprietary information

- Elicit reassurances on prospective commitments from the founders and key personnel/managers, especially if the transaction includes postclosing obligations or transitional support

These issues are more important in a transaction involving the purchase or investment in a business (Case Studies 3, 4, 7, and 8), but they can also be significant, for example, in transactions in which ownership of collateral for a loan or licensed technology needs to be verified (case studies 2 and 6). The concept of conducting due diligence relating to employment matters is introduced here, but I discuss it in detail in Chapters 7 and 8.

Conclusion

The due diligence questionnaire should incorporate the major issues outlined in the due diligence plan for the particular transaction at hand. The value of the questionnaire to the overall diligence review will largely depend on whether it seeks information relevant to the nature and the specific terms of the transaction rather than a generic set of questions. Nonetheless, the due diligence questionnaire also includes *standard questions* that are important to almost any business due diligence examination. These standard questions, which seek to confirm fundamental legal, financial, operational and personnel matters regarding the target business, have been the focus of this chapter. Chapter 4 considers two further sets of questions in the due diligence questionnaire that arise from the underlying facts of the particular proposed transaction: *deal-type questions* and *deal-specific questions*.

Tailoring Due Diligence to the Transaction

The purpose of the due diligence investigation is to gather the requisite information before the investor, purchaser, lender, entrepreneur, or potential business partner moves forward with the business transaction. Chapter 2 explained that the party conducting the review—for example, a purchaser, investor, joint venture participant, licensee, or professional advisor (lawyer, accountant, technology consultant)—seeks to verify facts and projections about the business cornerstones: the company, its business operations, the valuation given the proposed transaction, and the personnel that may be essential to achieving the goals of the business deal.

In addition, as described in Chapter 3, the party seeking the information poses a series of questions to the targeted business in the form of a due diligence questionnaire. Thus, before launching the actual due diligence review, it is essential to prepare the questionnaire to ensure it is designed to elicit information relevant to the proposed transaction. Although for most transactions the questionnaire includes a number of standard questions (as explained in Chapter 3), too often, the potential investor thinks it is sufficient to use a form questionnaire without regard to the nature of the potential business deal. This unsophisticated one-size-fits-all approach can result in failure to uncover legal or financial facts or information about the business that might otherwise lead the investor to terminate the transaction or demand substantial changes to deal terms.

The purpose of this chapter is to demonstrate how the nature and terms of the proposed business deal affects directly how you draft a due diligence questionnaire. First, it examines a variety of business transactions and the information that is almost always sought in the context of the specific type of deal, such as an asset purchase or a loan or a licensing agreement (common deal-type questions). Second, it explores how aspects of the questionnaire need to be adjusted if the structure or terms of the transaction are altered (deal-specific questions).

Due Diligence: Common Questions Based on Deal Type

As discussed in Chapter 3, there is a series of due diligence issues that applies almost universally, regardless of the type of transaction. The standard questions focus on basic information about the company, the company's ownership of key assets, financial and tax matters, contracts and undertakings of the company, common legal questions, and common employment and key personnel questions. Although the scope of the due diligence investigation and the specific due diligence questions must be prepared based on the particular terms of each transaction, there are also several common issues that need to be addressed based on the *type* of transaction being considered.

This section demonstrates how the type of the business transaction (for example, an asset sale as opposed to an investment) dictates that certain common issues must be examined separate from any specific due diligence that may result from variations in the actual business terms. A business deal can involve relatively simple or incredibly complex structures, but whether you are a novice entrepreneur or a seasoned deal professional, it is likely you may conduct due diligence for one of the following types of transactions:

- *Financing transaction*: A loan transaction, similar to the proposed loan to Overlook Inc. discussed in Chapter 3

- *Asset sale*: The purchase of all or some of the assets of a business, similar to the proposed purchase of ABB's key assets by Jack discussed in Chapter 3

- *Business buyout*: The purchase of a business, by purchasing all the ownership (stock, membership) interests in the company, similar to the SamGar transaction discussed in Chapter 3

- *Private placement*: An investment in a private company, by purchasing some of its stock, such as the private equity transaction involving the purchase of the Preferred A Shares in Karly Medical Device Co. described in Chapter 3

- *Commercial real estate transaction:* The purchase of commercial real estate, such as the purchase of the strip mall described in Chapter 3

- *Partnership:* Becoming a partner in a business or buying a piece of a business, such as Adrian's purchase of 50% of Rowland's music store, as discussed in Chapter 3

- *Material contract:* A long-term contract, such as a licensing transaction or even a franchise deal, similar to the patent license discussed in Chapter 3

These transactions involve the privately held (in other words, nonpublic) companies to which entrepreneurs and business owners are most likely exposed during the due diligence process. Therefore, it is instructive to break down the commonality of the issues that arise in each of these types of business transactions.

The Financing Transaction

The main focus of due diligence in a secured loan transaction is to obtain a sufficient level of comfort regarding the borrower's ability to repay the loan (financial due diligence) and to confirm the lender's rights to the collateral in the event of a loan default (legal due diligence).[1]

Common Financing Transaction Issues

Let's revisit the proposed loan between Lucy (the lender) and Overlook Inc. (the borrower) discussed in Chapter 3. In formulating an appropriate set of questions for the due diligence review, it is necessary to break down the transaction into the key facts:

Nature of the transaction: a secured loan

Borrower's business: a computer networking and repair business

Entity type: corporation

Amount of loan: $75,000

Material additional facts or issues: loan secured by assets and receivables of borrower

---

[1]Additional concerns arise if the loan is convertible into equity in the borrower. Then, the due diligence investigation should be expanded to include issues that are typically addressed by an investor in a private placement because the lender could potentially become a shareholder/member of the borrower if it decides to convert the loan into equity in the company.

In general, for any secured financing transaction, whether the loan is $1,000 or $1,000,000, or the term is 30 days or 30 years (as in the case of a mortgage), or whether the borrower is a multimillion-dollar manufacturer of widgets or a small computer company, the due diligence looks to confirm two things: (1) that the borrower can repay the loan and (2) that the collateral is sufficient. In other words, in the context of any secured loan/financing deal, regardless of the borrower's business, the size of the loan, or the nature of the collateral, the basic concerns are (1) an assessment of the probability that the borrower can repay the loan when it comes due and (2) if not, that the liquidation of the collateral is an adequate substitute in the event of a default by the borrower. If you take a look at Appendix C, the Sample Financing Transaction Due Diligence Questionnaire, you'll note that your job is first to ask the borrower to furnish information necessary to confirm the proper formation of the borrower's business entity, its legal authority to enter into the transaction, and proof that the borrower has an unencumbered title to the assets (these issues should sound familiar because they are part of the standard due diligence questions discussed in Chapter 3). The majority of the remaining questions should then examine the following:

1. Does the financial due diligence investigation satisfy the lender that the borrower's business will produce the income to pay the loan in accordance with its terms? In this regard, you revisit the issue of valuation, which was identified as one of the four cornerstones of due diligence discussed in Chapter 1. Often, with the assistance of a financial professional, financial due diligence examines the borrower's profit and loss (P&L) statements, tax returns, and other financial documents to gain an understanding, for example, of the borrower's

   a. Short and long-term liabilities

   b. Income vs. expenses

   c. Receivables

   d. Budgets and financial plans

   e. Assets, to determine whether they are of sufficient value to satisfy the borrower's financial obligations if the borrower cannot meet the loan terms

2. In the event of default by the borrower, does the collateral provide sufficient security to, at a minimum, repay the loan or, as preferred, allow the lender to realize the intended economic value of the transaction (the principal,

plus interest and costs of collection)? To this end, legal due diligence asks the borrower to confirm?

a. Does the borrower own the pledged assets?

b. Are the assets already pledged as collateral in a separate financing or otherwise encumbered?[2]

c. Are there circumstances that could result in the borrower losing its rights to the assets (such as an existing judgment, a tax lien, pending or threatened litigation, or a conflicting claim by a third party)?

Unique Issues in the Financing Transaction Case Study

Aside from the due diligence questions commonly raised in a secured loan transaction, the investigation should address any deal terms that could potentially raise additional financial or legal issues. One deal aspect that requires additional attention in the loan transaction between Lucy and Overlook Inc. is that the security for the loan includes accounts receivable. This fact does not alter the basic questions about the whether the borrower has the ability to pay the loan and, if not, whether the value of collateral is sufficient to satisfy the borrower's loan obligations. But it adds a layer of due diligence requiring the lender to determine if it will be able to enforce and collect the receivables in the event of a loan default. To determine if the receivables are collectible in the event of a loan default, the lender might ask a series of questions focused on the following issues:

- Does the company have documents evidencing the receivables, including without limitation, any contracts, purchaser orders, invoices, or legal documents creating a payment obligation.

- Does the company have any documents, reports, or summaries detailing the payment history with respect to each account, including the ages of the receivables? (If not, the lender might follow up with a request that the borrower prepare a detailed report of the receivables for each account.)

---

[2]Determining whether the company's assets have already been pledged as collateral is a significant issue in most business transactions. Agreements granting third parties secured interests in assets of the company affect a party's right to obtain the security it seeks in a loan transaction (Case Study 1) or buying the assets (as in the asset sale transaction of Case Study 2), and may affect the underlying value or raise issues of financial stability, as in a deal involving the sale of a business through a stock purchase transaction (Case Study 3); a license of the assets, as in an exclusive license agreement (Case Study 6); or a partnership or prospective owner in a business, as in the purchase of the music store (Case Study 7).

- Does the company have financials for the accounts? Has it run credit checks and collected any other background information on each account?

- Has the company received any letters, claims, notices or legal documents in which any debtor has or is threatening to dispute any of the receivables?

In the end, the lender needs to obtain a sufficient level of comfort regarding its ability to collect on the collateral—in this case accounts receivables—if the borrower defaults on the loan.

The Asset Sale

An asset sale is similar to the proposed transaction between Jack and ABB, a company that sells gift cards offered by a variety of major chain stores. Jack has offered to purchase certain assets of ABB, including its software, customer list, and contracts with the retail chains. Some issues are common to most asset sale transactions; others are unique to the particular transaction, the nature of the business, and the proposed deal terms.

Common Asset Sale Issues

As usual, the first step is to break down the transaction into the most important facts, which then dictate the structure of the due diligence examination:

Nature of the transaction: an asset sale

Assets being purchased: software, customer list, contracts with chain stores

Purchase price: to be determined

Material additional facts or issues: seller's ownership of the software, transferability of the customers to the purchaser, and the ability to assign the chain store contracts

Postclosing obligations of seller: to be determined based on the due diligence[3]

---

[3]Chapter 8 explores significant issues that the due diligence investigation may uncover and their possible solution.

The following are the due diligence issues common to most asset sale transactions:

1. Does the seller own and have the authority to convey the assets to the purchaser?

    - Can the seller prove ownership of the customer contracts, the software, and the contract rights being assigned?

    - Does the seller have the right to assign the customer list, software, and contracts to the purchaser or are there legal restrictions preventing the sale?

2. Do the assets work? Do they do what they are being purchased to do? This may require testing or an inspection of the assets by an expert familiar with similar products, goods, machinery, or technology.[4]

3. Does the valuation assigned to the assets as part of the deal support the purchase price? In the context of the ABB asset sale, questions include the following:

    - Do the customers generate sufficient revenue to justify the value assigned to the customer list in the context of the transaction?

    - Who are the biggest customers? Will there be a material impact from the loss of them? What does the purchaser need to do, or require the seller to do, prior to and after closing to retain these customers?

    - Does the ABB software provide a technology solution that supports its valuation?

    - Are the chain store contracts assignable to the purchaser? Are there any concerns about their future value? What does the purchaser need to do, or require the seller to do, prior to and after closing to retain these contracts?

---

[4]Are you or your financial and legal advisors qualified to test the key technology, machinery, or equipment? As discussed in Chapter 9, consider whether the assistance of an expert who understands the functionality and valuation of any of assets is necessary to complete the due diligence properly.

The Sample Asset Sale Due Diligence Questionnaire (Appendix D) includes the standard due diligence questions (see Chapter 3), which require the seller to confirm the proper formation of the seller business entity, the legal authority to enter into the transaction, and proof that the seller has the right and authority to transfer the assets to the purchaser. It also includes questions that are typical in the context of an asset purchase transaction, which are intended to confirm (i) seller's unencumbered ownership rights to the assets, (ii) the ability of the seller to legally transfer the assets, and (iii) the proper valuation of the assets.

Unique Issues in the Asset Sale Case Study

In this section, we look at the unique aspects of Jack's potential purchase of ABB's assets and what additional issues need to be considered in drafting the due diligence questionnaire. The ABB transaction involves the purchase of the seller's customer list, software programs, and certain contracts the seller has with third parties. The transfer of these types of asset is fairly standard in this digital age, so the ABB asset sale is not unique in that regard. The conveyance of these assets, however, does require a different focus than, say, the purchase of an auto body shop with no online presence. Compare the following:

1. *Software:* Does the seller own the assets?

    - *ABB:* Did Dana, developer of the software and a company founder, ever contribute the technology to ABB? If not, ABB has to resolve the ownership issue before the transaction can proceed.

    - *Auto Body Shop:* Assuming the auto body shop does not utilize any of its own proprietary technology, does the seller utilize third-party technology to operate the business? For example, it might rely on software for tracking sales and inventory, in which case the purchaser needs to determine if it wants to continue to use this third-party software and if so can it assume or obtain a wholly new license from the licensor.

2. *Customers:* Is the customer list assignable?

    - *ABB:* Are there any legal issues that may create problems because ABB retains credit card data or other personal information subject to privacy and data security laws?

- *Auto body shop*: Does the auto body shop maintain customer information, and if so what is the nature of this information? Assume the auto body shop only maintains basic customer information (name, address, model of car customer own, and previous work performed by the shop) but does not maintain customer e-mails or credit card information. The transfer of the customer list would not require the level of scrutiny or the focus on the privacy issues implicated by the ABB transaction.

3. *Material contracts*: Are the material contracts assignable?

   - *ABB*: Can the contracts between the major chain stores and ABB be assigned to the purchaser?

   - *Auto body shop*: What are the arrangements with the shop's suppliers, especially the parts manufacturers? Unlike the contractual relationship with the retailers in the ABB transaction, the auto body shop likely is on a cash basis or has a credit arrangement with suppliers – and thus there are no supply contracts to be assigned. The purchaser would set up its own relationship with these suppliers.

4. Do the assets work?

   - *ABB*: Does the ABB software function properly? The purchaser would want the software tested by an expert to ensure functionality since it is the crown jewel of the transaction.

   - *Auto body shop*: Do the licensed software programs that are to be transferred by the seller, if any, function properly? The level of scrutiny for standard software programs (like inventory tracking software) will be substantially less than in the ABB transaction, in which the proprietary, one-of-a-kind software application is the whole reason for the transaction. In contrast, the purchaser of the auto body shop needs to make sure the machinery, tools, and any diagnostic or other equipment are in good working order.

The Business Buyout

Let's use the SamGar Technology case study to examine a business buyout deal. To refresh your memory: SamGar Technology (the seller), which maintains a subscription gaming web site, wants to sell its business to Kobe Zander (the purchaser), a computer game developer. Zander wants to purchase all the membership interests of SamGar for $175,000, and is willing to purchase the equity in the company because he believes the value of the enterprise is closer to $300,000, less an outstanding loan, which SamGar has stated is $65,000. The key terms of the transaction for purposes of due diligence are as follows:

> *Nature of the transaction:* business buyout/purchase of the seller's total equity
>
> *Business to be purchased:* gaming web site with subscription-based customers
>
> *Type of entity:* LLC
>
> *Purchase price:* $175,000 plus assumption of a $65,000 loan.
>
> *Additional material facts or issues:* all of the company's revenues are derived from offering on-line, subscription-based services.

Common Business Buyout Issues

In contrast to the ABB asset sale transaction, in which the purchaser wants to buy select assets of the seller, the SamGar transaction involves a buyout of the entire business through a purchase of 100% of the membership interests of the LLC. However, many of the basic deal questions are similar to the questions in the typical asset purchase—namely, whether the company being sold owns the key assets of the business, whether the assets work, and whether the value assigned to the business is appropriate based on its financials. However, the major difference with a business buyout is that the purchaser is buying the company (acquiring its assets and assuming all its liabilities), which requires the purchaser to assess not just the assets but also the company's existing and potential financial and legal liabilities, and employment-related matters. The common due diligence issues for most business buy-out transactions include the following:

1. Does SamGar, a technology company, own all the assets necessary to operate the business?
   * Who owns the software platform and its applications?
   * Who owns the web site?

- Who owns any other assets necessary to operate the business?

- Are there any issues that could negatively affect the company's ownership rights in the assets?

- Are the domain names properly registered to the company?

- Does the company own any U.S. and international patents, trademarks or other intellectual property?

- Are there any licenses from third parties that may terminate on change of ownership?

- Are there any contracts, leases or other significant agreements that terminate on change of ownership?

- Does a change in ownership create any issues regarding existing customers with respect to privacy or other issues?

- Do the actual individual sellers of the membership interests have a free and clear title to the membership interests?

2. Do the assets work as represented (with a particular focus on technology, because it is the main component of the transaction)?

   - Should a professional be hired to test the functionality of the software and other technology assets?

   - Can the assets—in particular in this case, the software platform—be integrated with the purchaser's operations?

3. Is the purchase price supported by the actual value of the business based on past and projected financials? Specific to our case study, is there support for Zander's belief that the purchase price of $175,000 is significantly lower than the potential value of SamGar after it is integrated with Zander's business? Although this is an issue for financial due diligence, which likely will be conducted by an accountant, business evaluation expert, or other financial professional, legal due diligence also includes questions that focus on valuation:

   - Can the company provide current and historical financial statements supporting the purported revenues and net income?

- Does the company have purchase orders, invoices, sales contracts, receipts, subscriptions, sales tax documents, and other information that support the projected revenues that underlie the valuation of the transaction?

- Can the company provide information relating to expenses to test the reasonableness of operating expenses, cost of goods sold, and any extraordinary expenses?

- What are the short- and long-term liabilities or potential liabilities (such as leases, installment purchase agreements, legal judgments and settlement agreements, and conditional liabilities) associated with the buyout?

- What accounting methodologies or principles does the business use to record revenues and expenses? How do these principles affect financial results?

4. Are there any tax issues?

- Can the company provide documents relating to federal, state, local, and foreign tax returns (including income, sales, property, franchise, payroll, and other applicable taxes) that show it is compliance with all tax obligations?

- Are there any open tax issues (including failure to pay sales taxes) that can result in tax liabilities and liens?

5. What financial or legal liabilities arise, for example, through contracts, agreements, or undertakings of the company?

- What long-term commitments exist that could affect the financial and operational aspects of the business? For example, the company may have entered into a long-term contract with an employee or a marketing company that the purchaser would prefer to terminate on taking over the business.

- Has the company made any warranties with respect to its goods and services that the purchaser is obligated to honor?

6. What are the potential legal issues arising from the purchase of this type of business?[5]

7. Is the company in compliance with all laws and regulations that are relevant to its business?

8. Because the deal involves a buyout, the purchaser needs to include due diligence on the employees of the company. This is a major difference from an asset sale, in which employees and employment liabilities remain with the selling company. Therefore, what are the relevant employment issues associated with a business buyout?

   - What are the terms of employment and consulting agreements?

   - Are there any invention assignment obligations?[6]

   - Have the employees executed confidentiality and nonsolicitation agreements?

   - Does the business comply with employment and wage laws?

   - Has the company granted any options to employees, consultants, or other third parties to own a portion of the company?

9. What are the employment contracts, particularly of key employees and consultants?

   - What are the employment costs, including salaries and benefits?

   - Are there any obligations under collective bargaining agreements?

---

[5]As previously discussed, privacy and data security rules are implicated by the transfer of customers and may even arise from the functionality of the assets, such as software that captures personal information.

[6]The company should be able to provide invention assignment agreements that indicate that all employees and consultants have assigned all intellectual property to company. While the "work for hire" rules under U.S. copyright law grant employers ownership of works made during the course of employment, an invention assignment agreement prevents employees from arguing they created the technology previously or did so outside of the course of employment.

- Have employees, key personnel (upper level management, directors, and officers), or even consultants been granted options, profit shares, or other rights that may result in a dilution of the buyer's 100% ownership of the business?

- Do key employees, by contract or otherwise, have a legal obligation or a financial incentive to remain with the company following a change in ownership?

- Has the company complied with employment/labor laws (the noncompliance of which could expose the company to substantial financial or tax liabilities or administrative enforcement actions)?

- Do employment policies and records confirm compliance with employment and labor law rules, compliance with unionized labor force obligations, proper policies and procedures regarding payroll matters, proper classification of employees as employees (and not consultants, to avoid employment taxes), adherence to immigration laws, and compliance with all emerging health care laws?[7]

Unique Issues in the Business Buyout Case Study

A significant portion of the revenues of most retail businesses in this day and age is generated by online sales. The most significant aspect of the SamGar business is that all of its revenues are derived from customers subscribing to services offered through their web site and software applications. Therefore, in the context of this business buyout, particular attention needs to be paid to ownership of the intellectual property rights underlying the software applications, stability of the technology (including the software, applications, and website), financial value of existing customers, any concerns regarding the transferability of the customers based on a change in ownership of the business, and the legal obligations arising under privacy or other laws based on the functionalities of SamGar software applications.

Issues relating to the ownership and stability of the proprietary technology are common to any deal where the target business relies on its technology to generate income. Moreover, due diligence questions regarding the company's revenues would be common to any transaction involving the purchase of a

---

[7]These questions are important to ask when joining a business as a partner (Case Study 7) and even when investing in a company as a minority shareholder (Case Study 4).

business. Here, however, the diligence review must address concerns about the subscription-based revenues, including the following significant issues:

- What are the financial and legal terms of any membership or subscription agreements with SamGar's customers?
- What are the services that the company is obligated to provide its subscribers?
- Are the financial terms beneficial or do they lock the company into unfavorable terms?
- Are there unfavorable warranties or cancellation policies?
- Does the change in the ownership of the business raise any privacy issues or other legal issues with respect to the customers?
- What policies and procedures does the company have in place to protect customer information?

The Private Placement

Let's refer back to the appropriate case study to review a private placement business deal. In this transaction, an investor is considering investing in a private company by purchasing 5% of its issued shares. The transaction involves the purchase of Preferred Series Class A stock in a private equity offering by Karly Medical Device Co., which has developed new technology for exploratory surgery that also stores information in the cloud. The key deal terms are as follows:

Nature of transaction: purchase of preferred stock in a private placement

Type of business: developer of a new medical device

Entity type: corporation

Consideration: agreed per share purchase price

Additional material facts or issues: issues raised by the fact the company is, essentially a startup, offering a new technology, and in the medical field

Common Private Placement Issues

A private placement is a transaction in which an investor purchases unregistered shares in a nonpublic company. If potential investors are *accredited investors* as defined under the Securities Act of 1933—basically, well-off people considered to be sophisticated in financial matters—the issuer of the shares is not required to provide potential investors any specific information or disclosures. The burden is on investors to ask for information they deem important to assess whether they want to proceed with the investment.[8] Getting the appropriate information via the due diligence questionnaire is crucial to evaluating the investment. The due diligence questionnaire for a private placement transaction would resemble the questionnaire for the business buyout in many ways, because both involve the purchase of equity interests in a business. As with the purchase of a business, due diligence in the context of a private placement should be a comprehensive analysis of the company; the company's products, services, and technology; along with its valuation and personnel. The due diligence questionnaire therefore consists of a comprehensive set of questions designed to elicit sufficient information regarding all four business cornerstones.

However, unlike a complete buyout of all the ownership interests of the company (as in the SamGar transaction), the purchaser may only be purchasing a minority interest in the company. The purchaser generally will not have say in how management operates the business. Further, the purchaser will be bound by any existing shareholder or investor agreements. In addition to many of the same issues in a business purchase, due diligence in a private placement transaction will also focus on the following issues:

- Do shareholder or investor agreements exist? If so, what obligations do they impose on, and what rights are granted to, shareholders?

- Is there a right of first refusal requiring the company to first offer shares to shareholders before any third parties?

- Are there rights to purchase shares that could result in dilution of the shareholders ownership in the company?

- Are restrictions on ownership or obligations imposed on shareholders under the company's certificate of incorporation/corporate charter and bylaws (or operating agreement, in the case of an LLC)?

- What are the terms of any options, warrants, or other rights granted employees, consultants, existing shareholders, or third parties to purchase shares in the company that would result in dilution of the investor's ownership in the company?

---

[8]Often, the company issuing the shares or membership interests provides a private placement memorandum (PPM) that contains a deal summary, overview of the company's business, standard risks associated with purchase of unregistered shares, and the financial, legal, and operational risks relating specifically to the issuer. The PPM, however, is *not* a substitute for due diligence by the potential investor.

- What are the limitations on the rights of shareholders to dispose of shares in the company, such as a co-sale obligation requiring a seller to first offer its shares to the other shareholders?

- Are there specific rights granted only to a certain class of shareholders, including a liquidation preference, right to dividends, or election of one or more board members?

These questions, designed to draw out information about obligations of shareholders and limitations on their rights, are commonly included in a due diligence questionnaire for a private placement.

Unique Issues in the Private Placement Case Study

Looking at our case study of a private placement transaction, we note that the medical device offered by Karly Medical incorporates a system that stores patient medical information in the cloud for access by healthcare providers and insurers. The success of the business depends on whether the device works but equally important whether a healthcare provider can utilize the technology without running afoul of the Health Insurance Portability and Accountability Act (HIPAA) and privacy laws. An investor needs to confirm that the Karly Medical technology complies with these laws regarding storage of private medical information. Failure to comply with HIPAA and privacy rules would be devastating for the company.[9] Compliance with privacy laws is of paramount concern in this private placement transaction and therefore the due diligence questionnaire should include questions specifically aimed at privacy, data storage and back-up issues:

- How does the technology ensure that private medical information is secure?

- What written policies and protocols have been implemented to protect private information and ensure compliance with company internal policies?

- Have there been any breaches or unauthorized releases of private information by the company or resulting from a use of its technology?

---

[9] The legal obligations created by storage of information in the cloud are not limited to medical companies. Investors in any company using the cloud should be concerned about privacy and proper data security, information storage policies, and backup and redundancy of systems to store critical company, customer, and/or user information.

- What policies and procedures have been implemented regarding data back-up?

- What disaster recovery and system redundacies are in place?

The Commercial Real Estate Transaction

To examine the commercial real estate transaction deal type, let's recur to the applicable case study. The transaction involves a nonbinding letter of intent to purchase a strip mall for $1.2 million; this is a standard deal with a few wrinkles. The first wrinkle is that the strip mall consists of five stores, one of which is vacant. The vacant store was leased previously by a dry cleaner. The second wrinkle is that the purchaser wants to expand the strip mall by adding four more stores on a portion of the property that is undeveloped, including a fast-food restaurant with a drive-thru window.

Let's break down the key facts:

> *Nature of the transaction:* real estate purchase

> *Assets purchased:* strip mall with five storefronts, one of which is vacant

> *Entity Type:* Corporation

> *Purchase price:* $1.2 million

> *Additional material facts or issues:* vacant store previously leased by a dry cleaner; purchaser wants to expand by adding more stores

Common Commercial Real Estate Transaction Issues

Because the transaction involves the purchase of real estate, the purchaser will engage a title company to perform a title search and prepare a title report. A title search is one aspect of due diligence that should always be conducted in a real estate purchase transaction. The focus of the commercial real estate transaction is on the following issues:

- Is the seller in good standing under the laws of the jurisdiction where it is registered and does the seller have the authority to sell the property?

- Does the seller own the title to the property free and clear of any competing title claims?

- Are there are any title defects that may affect the ability of seller to convey the property?

- Are there other encumbrances?

- Are there are any mortgages on the property?

- Are there are any liens or judgments against the property?

- Are there any restrictions on the use of the property, including restrictions in a deed or imposed by zoning or other municipal laws?

- Have any rights been granted to third parties by easement or otherwise?

- Does the seller owe real estate taxes?

- Have any lawsuits or notice of lawsuits have been filed against the seller

The title search in a real estate transaction is, therefore, aimed at obtaining much of the same information as the due diligence done for other business transactions.

Unique Issues in the Commercial Real Estate Transaction Case Study

Along with the title search, the purchaser should perform due diligence similar to that conducted for an asset sale, because the buyer in a commercial real estate transaction is not only purchasing real estate, but also the assets of the seller's business. A due diligence questionnaire therefore includes many of the same standard questions raised during in the due diligence investigation for an asset sale: corporate authority; ownership of the assets being sold; restrictions on use by law or by contract; issues regarding taxes, liens, encumbrances, judgments, or pending lawsuits; and so forth. However, the questionnaire also should include financial and legal questions specific to a commercial real estate transaction:

1. What are the financial terms of the leases? This information is important in determining the appropriate valuation of the property and whether the purchase price, in our example case study, of $1.2 million is supported by the income generated by the property.

   - Are the rents are at market rates? If not, what are the remaining lease terms?

   - Are there reasonable rent escalations?

- Do tenants have the option to extend their lease? If so, what are the financial terms?

- What are the carrying costs, including real estate taxes and property maintenance costs?

- What are the costs of construction and carrying costs associated with building the new stores?

- Does the purchaser have commitments in place to lease the new stores, including the fast-food franchise, which may be jeopardized if zoning or other restrictions on property use require her to change her plans?

2. Does the commercial property appraisal report commissioned by the purchaser support the purchase price for the property?

3. Has the seller granted any tenant or third party a right of first refusal to purchase the property?

4. Do the leases grant any tenants the right to prevent the owner from leasing the other stores or any new stores to potentially competitive businesses? For example, a tenant who operates a deli may have a right in its lease to preclude the owner from leasing to other stores selling food, or a shoe store may have been granted the right to object to a clothing store that sells footwear.

5. Are there any potential environmental issues? A buyer of commercial real estate generally requires an environmental assessment (Phase I)[10] to determine whether the property is contaminated or otherwise in violation of federal or state environmental regulations. The concern in our case study is even greater because a former tenant was a dry cleaner, which is a red flag because dry cleaners use chemicals that are subject to environmental regulations. Environmental issues are a concern not only because the site can be contaminated, but because the purchaser has successor liability and is responsible for the huge costs of cleaning up the property, even though the contamination occurred prior to the transaction.

---

[10]A Phase I environmental site assessment (ESA) is the first step in the process of environmental due diligence. The ESA report is prepared by an environmental consulting firm that identifies whether there are any existing or potential environmental contamination liabilities. If the ESA discloses contamination issues, a Phase II assessment may be conducted, which is a much more detailed environmental investigation.

6. Do any regulations exist on the use of the property, such as those contained in leases, deeds, or easements? For example, in our case study, the purchaser intends to develop additional stores; however, local zoning laws or other restrictions may preclude the intended development.

7. Are there any regulations that could restrict further development of the property? This information must be acquired by examining local zoning and other laws. Some of these issues include the following:

   - Are there zoning laws that prescribe the amount of frontage required that would seriously alter the planned use of the site?

   - Are there zoning regulations or the right of other municipal authorities to prohibit additional construction because of concerns about the effect on traffic patterns?

   - Are there restrictions on drive-thrus?

   - Are there restrictions on fast-food restaurants?

   - Are there restrictions on the type of signage the fast-food restaurant requires of its franchisees?

   - Are there restrictions on hours of operation and local noise ordinances?

   - Are there parking requirements that reduce the intended square footage of the additional rental properties (thus changing the economics of the deal)?

8. What are the results of the property inspection?

   - Does the building meet all building codes?

   - Is the building structurally sound?

   - Are the equipment, fixtures, and building systems (heating and cooling, alarm) in good working order?

In summary, a commercial real estate transaction involves four separate due diligence investigations that run in parallel: (i) an appraisal to determine the value of the property; (ii) a title search performed by the title company (or, in some states, by a the lawyer) for the purchaser; (iii) the examination conducted by the purchaser through the due diligence questionnaire, professional advisors, and consultants; and (iv) the property inspection.

The Partnership

Recurring to the partnership case study, remember that the buyer is considering the purchase of a 50% interest in an LLC that is a music store. The material facts of the partnership are as follows:

>*Nature of the transaction:* purchase of a 50% interest in a business
>
>*Type of business:* music store
>
>*Entity type:* LLC with one owner
>
>*Consideration:* $35,000
>
>*Additional material facts or issues:* (a) the buyer is concerned about current owner's long-term commitment to the business; (b) the current owner has expertise the purchaser does not regarding a major source of revenue for the business; (c) there is a potential retention issue regarding a key employee; and (d) the purchaser is being asked to become the personal guarantor on the LLC's credit line.

Common Partnership Issues

In our case study, Adrian's proposed purchase of 50% of Rowland's equity in the music store raises financial, legal, and operational issues similar in nature to diligence conducted for a private placement or business buyout:

1. Is the $35,000 a fair purchase price for 50% of the LLC based on past and projected financials?

2. Does the LLC own all the assets necessary to operate the business?

3. Are there any concerns raised by the contracts that are material to operating the business, including the pending expiration of its lease?

4. Are there any concerns with respect to relationships with suppliers and vendors of inventory (in our case, instruments, instrument parts, music books, sheet music, and so on)?

5. Does the company have licenses to key operational systems that include a point-of-sale system that tracks customer purchases and inventory (and, in our case study, a system for scheduling music lessons)?

6. What are the terms under which the employees were hired?

7. Is the business in compliance with employment laws?

8. Does any employee, consultant, or third party have an option or warrant to purchase an interest in the LLC, or a right of first refusal?

9. What are the terms of the operating agreement or any other governance documents?

10. Are there agreements that grant third parties any rights in the business or its assets?

11. Do any agreements

- Include restrictions and obligations that affect ownership, management, and control rights?

- Need to be amended to eliminate the owner's unfettered management authority?

- Need to be amended to protect the purchaser's economic, management, and ownership rights?

- Need to be executed, including a new or amended operating agreement, setting forth the rights and obligations of the partners?

Unique Issues in the Partnership Case Study

As with all deals, the nature of the transaction dictates how the basic due diligence investigation should be structured, and the particular facts of the deal expand the scope of the basic due diligence to address unique aspects of the deal. In our case study, three facts are screaming for attention: (1) Adrian's replacement as a guarantor of the line of credit; (2) Rowland's desire to focus substantial time on a new business venture and, apparently, step out of his day-to-day management of the music store; and (3) the importance of one of the employees to the success of the business.

The requirement that Adrian replace Rowland on the personal guarantee mandates that Adrian not only pay particular attention to the terms of the credit line, but also the finances of the business. Although he is investing $35,000 for 50% of the business (membership interests), his total exposure is currently another $20,000 and up to $50,000 if the entire line of credit is drawn down. The due diligence will already include a number of questions relating to the financial condition of the business, but the potential personal liability arising from the guarantee heightens the level of scrutiny.

The questionnaire needs to consider the following additional issues:

- Do the financials support not only an investment of $35,000, but also a potential additional personal exposure of $50,000 under the line of credit?

- Will the Operating Agreement give purchaser sufficient authority with respect to financial matters?

- Should the purchaser demand, as a condition of the investment, that the operating agreement provide a veto authority on additional credit line draw-downs?

Rowland has been clear about his intention to focus half his time on his new bar. What is unique about this fact is that it is not an issue that is revealed through the written due diligence questionnaire, but through the purchaser's discussions with the seller. However, once this fact is known, the due diligence needs to address:

- What authority will the purchaser have relating to the operation of the business?

- Does an operating agreement or other documents need to be executed or amended to give the purchaser control over the business operations?

- Are any of the current employees capable of managing the daily operations of the business?

Rowland's departure as the full-time manager of the music store raises the issue of whether he will still provide sufficient time to repair instruments, which has been a major reason for the success of the business. If it appears that he will not have the time, the deal may no longer hold its value. There are solutions, the most obvious is to ensure the employee, Joel, whose reputation is growing and drawing an increasing number of customers, remains with the business. If Joel is a possible answer, the due diligence requires extra attention:

- Is Joel an employee at will (and therefore can he leave at any time)?

- What can the store do to retain Joel?

- If there are additional employment expenses to retain Joel, what is the impact on the business's financials?

The Material Contract

Material contracts come in many different forms, such as joint venture, development, co-marketing, and distribution and licensing agreements. Our case study is concerned with a licensing agreement: Kilbourn Pet Toys wants to license three patents from Jordan Creatives Ltd., a company incorporated in the British Virgin Islands and headquartered in Hong Kong. The key facts of the deal are as follows:

Nature of the transaction: exclusive patent license

Type of business: intellectual property holding company

Entity type: British Virgin Islands (BVI) limited company

Consideration: royalties

Additional material facts or issues: the licensor is a foreign company formed in the BVI; the company is headquartered in Hong Kong; and the company has no business operations other than as a licensor of intellectual property.

Common Material Contract Issues

Although the scope of this investigation may be limited compared with other deal types, the intent is the same: verification that the transaction is a good idea financially and legally. The potential licensee must address financial and legal concerns similar to other business deals:

1. Is the licensor duly organized and does the licensor have the authority to enter into the license agreement?

2. Does the licensor have all rights, title, and interest in the assets (in our case study, the three patents)?

3. Has the licensor pledged the patents as security for a loan?[11]

4. Are there are liens, judgments, or pending or threatened claims against the company or the patents?

5. Are there existing licenses, options, or other rights that can be asserted by a third party with respect to the patents?

6. What is the potential value of the license?

7. What is the financial status of the licensor (as a bankruptcy could disrupt the rights of the licensee)?

---

[11] The license agreement needs to address licensee's rights in the event of a default on any loan secured by the patents or of licensor's bankruptcy.

Unique Issues for the Material Contract Case Study

In the context of a potential license agreement, the licensee should ask the licensor to provide the legal and financial information necessary to establish ownership of the intellectual property and its financial ability to both maintain the patents and meet its obligations under the license agreement. The licensee should not rely solely on the licensor's responses to the due diligence questions. The licensee should also independently investigate issues that arise based on the specific facts underlying the proposed agreement.

Here, the licensee needs to address the following issues:

- Has a patent search been conducted in the USPTO and any foreign jurisdiction where the patents have purportedly been granted to confirm the issuance of the patents to the licensor and thus the ownership rights?[12] If the licensee cannot confirm licensor's right to grant the license, the exposure to the licensee can be substantial, including a claim for royalties from the rightful patent owner or manufacturing and marketing costs for products it cannot sell legally.

- Has a search been conducted under the Uniform Commercial Code (UCC), because there are conflicting views regarding the proper method for a lien holder to file a security interest in patents?[13]

- Since the licensor is not based in the United States, how can the licensee verify the license is enforceable in the event of a breach and that it will be able to pursue and collect on any action against the licensor?

- How can the licensee verify that the licensor has not granted licensing rights to any other persons or entities? The licensee is paying for an exclusive license, and does not want a lawsuit in the future from a previously undisclosed licensee who claims to have rights to a particular market.

---

[12]The importance of conducting public record searches, including a search of patent and trademark information available at the USPTO, is discussed in Chapter 9.

[13]The consensus is that, to perfect a security interest in a patent against subsequent lien creditors, the secured creditor must file a UCC financing statement with the secretary of state of the state where the debtor is located. To perfect a security interest in a patent against subsequent bona fide purchasers, the secured creditor must also record the security interest with the USPTO. In our case study, there is the additional issue that the licensor is located in Hong Kong and incorporated in the BVI, and some of the patents may be foreign registered. If so, the licensee needs to engage the assistance of foreign patent counsel to verify licensor's unencumbered title to the foreign patents.

Conclusion

This chapter looked at several different types of business transactions to distill the aliquot of universal deal-type questions in the due diligence questionnaire. In addition, this chapter examined deal-specific questions that are formulated to address issues arising from the terms of the transaction and significant facts relating to the business and material aspects of target company's operations. I dissected several typical transactions to identify their basic facts, then highlighted significant due diligence issues that are common and unique for each deal type. I interwove examples from our case studies to show some of the unique types of questions that should be asked during the due diligence investigation.

A Material Legal Issue Can Kill the Deal

The previous chapters examined the role of the due diligence process in a business transaction, the importance of preparing a due diligence plan as a road map for the investigation, and formulation of the due diligence questionnaire, which should include standard questions common to almost all business transactions, and deal-type and deal-specific questions that depend on the nature and terms of the proposed business deal. Although the target company hopes no negative issues are discovered, due diligence can uncover a variety of issues. Some can be resolved with a relatively easy financial or legal fix, others by renegotiation of the deal terms, and still others are so serious that termination of the proposed transaction may be the only option.

This chapter discusses several issues that result in the termination of a potential transaction because the deal terms cannot be met; resolution of the issue will take too long, is too uncertain, or will be too costly; the risks of proceeding are deemed too great; or the deal is unpalatable because of an unexpected issue discovered during the due diligence investigation.

Material issues uncovered during the legal due diligence investigation can kill a deal. Termination of a deal can arise for the following reasons:

- A party conducts due diligence after executing a non-binding letter of intent or memorandum of understanding, discovers fundamental issues relating to the business, and—because the party has no legal obligation to proceed—simply decides not to pursue the transaction.[1]

- In the absence of a binding agreement, the parties are unable or unwilling to renegotiate the terms to address issues discovered in the due diligence process.

- A binding agreement has been entered into but the closing of the transaction was contingent on the absence of any material due diligence issues, and the due diligence investigation uncovers several material financial, legal, operational, or personnel issues.

- A binding agreement exists but the due diligence investigation reveals that the borrower, seller, or potential deal partner cannot fulfill the financial or legal preconditions required to close the transaction.

Given the plethora of issues that can lead to the termination of a business deal, the focus here is on many of the material issues commonly discovered through due diligence.

Legality and Compliance with the Law

A transaction cannot proceed if it is illegal. Hiring a hitman to kill your business partner, even if arguably deserved, is not only a crime but also voids the agreement from its inception (void *ab initio*). No due diligence or legal research is necessary to tell you this, presumably. There are less obvious hurdles that can delay considerably or altogether preclude completion of a business deal because they require government approvals or permits, or may even be prohibited by the laws of the relevant jurisdiction. Although any number of examples illustrate situations when a legal issue precludes the completion of a transaction, the following are intended to provide a flavor of the variety of legal roadblocks that can be discovered during the due diligence process.

One issue that can arise in a cross-border transaction is the application of foreign law to one or more aspects of the deal. Foreign law obviously is relevant when the company that is the subject of the transaction is headquartered

---

[1]As discussed in Chapter 9, a nonbinding letter of intent or memorandum of understanding often precedes a binding agreement.

outside the United States. However, it also can affect the transaction when the company has been formed under foreign law, even if it operates solely in the United States, or there are subsidiaries or other business operations abroad. For example, consider a deal involving the purchase of a U.S. business that purportedly owns real estate in a foreign country. A review of the law where the real estate is located might reveal that only citizens of that country can own real property or certain types of businesses. A lawyer from the country where the property or business is located would need to be engaged to review and opine on foreign legal issues. The U.S. purchaser might learn that he or she cannot own the foreign real estate or can only own a noncontrolling interest, such that the property would be legally owned by a foreign partner. Under such circumstances, the U.S. buyer may no longer be interested in the transaction because of the difficulties and potential risk of having no or limited control over a material business asset located in a foreign jurisdiction.

Another potential legal obstacle arises if there are aspects of the deal that require approval from a federal, state, or local agency or government authority. The inability to obtain such approval could lead to termination of the transaction or a significant downward valuation if, for example, the purchaser or investor was planning on a business expansion that was dependent on obtaining certain government approvals. For example, the strip mall transaction (Case Study 5) may not be of interest to the potential purchaser if she learns that zoning and other local board approvals for a planned expansion could take many months, could require significant alteration of the planned structure, or could result in a reduction in the permitted size of the expansion, or that there is a possibility the authorizations won't be obtained at all. The inability to obtain the necessary approvals may render the economics of the transaction completely uninteresting, leading the buyer to terminate the deal.

A permit or license may be required to operate all or a part of a business. A change of ownership of a business or its assets may require the company to acquire a new license, or the previous permit may be assigned to the new owner subject to certain conditions. Due diligence in this situation would include inquiries about the necessity of any licenses to operate the business, and whether permits and licenses can be reassigned. A restaurant owner that has a large outdoor meal service would want to make sure the outdoor café permit can be assigned and that the conditions for approval of the assignment are met. A liquor license cannot be assigned; thus, if the new owner of a bar-cannot qualify for the license for whatever reason, pursuing the transaction does not make sense. The purchaser of a manufacturing business would inquire whether the business is in good standing with respect to the permits related to the disposal of hazardous materials or pollutants. An investor in a staffing agency would make sure the agency has the state mandated business licenses. The buyer may even discover that the business never had the requisite licenses or permits to operate in the first place. The absence of or inability to obtain required licenses can leave a purchaser no choice other than to terminate the transaction.

Separate from the need to obtain licenses or approvals, some businesses are heavily regulated and are subject to substantial compliance with a detailed set of laws and regulations. For example, manufacturing companies are subject to safety and health regulations, including those under the Occupational Safety and Health Administration (OSHA), and *any* business that collects customer information is subject to privacy and data security laws. The failure to comply with these laws can result in substantial fines or even lead to the closure of the business. If, during the course of the due diligence process the buyer of or investor in the business learns the prospective company has numerous OSHA complaints, is in violation of environmental laws, or has no policies or procedures to ensure compliance with privacy rules, the risks created by these legal issues may override the desire to own or invest in the business.

Last, there are simple administrative, licensing, or other fees that, if not paid, can result in the dissolution of a business entity, loss of a key business license, or even loss of the rights to a valuable asset. For example, failure to pay annual state corporation fees (referred to in some jurisdictions as a *franchise fee*) can result in eventual dissolution of the entity. Although reinstatement may be possible, until the matter is resolved, the transaction cannot proceed. As another example, if a patent holder fails to pay maintenance or renewal fees in each jurisdiction where the patent is issued, the patent will be forfeited (Case Study 6).

These are just a few examples of conditions under which a transaction may be precluded by law altogether or cannot proceed until issues relating to legal compliance, licensing, or other government approvals are resolved.

Ownership Issues Relating to Assets

As discussed in previous chapters, a fundamental aspect of due diligence in most transactions is establishing the other party's ownership or rights to the key business assets. Consider the following examples:

- In a secured loan transaction (Case Study 1), the lender would never agree to make the loan if due diligence disclosed that the borrower did not own the assets offered as collateral for the transaction. If it is discovered that the borrower does not own the assets, the lender has no security for the loan in the event of a default.

- A deal involving the purchase of a business, whether structured as an asset sale or as a stock purchase deal, obviously cannot proceed if the seller does not own the material business assets (Case Studies 2 and 3).

- An investor would not proceed with the purchase of interest in a company if it is determined the company does not own or have the rights to key business assets (Case Studies 4 and 7).

- A buyer would not purchase commercial property if the seller cannot convey the title to the property (Case Study 5).

- A license of intellectual property is an illusory agreement if the licensor does not own or have the right to license the intellectual property (Case Study 6).

In many transactions, proving ownership or rights to the assets of a business is fairly straightforward—a bill of sale, a purchase contract, or a title demonstrates ownership. A patent issued by the relevant government patent office in the name of the licensor generally establishes ownership for purposes of a license agreement. However, in other transactions, due diligence may reveal that the target company either cannot or may have difficulty proving ownership of material business assets. The purchaser of the strip mall (Case Study 5) would not move forward with the deal if the title report discloses there is a defect in the seller's title to the property that cannot be resolved. A licensee would not enter into a license agreement if he or she learns there is a pending lawsuit by a purported inventor challenging the validity of the patent.

The ABB transaction (Case Study 2) is an example of the due diligence process leading to a discovery of a serious concern regarding the seller's ability to prove it owns the material assets to be conveyed in the proposed transaction. Recall that, during the course of the due diligence investigation, Jack's lawyer learns that Leah's former business partner, Dana, never contributed the ABB software—which she developed—to ABB. Without an assignment from Dana to ABB of all intellectual property and other rights, the ownership of the software remains in question. The lawyer has, therefore, advised Jack correctly in not to proceed with the transaction unless Dana executes an assignment of the software to ABB.

Ownership of important tangible or intangible assets is a major aspect of a due diligence investigation. The inability to demonstrate sufficiently the ownership of or the rights to use such assets, or to resolve any issues if discovered, inevitably results in termination of a proposed purchase, investment, license, or partnership transaction.

Encumbrances

Another issue discovered during the due diligence investigation that may lead to termination of a proposed deal is the existence of liens or other encumbrances on the assets of the business. Encumbrances occur with the consent of the company, such as a mortgage on real property or the granting of a security interest on tangible or intangible assets in connection with a loan. Liens or other encumbrances can also attach to the assets of a business without consent (for example, as a result of a creditor's enforcement of a judgment or the failure to pay local, state, or federal taxes). In some circumstances, the discovery of a lien or other encumbrance on the assets of a business necessitates termination of the transaction.

For example, a lender in a secured loan transaction would not want to make a loan if he learned that (i) the state tax authorities have a lien for the full value of the collateral, (ii) the assets are fully collateralized in connection with an existing loan, or (iii) a judgment creditor has obtained a lien in an amount that exceeds the value of the collateral (Case Study 1).[2] A potential investor may discover through due diligence that a large-judgment creditor has commenced proceedings to collect on its judgment and is seeking enforcement against all the assets of the business. Similarly, the due diligence investigation could uncover a pending foreclosure action by a judgment creditor against patents that a company needs to license to manufacture and sell its new product (Case Study 6).

The strip mall transaction (Case Study 5) is a good example of a nonmonetary encumbrance that cannot be resolved and could therefore cause cancelation of the proposed transaction. In the strip mall transaction, the buyer has determined there is a good financial opportunity in purchasing the strip mall not only because of the existing rent roll but also because of the potential to develop additional stores on the undeveloped land. If the title search discloses an existing mortgage or unpaid real estate taxes, the transaction could proceed, as long as the liens are satisfied at or before the closing. However, what if the title search discovers an easement that gives an adjacent land owner the right of ingress and egress to the undeveloped land and he is demanding a ridiculous sum to relinquish the easement? In this case, the existing easement would preclude the purchaser from pursuing additional development of the property and, most likely, she would not want to proceed with the transaction.

Third-Party Rights

An effective due diligence questionnaire includes questions designed to determine whether any third parties have rights that can affect transaction completion or significantly undermine the transaction valuation. Sometimes a third

---

[2]As discussed in Chapters 6 and 8, material due diligence often can be resolved. For instance, in this case, the lender's funds could be used to satisfy the existing lien. On the other hand, if the lender intended the loan for a specific purpose, such as the development of a software application, use of the loan funds for a different purpose is not a solution.

party holds rights with respect to the business or its assets and, in the absence of a waiver of that right, the purchaser or investor should not risk proceeding with the transaction.

A common issue that can be overlooked is a third party's right of first refusal, or an option to purchase the assets or stock of a company. In the strip mall transaction (Case Study 5), the buyer's interest in the deal is largely based on her desire to use an undeveloped lot to expand the footprint of the mall. If she discovers that the seller granted an adjacent land owner an option to purchase the undeveloped lot, she would most likely walk away from the deal. In the example of a patent license (Case Study 6), if the licensor granted a third party the option to the license for a particular country, the licensor could not grant a worldwide patent license without securing a waiver of the option.

Rights of first refusal are often granted investors in private-equity financing transactions as further consideration for an investor's participation in early financing rounds. In addition, owners of a class of preferred stock may have obtained the right to approve the terms of any subsequent offerings below a certain valuation to prevent excessive dilution of their ownership interest. The failure of to obtain the approval of the preferred stockholders to issue the additional shares would require termination of the proposed subsequent financing round.

Third-party rights may be as obvious as a right of first refusal or they may be buried in a contract clause prohibiting an assignment of a contract that is an essential aspect of the transaction. In the ABB asset sale (Case Study 2), the assets to be purchased include contracts with major retail chains. However, Jack's lawyer discovered that several of the contracts contain antiassignment clauses that prohibit transfer of the contracts absent the approval of the retailers. Jack's lawyer discovered this issue because the due diligence questionnaire expressly asked for a copy of each contract with the chain stores. To address this issue, during negotiation, Jack should demand that the seller obtain all consents from the chain stores. Absent the written approval of the retailers, a material aspect of the ABB transaction cannot be satisfied and Jack most likely won't go ahead with the deal.

The right of first refusal, an option, or an approval right may be in any number of agreements or documents, including, for example, an investor rights agreement, an operating agreement, a shareholders agreement, a loan document, a license agreement, or the (anti) assignment clause of a contract. If the rights holder is given notice of the proposed offer and then exercises his or her rights (or, in the case of an approval right, refuses to give consent), the potential deal may terminate. What is substantially more problematic is failure to give notice to the right holder, who subsequently learns of the deal and then sues to enforce his or her rights.

Lawsuits and Judgments

Another issue that can give rise to cancelation of a proposed transaction is the existence of a pending, or even threatened, lawsuit, or administrative (government) or criminal action against the company, its assets, or its key personnel. The due diligence questionnaire should include requests for information about pending or threatened lawsuits or claims (see Chapter 7 and Appendix B). The discovery of a material lawsuit or claim can render the transaction too risky or even legally incapable of being completed. The following situations demonstrate how a lawsuit or claim can lead to termination of a business deal.

A company would not want to make a secured loan if it learns there is a pending lawsuit regarding rights to the collateral (Case Study 1). A lawsuit that seeks substantial monetary damages could raise issues regarding the valuation of the business and thereby create an insurmountable risk for the lender.

If, in the context of the ABB asset sale (Case Study 2), Jack discovers through due diligence that Dana filed a lawsuit seeking a declaratory judgment that she owns the ABB software, Jack would not want to close the transaction until there is a final court decision. If the court rules in favor of Dana, it would be legally impossible to proceed with the sale of the asset to Jack.

The investor in the private placement transaction involving Karly Medical (Case Study 4) probably would not want to proceed if, during the course of a due diligence investigation, the investor discovers that the company had received inquiries from the Food and Drug Administration (FDA) about some of the medical claims made by the company regarding its new medical device. Along the same lines, the discovery of a fraud investigation against a company and/or a founder by the Securities Exchange Commission would certainly scare off any potential investor. As noted in previous chapters, due diligence should include not only a search for civil lawsuits, but also claims or threatened actions by administrative agencies that may govern an aspect of the company's business, as well as searches for pending or threatened actions against key personnel.

It is important to inquire about pending and threatened lawsuits or administrative actions. A letter from the Environmental Protection Agency (EPA) or a state's department of environmental conservation inquiring about the activities of a tenant that operates a laundromat should raise red flags for the potential purchaser of a commercial property (Case Study 5). The inquiry eventually could lead to tremendous financial exposure and a nightmare of obligations relating to remediation of the environmental issues. A buyer cannot legally avoid responsibility simply because the environmental issues arose before purchase of the property.[3] Unless the potential claims are resolved or the purchaser obtains a clear picture of the financial exposure and legal obligations of moving forward, proceeding with the transaction would be foolhardy.

Employment or labor issues can also create significant obstacles for any business. Suppose that, during the course of a due diligence investigation relating to the purchase of an interest in a business, the buyer learns there are numerous wage claims and the business is being audited by tax authorities for improper classification of employees as consultants, and that there have been sexual harassment complaints against the owner filed with the Equal Employment Opportunity Commission. A new partner would most likely not want to become an owner in a business is under fire from the EEOC or the IRS that could lead to substantial liability or the risk of recurring audits by employment or tax authorities. The existence of sexual harassment complaints may not alone be a legal obstacle to entering into a partnership, but they should cause the potential investor to question whether the business owner would make a good business partner.

If the due diligence investigation uncovers an impending or threatened lawsuit or administrative action, the nature of the existing or potential claims needs to be understood thoroughly. Additional information and documents relating to the claims should be requested, and a determination regarding the legal, financial, and other potential issues should be vetted, which may require engaging professionals with the expertise to provide advice on particular claims. For example, in Case Study 5, an environmental consultant could advise on an EPA claim; or in Case Study 4, a regulatory lawyer could render an opinion on an FDA inquiry. An impending lawsuit or action may necessitate a transaction delay until the matter is resolved, or an outright termination of the transaction because the claim renders completion of the transaction impossible or destroys the financial underpinnings of the deal.

Employment and Personnel

The disclosure of employment or personnel issues can result in termination of a deal. The due diligence questionnaire therefore will include questions with respect to personnel matters, including fundamental questions relating to employment terms of key personnel; compliance with labor laws; existence

---

[3]One solution, which is discussed in Chapter 8, is to obtain an indemnification from the seller. Leaving aside the question of the seller's ability to meet the financial obligations of the indemnification, the remediation could be so disruptive to the other tenants or so extensive that it renders indemnification meaningless.

of employee stock pools; whether personnel have signed confidentiality, invention assignment, and noncompete agreements; and employment/wage claims. Employment issues can affect a company's finances and overall operations in various ways, such as the following:

> *Ownership of assets:* If employees, including founders, have not signed an invention assignment agreement, there could be issues regarding ownership of a company's intellectual property.

> *Noncompete/nonsolicitation:* If employees or partners are not required to sign nonsolicitation and noncompete agreements, or the noncompete is unreasonable and therefore cannot be enforced, the company risks competition from former employees or partners who have valuable business information.

> *Capital structure:* Stock options or profit share rights may be a good method for retaining key personnel, but they also affect a company's capital structure. If the potential dilution from issuance option-related shares is too great, potential investors may decide not to invest.

> *Reasonableness of compensation terms of directors and key personnel:* A purchaser of or investor in a company, or a new business partner should review carefully the terms of all employment agreements with directors and key employees to verify the reasonableness of compensation, benefits, and other the financial obligations.

> *Employee retention:* An investment in a new-technology company can be too risky if a key employee who does not have an employment agreement has expressed an intention to leave, or the pivotal inventor who is responsible for developing the company's new medical device has a terminal illness, or if the contract of an important manager is expiring.

> *Compliance:* The failure to comply with employment laws can expose the business to substantial financial risks, including large civil judgments; obligations to pay back-wages and additional taxes, interest, and penalties under state and federal tax laws.

Personnel vetting: It is not unusual to require founders and potential partners to submit to a background check and credit report. Investing in a company in which the founder has filed for bankruptcy may not be an appealing investment. Nor would you want to become a partner in a medical practice in which the current partners failed to discover the billing manager had been convicted of Medicaid fraud.

Due diligence can lead to the discovery of a variety of personnel matters that may result in cancelation of a business deal either because of existing or potential issues that create financial or legal risks for the company.

Structural Issues

The diligence review may reveal that the target company or potential business partner purposely or unintentionally misrepresented information about the company that destroys the financial or legal underpinnings of the deal. Consider how altering facts relating to the structure of the business affects the following example transactions negatively:

Loan transaction/corporate name change: During the course of the due diligence process in connection with a secured loan, the lender learns the name of the business was changed a year earlier and a UCC-1 (security interest) was filed on all the assets under the old business name. The lender would not want to make a loan to the company under these circumstances.

Stock buyout/annual corporate compliance: A company selling its stock in a buyout unknowingly failed to pay annual state fees. As a result, the company was dissolved administratively—meaning, the purchaser would be buying stock from a nonexistent corporation.

Stock investment/capitalization: On reviewing the capitalization table (commonly referred to as the *cap table*), an investor intending to purchase Series A stock realizes the number of outstanding (issued) shares in the company is 15% more than originally believed, as a result of uncovering existing employee stock options and a convertible loan held by a founder. With this dilution, the valuation of the business is no longer in line with the investor's view of the company.

Stock purchase/tax status: A company elected for S Corp status, allowing for tax treatment as a partnership rather than a corporation, to avoid double taxation. The problem is the potential investor is not a U.S. citizen and cannot be a shareholder in an S Corp.

Partnership/business structure: The purchaser of 50% of a music store finds that the same LLC that operates the music business owns the building where the business is located. The purchaser's lawyer and accountant strongly urge transfer of the real estate to a separate entity that charges the music business rent. The restructuring ensures that the real estate is no longer exposed to the liabilities of the business, and allows the entity that owns the operating business to have a write-off relating to the payment of rent to the real estate entity. The owner refuses, claiming that maintaining two businesses is a hassle, doubles bookkeeping obligations, and increases accounting costs unnecessarily. The accountant and lawyer might advise the purchaser against proceeding with the transaction because they are uncomfortable with the legal and tax structure of the business.

Partnership/governing documents: A review of the operating agreement for an LLC with six members reveals that the business is member managed and, as a result, each member has the authority to manage the business and bind the company to contracts, loans, and any other agreements and undertakings. The potential new member realizes she does not want to become a partner in a business in which the disengaged member who holds 5% of the membership interests has the same authority to bind the company as majority member and founder. Although she asks for a revision of the operating agreement to create a manager-managed entity, the existing agreement expressly requires unanimous approval of any amendment—and it is easy to guess who won't approve the change. The potential new member does not pursue the deal.

Structural issues can create financial or legal risks that are simply too great for a deal to survive. There also can be circumstances when the structural issue can be addressed—for example, through an amendment of governing corporate documents—but the ability to make the change may be thwarted by other factors, such as the unbending shareholder who can veto the easy fix.

If issues relating to the structure of the business or affecting the structure of the deal cannot be resolved, termination of the transaction may be the only option.

Intangible Issues

There are some due diligence issues that do not raise legal or financial concerns, but nevertheless may cause a party to decide against a proposed business deal. These issues can manifest themselves as moral or other concerns that cannot be categorized and are, essentially, intangible factors that are important enough to the particular buyer or investor regardless of how others may see the issue.

A plethora of intangible factors can result in termination of a deal. For example, the purchaser of the strip mall might find it objectionable that current owner signed a lease with an adult book store one week after the letter of intent to purchase the property was executed. A person buying into a business partnership might disagree with the continued employment of a manager who is the subject of a pending sexual harassment lawsuit and whose presence is creating issues for other female employees. A patent licensor might decide not to proceed with a license if the licensor learns the potential licensee, who intends to make dog toys, has contracted with a foreign manufacturer accused of using lead-based products in the production of cat toys. Or, as final example, a potential partner in an indoor flea market venture may be opposed to including a person in the partnership who has a very poor reputation among vendors at another location owned by the potential partner. None of these examples creates an actual legal or financial due diligence issue, but each could still result in a party backing out of a proposed deal because the issue renders the transaction unappealing for moral or other intangible reasons.

Conclusion

There are numerous issues that can ultimately result in cancelation of a transaction at any stage during the due diligence investigation. Termination of the transaction may become necessary because there is no way to resolve the issue, or any possible resolution of the issue is so risky or costly that it is not really a resolution at all. In the next chapter, we explore two concepts: (1) possible fixes for many common due diligence issues and (2) circumstances when the due diligence investigation creates an opportunity for a party to negotiate a more favorable transaction by altering the financial terms or deal structure, or by demanding additional rights from, or imposing additional obligations on, the target business.

Has Due Diligence Created an Opportunity to Improve the Deal Terms?

An overarching theme of the due diligence investigation is an attempt to verify the business story as told by the seller, potential partner, or the company seeking financing (hereafter, "the seller"). Chapter 5 discussed examples of how the discovery of certain types of legal issues results in termination of a proposed deal because they undermine the business story. Some deals fail because they are legally impossible to complete or simply too risky, costly, or uninteresting from a financial or business standpoint. Not all issues discovered during the due diligence process end in termination of a proposed transaction, however. Rather, there are usually financial, legal or business solutions that can remedy the issue or issues. For the party conducting the due diligence investigation (hereafter, "the buyer"), the discovery of information challenging a seller's story can create an opportunity to renegotiate financial or legal terms, or aspects of the proposed deal, or may require the seller to make changes to its business operations. Any solution proposed by a buyer must still be acceptable, of course, to the seller. In many cases, however, the seller may have no choice but to accept revisions to the original deal terms if it wants the transaction to proceed. This chapter explores common due diligence issues that can create an opportunity for the party conducting the due diligence investigation to negotiate more favorable financial terms, deal structure, or rights when the other party is motivated to move forward with the deal done.

First we examine whether the other party to the transaction is a *motivated seller*. In others words, the seller is willing to renegotiate the initial terms of the deal to address issues discovered by the buyer during the due diligence. Second, we take a look at some of the more common issues that provide a compelling basis to renegotiate deal terms: unsupportable valuation assumptions, management and governance issues, operational weaknesses, personnel issues, and concerns relating to corporate structure.

Is the Other Party a Motivated Seller?

It does not matter how minor or significant the issue, if the other party to the transaction is not interested in revisiting pre-due diligence deal terms then there is no chance to negotiate based on issues discovered during the investigation. At some point during the deal, the buyer, who is conducting the due diligence investigation, advises the seller about any financial, legal, or other issues that were discovered. If the issues do not undermine the fundamental assumptions of the transaction—and thereby mandate deal termination (as discussed in Chapter 5)—then the next step is to consider available options to address issues disclosed by the investigation. Sometimes the fixes are quite simple and do not provide a legitimate basis for demanding changes to previously negotiated terms. Other times, a buyer may have reasonable grounds to argue for renegotiation of the original deal terms. Regardless of the nature of the issue, the seller must have a motivation for making the deal happen. Absent some motivating reason to complete the transaction, resolution of issues is unlikely to occur.

The target of the due diligence investigation (the seller) can be motivated by financial or a variety of other reasons to agree to revise deal terms based on the due diligence findings. If you wish to renegotiate material deal terms, to request additional rights, or to ask the seller to accept pre- or postclosing obligations,[1] it is important to understand what might motivate the seller to accept the revised terms. The potential reasons why a seller might be motivated are numerous and may include the following:

- The potential for the seller to realize a large financial gain that, even under any proposed revised terms is still substantial enough to motivate him or her to accept revised deal terms

- A limited window for the seller to take advantage of a closing tax loophole, change in tax law, or other favorable tax treatment

- The existence of substantial liabilities that cannot be satisfied without disposing of all or some of the assets of the business

- The seller's need for funds to pursue other business plans

- Current business partners who disagree on important issues that affect the business negatively

- The acquisition of a new partner who brings a skill set or particular assets that provide an opportunity for dramatic growth of the business

- The death, disability, imminent retirement, or personal issues of the seller

If the buyer understands that the seller is motivated and, even more important, knows the factors driving the seller, the buyer can leverage that knowledge to rework the terms of the deal. Contrast the motivated seller with a company that is not burdened by external factors to achieve a deal; their response to due diligence issues raised by the buyer—and any attempts to revise the deal terms—may be "Take it or leave it."

Unsupportable Valuation Assumptions

The valuation of a business or its assets ultimately determines the amount a lender is willing to loan a business (loan transaction, Case Study 1); the price a buyer is willing to pay to purchase a business or its assets (asset sale, Case

---

[1]Most transactions have a few standard preclosing conditions, such as a board resolution authorizing the transaction or certification by the company regarding the continuing validity of the representations and warranties contained in the contract. The preclosing conditions referred to here (and discussed in detail in Chapter 8) are specific conditions incorporated in the definitive agreements to address issues discovered during due diligence.

Study 2; business buyout, Case Study 3; and commercial real estate transaction, Case Study 5), or to pay the fees that are reasonable in connection with an intellectual property license (Case Study 6). When a buyer learns that the due diligence investigation does not support the deal's valuation assumptions, his reaction should be the same as if he was offered a used car for a price that exceeds the Bluebook value: negotiate new terms or strongly consider walking from the deal.

What, then, are reasonable grounds for renegotiating deal terms based on valuation concerns? The legal, financial, operational, or other issues that can negatively affect the valuation of a business are wide ranging, especially because valuation is not only a factor for determining what is fair consideration (e.g., the purchase price), it also can influence other deal terms. This section presents several examples in which (1) due diligence issues call into question valuation assumptions and (2) how this might affect not only the financial terms, but also how it can result in reconsideration of other aspects of the deal.

Financing Transaction (Case Study 1)

The lender in a secured loan transaction is trying to determine whether the borrower has the financial ability to pay the interest and repay the principal and, if not, whether the collateral is sufficient to satisfy the loan obligations. The due diligence investigation will focus on evaluating the borrower's current and projected financial situation as well as the value of the assets offered as collateral for the loan. Examples of common issues that are apparent from a company's financials and that affect the valuation of its business or assets negatively include a finding that the borrower's

- Liabilities are greater than represented, whether because of previously undisclosed loans, the existence of a substantial legal judgment, a large potential for warranty claims resulting from an issue with one of its products, unresolved tax issues, or any number of other financial obligations

- Revenues are declining

- Operating expenses have increased and profit margins are shrinking

- Original assumptions about the fair market value of the collateral are not supported by an actual appraisal

The valuation of the borrower or the assets of the borrower can also be called into question other than through a review of the company's financials. For example,

- A concern that profit margins will be affected by regulatory changes, requiring costly changes to the products or services

- The announcement that a competitor plans to open up a store nearby

- The possibility of a substantial decline in revenues resulting from the loss of a major client, the pending termination of a significant contract, or the departure of a key employee

- The filing or several lawsuits against the company claiming substantial damages

- The owner's key man insurance policy is expiring and health issues have created serious questions about the ability to renew[2]

If, during the course of the due diligence investigation, the lender learns that the valuation of the borrower's business or the collateral is less than initially believed, the borrower needs to reconsider the terms of the loan in light of the increased deal risks. The lender can choose to walk if itdeems the risks too great or offer to proceed only if the borrower accepts new loan terms aimed at ameliorating the increased risk.

Possible solutions are as follows:

- Reduce the amount the lender is willing to lend the company or divide the loan into multiple advances and condition each advance on the company satisfying defined milestones. The milestones could include revenue targets or a reduction in operating expenses.

- Revise payment terms. For example, the lender may originally have been willing to grant an interest-only loan with a balloon payment at maturity; however, given the increased financial risk, the lender could instead require monthly payments of principal as well.

---

[2]A key employee insurance policy provides the company insurance proceeds on the death or disability of a significant business partner or employee. The insurance is intended to address at least the initial financial impact from the death or disability of the key partner or employee.

- Include additional grounds for default and acceleration of the loan, such as the failure to meet certain revenue milestones or the reduction of expenses.

- Consider whether the company has other collateral to offer, such as receivables and demand personal loan guarantees.

- Include terms that require management to provide financial information (e.g., balance sheets and sales figures) on a monthly basis so that the lender can monitor the financial condition of the company.

- Impose financial controls on management or require management to seek lender approval for certain expenses.

- Require additional insurance while the loan is outstanding.

Asset Sale and Business Buyout (Case Studies 2 and 3)

The information obtained during the due diligence investigation will aid the buyer in determining whether the valuation of the business assets, as in the case of ABB's sale of its software and material contracts (Case Study 2), or of the business itself, in the case of a business buyout (Case Study 3), is reasonable. If the due diligence investigation uncovers facts raising legitimate questions regarding the valuation of particular assets or of an entire business, the purchaser then has just cause to demand reduction of the purchase price or other changes to the deal terms. In an asset sale or business buyout, the valuation of the assets to be acquired or of an entire business can be called into question as a result of due diligence. First, there may be financial issues disclosed by the seller's financial documents:

- Revenues of the business or, in effect, those generated by the assets, are less than the buyer understood when the deal was originally negotiated

- Revenues generated by the business or the assets are declining

- There is a high volume of customer refunds or product warranty claims

- Operating costs of the business or the costs to maintain and exploit the assets are higher than originally believed and cannot be reduced by the buyer

Possible solutions are as follows:

- Demand a reduced purchase price.

- Pay the purchase price in installments based on the seller achieving specifically defined milestones.

- Reduce the initial purchase price but give the seller the opportunity to receive additional payments if certain financial milestones are achieved—typically referred to as an *earn-out*.

There also may be legal, financial, or other issues that affect valuation of the business or the assets that cannot be gleaned from the company's financial statements. For example,

- A pending or threatened lawsuit seeking significant monetary damages

  Possible solution: Require an indemnification and escrow a portion of the purchase price to cover any potential claim.

- Questions about the efficiency of the structure of the business from a tax standpoint

  Possible solution: Restructure the business to address tax issues and, if not possible, reduce the purchase price.

- An ongoing tax audit or even a change in tax regulations that could affect the business going forward

  Possible solutions: Require indemnification, escrow a portion of the purchase price, restructure the business, and/or adjust accounting policies.

- The highest grossing salesperson is retiring or is demanding substantial changes in how commissions are structured

  Possible solutions: Reduce the purchase price, structure part of the purchase price as an earn-out, require the seller to hire and train a new salesperson prior to closing, or cooperate in the process after closing.

- The entry of one or more competitors into the same business or market

  Possible solutions: Adjust the purchase price or structure payments of the purchase price in installments that depend on revenue targets.

- A pending or proposed change in the law or the recent adoption of new regulation that makes it more expensive to operate the business or require a change in how the assets are exploited or products are marketed

  Possible solution: Adjust the purchase price.

- The expiration of a major cross-marketing agreement that generates a large percent of seller's revenues

  Possible solutions: Adjust the purchase price, require the seller's postclosing assistance with the negotiation of a contract extension and/or approaching new marketing partners.

A buyer who discovers that valuation assumptions are not supported by financial due diligence or are questionable because of potential legal or other issues should require renegotiation of the deal terms before proceeding with a transaction involving the purchase of a business or its assets.

Private Placement and Partnership (Case Studies 4 and 7)

Similar to the business buyout, in a deal involving the purchase of a noncontrolling interest in a company, there should be a baseline valuation of the business borne out by the due diligence investigation below which the investment would not make sense to the potential investor. As discussed previously, the same concept applies to the purchase of a business or its assets. However, what differentiates the valuation issue for a total business buyout versus a the purchase of a minority interest in a company is the investor's lack of any authority with respect to control and governance of the business. A buyer of a business may have plans for changing the business to increase revenues, cut expenses, improve profitability, or even expand product lines. Therefore, even if the valuation is less than initial expectations, it still may be sufficient to proceed with the transaction. In contrast, a noncontrolling investor needs to be extremely comfortable with the valuation because, unlike in a buyout, the buyer often can do little to improve the business. Therefore, arguably, the purchase of a minority interest requires a somewhat different approach to valuation than the approach a buyer may adopt in the context of a business or asset purchase. The due diligence conducted by a passive investor or a partner buying a minority stake in a business arguably should involve a level of scrutiny that exceeds the business or asset buyout transaction.

For example, assume the investor in the Series A Stock of Karly Medical has been offered 33% of the company for $1.5 million, antidilution rights that are limited to the next financing round, but no rights to be involved with the management of the business (Case Study 4). Similarly, consider Adrian's offer to become a 50/50 owner of a music store (Case Study 7), whose proposed terms would leave the current owner in control of the day-to-day operations. In both circumstances, the investor or new partner is making a decision to become an owner because he or she believes the investment is consistent with the valuation at the time of the investment or the growth of the business as projected by the company's management. If the investor discovers weaknesses in the financials, growth assumptions, or business operations at a later point, he will be at the mercy of the controlling partners, who may have no interest in changing the course of the business.[3]

Accordingly, before proceeding with the purchase of a noncontrolling position in a company, the investor is cautioned to apply a heightened level of scrutiny with respect to, among other aspects of due diligence, the valuation. As with a business purchase, the investor should examine whether the financials support the valuation and whether there are any legal issues that may undermine valuation assumption. In the event the due diligence investigation leads to concerns about the value of the company, the investor must decide whether the deal still makes financial sense, determine whether the company is willing to renegotiate the terms, and, if so, what changes should be requested to address the financial issues.

Possible solutions include the following:

- Adjust the valuation downward, thereby increasing the investor's ownership interest in the company.

- Grant the investor the right to participate in management of the company or at least have a veto on major financial or other business issues.

- Impose financial controls on expenses, and preparation and imposition of business plans with periodic updates.

- Penalize the controlling partner through a reduction of compensation or ownership interest in the business if the company fails to meet financial plans.

On the other hand, if the company is not willing to address the problems highlighted by the due diligence investigation, the only alternative for an investor considering the purchase of a minority stake is to walk away from the deal. Otherwise, she will be at the mercy of the controlling shareholders and has no ability to protect her investment.

---

[3]If there material misrepresentations by the seller that come to light only after the closing, the investor may have legal claims. Enforcing any claims, however, can be costly and may not provide a timely solution if the company needs to restructure operations immediately.

Commercial Real Estate Transaction (Case Study 5)

In a simple purchase of undeveloped real estate, it is easy to see how valuation is generally the most common issue in the transaction. The buyer will obtain an appraisal and will likely not proceed with the transaction if the comparable properties (commonly referred to as *the comps*) are less than the proposed purchase price. However, the appraisal is not the only basis for determining the appropriate valuation of undeveloped or developed commercial real estate. Case Study 5 illustrates other due diligence issues that can affect valuation in the context of the purchase of commercial real estate. Recall that the purchaser is interested in buying the strip mall based on the income it generates as well as the potential to increase the cash flow substantially by adding store fronts on the undeveloped portion of the property. If the assumptions about what the property currently generates and has the potential to generate are wrong, then the valuation on which the purchase price is based is also incorrect. Issues regarding the proper valuation of commercial real estate can arise because

- The value of comparable properties is lower

- Rents generated by the stores are less than represented by the seller

- Rents are likely to decline because of upcoming lease expirations or a tenant is closing her store and is in breach of the lease

- Real estate taxes, insurance, and property maintenance costs are increasing substantially, and the cost cannot be passed onto tenants under existing leases

- A building inspection has been performed and disclosed a leaking roof and the need for a new heating, ventilation and air-conditioning system, all of which will be extremely expensive to resolve

- The owner has received notice of a possible environmental claim and the scope and potential cost of remediation remain unknown

- The proposed development and expansion of the strip mall has been opposed by the local zoning or planning board or will only be approved with substantial revisions that will mean fewer stores can be added, thereby undermining the projected cash flow assumption

The buyer in a commercial real estate transaction will rely on various assumptions about the value of the developed or undeveloped property to be purchased. The assumptions are usually premised on (1) how similar properties are valued in a comparable geographic area; (2) the revenues generated, the operating expenses, and ultimately the cash flow produced by the property; and (3) whether there are plans to develop vacant land or expand the footprint of existing buildings and whether there are any obstacles to the development of the property. These are just some of the issues that could be brought to light as a result of due diligence and would affect the valuation of a commercial real estate transaction negatively. If the due diligence investigation exposes these or other issues undermining the valuation, the purchaser may consider the following solutions.

Possible solutions include the following:

- Renegotiate the purchase price to bring it into line with comparable property values.

- Renegotiate the structure of the purchase price, which can include a partial cash payment at the closing, with the remainder paid in the form of an earn-out based on revenues or profits generated by the property.

- Reduce the purchase price but include a payment to the seller if he successfully assists the purchaser in obtaining the necessary approvals for the development of a vacant portion of the property.

- Include indemnification and escrow clauses that address pending litigation and potential environmental claims.

To reiterate an important theme, a major function of the due diligence examination is to test the valuation assumptions on which the parties initially agreed during their negotiation of the deal terms. If these assumptions are not supported by the due diligence investigation, the buyer may still be willing to continue with the deal subject to revised deal terms reflecting an appropriate valuation of the business.

Operational Issues That Can Undermine Assumptions about the Business

The financial due diligence in a business transaction asks a series of questions designed to determine whether the financial assumptions about the subject business are correct. Put simply, do the financials support the valuation underpinning the transaction? If a company is borrowing money, does the lender have a sufficient level of comfort regarding the borrower's ability to repay (or at least offer sufficient security) in connection with the loan? If a purchaser is buying a business or its assets, or is investing in a business, is the company proposing a fair purchase price in light of its current or projected financial situation? Legal due diligence asks a series of questions seeking to confirm that the business complies with legal obligations; owns or has a right to use its material assets; is not the subject of material civil, administrative, or criminal proceedings; can legally enter into and meet the terms of the proposed transaction; and that there are no major obstacles to timely fulfillment of the deal terms. Whether through the rubric of the financial or legal due diligence, the overall process also elicits information about business operations and how well the business is managed. The discovery of a significant weakness in the business operation or in how the business is managed by its officers, directors, or controlling members next leads to the question of whether there are any reasonable means to address operational or management issues. If there are reasonable fixes, the deal structure, terms, valuation, and postclosing obligations should reflect how operational or management problems are to be addressed. This next section first reviews a few examples of common issues discovered during due diligence arising from weaknesses in the management of the business and then suggests deal terms that can be offered to address these issues.

Operating Expenses and Liabilities Are Excessive

The purchaser of a minority interest in a company or a potential lender should be concerned if financial due diligence exposes that the company does not manage operating expenses well or has substantial unjustifiable liabilities. When the purchaser becomes an owner of a minority interest or the lender makes the loan, he or she will not have the ability to control spending by the company.

Possible solutions include the following:

- Demand a board seat. In the case of the purchase of an ownership interest in a company (Case Study 4), if the investment is significant enough, investors might consider asking for a seat on the board of directors. The directorship would provide an opportunity to participate in major decisions and keep an eye on significant aspects of the financial and business operations.[4]

---

[4] A board seat can also bring risk, especially when there are several other members or shareholders. If a shareholder believes she has a claim against the company, she might join the directors. Some, but certainly not all, closely held companies have Directors and Officers Insurance (D&O), which provides indemnification for liability and litigation costs in many cases. Even if there is a D&O policy, the investor may not want to the potential exposure and hassle of being a defendant in a lawsuit.

- Include an expense covenant. As part of the investment documents or the loan documents, include a covenant that precludes the borrower from taking on more debt and requires the company to obtain investor/lender approval for expenses or an aggregate of expenses in excess of a defined amount. Be aware, however, that drafting the expense covenant can be a bit tricky because it needs to give the investor the authority to approve certain expenses, but cannot constrain management to the extent that it interferes with their ability to run the business.

- Include a covenant that requires management to provide a business plan and periodic budgets with updates. If the company deviates substantially from the business plan or budget without a good justification, a breach of the covenant can trigger additional controls on management.

Management Salaries/Benefits Are Excessive

During the course of due diligence relating to a private equity investment in an early-stage company, it is astonishing how often potential investors discover that management is receiving salaries and benefits that are inconsistent with the financial condition of the business. The founders may view the compensation as necessary to retain key employees, and members of management will argue their compensation is consistent with market rates or that they are sacrificing opportunities by staying with a startup. Compensation-paid management often may be justified; however, investors or new partners may see it differently. They will assert that the proceeds of their investment should be used to address various business needs (e.g., product development, marketing, additional hiring), and that sacrificing compensation now is the trade-off for the potential of a much larger payoff down the road.

Possible solutions include the following:

- Include a use of proceeds provision that limits how the investment (or loan) proceeds can be spent by the company.

- Reduce salaries or benefits. Management obviously may object to a reduction in salary, but if investors feel strongly enough, they may decide to demand the change in management salaries as a condition of the investment.

- Defer salary. A compromise for immediate salary reduction may be a deferral of a portion of the salary, with payment of the deferred amount based on a triggering event. Triggering events can include a change in control/buyout, sale of a majority of the assets, a financing round in which a defined amount needs to be raised, or attainment of revenue or profit targets, or even business milestones (e.g., a product launch). The downside is that the deferral is still an obligation of the company and a liability that affects the company's balance sheet negatively.

- Grant options or an outright issuance of stock to compensate management and key employees, and avoid an immediate drain on the company's finances. The argument against stock options or the issuance of stock is that it dilutes the existing ownership of equity holders, and therefore current and any potential future investors will not be in favor of replacing an undesirable salary structure with substantial dilution. If the parties agree to stock options or an outright grant as a replacement of a portion of salary, the next key issue is to determine how to calculate the amount of options or stock to be granted. The investor may argue for a right to approve grants in excess of a threshold amount to avoid replacing a short-term cash management issue with a long-term concern about dilution.

- Offer key personnel a share of the profit or a bonus when the business achieves defined milestones, in exchange for a near-term reduction of salary. Personnel will be rewarded when the company achieves defined goals without depleting finances at critical development stages of the business. As with stock options or equity grants, the investor should require a clear definition of the triggering milestones for profit share or other bonuses.

Tax Policies and Efficiencies

The due diligence investigation often leads potential investors or buyers to a discovery that the company does not manage tax matters efficiently, creating unnecessary and additional tax liabilities for the business or its members. Mismanagement of tax matters can arise from misapplication or the failure to take advantage of favorable tax rules and regulations. Tax issues can be a result of a variety of problems, including whether the company chose the right corporate structure at the time it was formed (e.g., would an LLC have been a better choice than a corporation or vice versa); whether management understands short- and long-term tax structuring issues; whether management has retained an accountant and is the accountant being used to reduce or defer tax liabilities; whether the company has procedures in place to collect and remit state and local sales taxes; whether the company records revenues and expenses, and maintains its financial records; or whether the governing documents include provisions that create an unfavorable tax obligation for its members.

Possible solutions include the following:

- Reorganize the business in a more tax-efficient manner. This may be a good solution if the corporate structure does not provide the most favorable tax treatment or increases the tax liabilities of the owners unnecessarily.[5]

- Require the company to engage an accountant or hire a financial officer who can manage tax issues properly.

- Obtain the opinion of a tax advisor to determine whether there are accounting or other changes that would improve tax efficiencies, and then require adoption of those changes as part of the deal terms.

- Require the company to put policies and procedures in place for proper recording of transaction and maintenance of financial-/tax-related documents.

- Insist on revisions to corporate documents to eliminate provisions creating additional tax obligations on owners.[6]

No Financial Controls Are in Place

Businesses can suffer from the fact that management has not put adequate financial controls in place. In the absence of financial controls and clear operating policies, employees and officers may have too much latitude when making financial decisions. Obviously, companies need to be concerned about unjustifiable expenses incurred by employees and officers. An equally important issue is the negative effect on revenues when the company either lacks or fails

---

[5]Reorganization can include, for example, the conversion of the entity to a different business entity form, formation of an entity in a tax-efficient jurisdiction, or use of a licensing, service, manufacturing, marketing, or distribution entity to reduce the taxes of the parent company by shifting some of the income to the subsidiary.

[6]As an example, an operating agreement can contain a provision that requires the company to make distributions to members to cover any tax obligations arising from the ownership of the LLC (a "tax distribution").

to enforce policies regarding pricing and other purchase terms relating to its products or services. It is not unusual to see situations when one or more employees or officers have unrestricted access to a company's bank accounts. Any number of other financial issues can arise when management does not incorporate financial controls in its business operations.

The existence of sufficient financial controls is a concern for sophisticated investors buying an interest in a company (like the Series A Stock Purchase involving Karly Medical) as well as entrepreneurs considering a partnership in a small business, such as the music store in Case Study 7.

Lets consider an example of the impact on a company's finances arising from the absence of sufficient financial policies and controls. During the course of due diligence, suppose Adrian's accountant notices that the rate for music lessons varies quite widely among customers. Initially, Adrian thinks that different teachers may have different hourly rates based on experience or other factors. When he asks Rowland about this, he is surprised to learn that Rowland is not aware of the issue. It is later determined that one of the employees has been giving discounts to entice customers to sign up for lessons and had no idea he should have cleared it with Rowland first. The pricing issue highlights two problems: (1) the absence of written policies or clear directives has cost the music store significant revenues and (2) the lack of financial controls created a situation in which not even the owner was aware of the pricing issue and the impact on the income of the business.

Possible solutions include the following:

- Require the company to put important business policies in writing so all employees are aware of the policies relating to matters such as expenses or pricing; and, if possible, add controls to ensure the policies are being followed.

- Determine where financial controls are needed and require implementation of the controls as a condition of the deal.

- Create separate master and operating accounts, and restrict employee or officer authority to the operating bank account that has a limited amount of operating funds.

- Require the company to implement financial checks so illegal or purely negligent activities can be discovered in a timely manner or even before they can occur.

No Documented Workflow and Operating Processes

Businesses of all types should document workflows, organizational structure, and general operating policies and procedures. Workflow documents detail the process by which significant business functions are carried out, such as how customer orders are entered into the system, how customer orders are filled, how inventory and supplies are ordered, how returns or exchanges are processed, and how or customer service is provided. Organizational charts detail the job titles and responsibilities of employees. Written manuals of policies and procedures should detail material business operations. The failure to document sufficiently policies and procedures related to major business functions can result in a number of issues, including the following:

- *Revenue leakage, loss of inventory, or incorrect booking of revenues when customer orders are not entered properly by employees or returns are not processed in accordance with clear policies.* For example, if the employee of the music store improperly enters the return of a rented instrument because there was no clear procedure on how to handle returns, there may be no way to track what, in fact, happened to the instrument.

- *Complaints from customers when standard policies are not followed regarding orders, exchanges, or refunds.* For example, consider how the reputation of the music store is affected if an employee refuses to honor a music lesson refund that another employee allowed under similar circumstances.

- *Inability to fulfill orders or meet customer demands because of poor inventory management.* For example, the effect on the sales of an emerging medical device manufacturer (Case Study 4) could be devastating if the manufacturer does not have clear protocols in place for ensuring timely manufacture so that customer orders can be filled based on demand. The failure to fill orders in a timely manner could result in the loss of customers, and the overproduction of inventory can create unnecessary expenses for a cash-strapped company.

- *Mismanaged supplies, resulting in overordering and unnecessary expenses, or underordering, creating potential business disruptions.* For example, if a restaurant runs out of beer, the ingredients to prepare the most popular menu items, or even delivery containers, its sales will be affected.

- *Violations of law or internal company policies by employees who are never advised of the policies in writing.* For example, if a business relies on internal call operations to solicit or process orders, but the employee operators are not coached on the standard sales pitch or calling guidelines, or there is no regular supervision, the call center operations can be ineffective. Even more troubling, if call operators are not properly educated on telemarketing laws and regulations, the company could be exposed to substantial claims by the Federal Trade Commission.

- *Issues that arise when companies engage third parties to manage aspects of their business but fail to provide clear rules and regulations regarding the business operations or oversight to ensure these third parties follow company rules.* For example, the owner of commercial real estate might hire a management company to oversee its properties, collect rents, and ensure tenant compliance with rules and regulations. Suppose one of the tenants, a dry cleaner, is not disposing properly of the chemicals used in the dry cleaning process, and the management company does not know because it does not check the property regularly. Proper management of the commercial property could have prevented serious environmental issues and potentially a huge liability for the seller and any subsequent owner of the property.

- *Issues that arise from the failure to document procedures relating to computer networks.* For example, a buyer of a business takes over operations after closing the transaction and realizes he does not have passwords for the computers, does not know how to enter customer orders, does not know the name of the company that manages the computer systems, and does not know the name of the contacts for key customers because they are stored in the Cloud. Moreover, when customers try to make purchases or use the company's Web-based applications, the application freezes. There is no written documentation detailing information about the computer system, and the seller is spelunking in Iceland. Sales would come to a standstill until a computer expert is engaged to resolve all the technology issues.

- *Failure of a business to protect proprietary information as well as the private information about its customers.* For example, if a business fails to adopt measures to protect proprietary information, a court may reject a claim for damages based on the release of the information (by an employee or other person), finding that the lack of safeguards meant the company did not see the information as important enough to protect. Worse, a court could find substantial liability from release of customer or client information if the business failed to adopt and enforce policies designed to protect the privacy of its clients or customers.

A myriad of issues can arise when management does not invest the time to document important operational, financial, or legal policies and procedures for officers and employees to follow. The costs can be tremendous, not only in terms of loss of revenues, but also from potential damages, fines, or penalties arising from violations of internal company policies or external laws and regulations.

Possible solutions include the following:

- Document in writing policies, procedures, protocols, and rules related to key aspects of the business that employees at all levels must follow.

- Prepare work flowcharts that illustrate clearly the company's major business processes.

- Maintain organizational charts that describe the responsibilities of staff.

- Secure document access codes, passwords, and other sensitive information.

- Ensure there is regular supervision of company employees, third–party service providers, and managers to make sure all policies, procedures, and relevant laws and regulations are being followed.

- Require that the sellers (in a business buyout or asset sale) provide postclosing support for transition of the business to the purchaser.[7]

- Engage a third-party consultant to document processes and procedures relating to significant aspects of the business, and require that the documentation be delivered to the purchaser as a condition of the closing.[8]

---

[7]Chapter 8 includes a discussion of clauses that can be added to a purchase agreement requiring postclosing cooperation from the seller.
[8]Documenting workflow and company policies and procedures makes excellent business sense even if a company is not considering a sale, given just some of the potential operating risks discussed in this section.

No Disaster Recovery Plan

Companies of all sizes must have policies and procedures that enable the business to respond to a catastrophic event. Implementing and following a disaster recovery plan may save a business if a disaster or even a short-term business disruption occurs. A disruption of the business can result from weather or other natural occurrence (e.g., hurricane, tornado, fire, earthquake, blizzard, flood), third-party negligence (e.g., a flood caused by another tenant), a disruption of basic services (e.g., loss of electricity), or other events out of the control of the business (e.g., a labor dispute or business failure involving the company's offshore manufacturer). The due diligence investigation should include determining whether the target business has a disaster recovery plan and whether has it been implemented and followed by the company.

The party conducting the due diligence should understand that the nature of the business can affect whether any disaster recovery plan that may have been adopted is, in fact, suitable. By revisiting several of the case studies, we can see how the nature of the business determines whether the disaster recovery plan is appropriate for the business that is the subject of the due diligence review.

Financing Transaction (Case Study 1)

The loan transaction case study is an example of a small business, in this case an owner of an computer repair business that is borrowing money to expand. The potential lender needs to be concerned that a business disruption will affect the ability of the borrower to meet the loan terms. Obvious concerns include, for example, catastrophic weather events, a fire, or flood that destroys the building where the business is located, or its tools, equipment, or inventory. A company that relies primarily on its location, equipment, and inventory to create revenue may be able to do very little advance planning to aid in post-disaster recovery. Ensuring that the borrower has adequate insurance may be the most important preparation the company can do to ameliorate the affects of a disaster. However, the business should ensure sufficient network backup systems are implemented.

The Asset Sale (Case Study 2) and Business Buyout (Case Study 3)

The ABB and SamGar case studies are examples of Internet-based and technology businesses that rely entirely on the seamless operation of its software applications and/or the uninterrupted operation of the Internet. For ABB, customer orders are processed and customer data are stored electronically.

SamGar, a developer of software, also relies on its computer networks, the cloud, and electronic data storage systems. Obviously, any event that affects the ability to process the orders, store or access client information, or use the computer network can ruin the business. The buyer of ABB's assets or all of SamGar's assets wants to make sure the company has its customer information backed up in several locations and perhaps through more than one type of electronic storage methods (such as offsite servers or the cloud).[9] The buyer of a business needs to be concerned about how the business can respond to disruption of the Internet and its computer network. In addition, the relationship and contracts with key vendors (hosting, technology, telecommunications, electronic storage, and so forth) must be reviewed to determine whether they have adequate system redundancies in the case of a disaster that affects their operations.[10]

Internet-based companies no longer are the only businesses that rely on electronic data. Businesses of all types store documents, customer files and information, client data, trade secrets, and other proprietary information electronically. If there is any concern the target business lacks adequate backup storage systems and protocols, the buyer needs to request that a disaster plan be put in place before closing the deal.

Private Placement (Case Study 4)

The transaction involving a private equity investment in the medical device maker Karly Medical raises many of the previously discussed concerns regarding electronic data storage and access to backup computer systems in the event of a disaster. This case study is especially instructive because the business is involved in the heavily regulated field of health care. To the extent Karly Medical's groundbreaking medical technology involves the access, storage, or transmission of patient information and data, it will be subject to privacy and other laws relating to electronic health records. Business risks can arise from the failure to back up data adequately, and also from the failure to safeguard and protect that data from being accessed or released without patient (customer) consent. Access or release of customer private information can occur by accident or it can be a result of intentional access (hacking) of a business's computer files.

---

[9]In the ABB transaction, the buyer is purchasing all of the assets, including customer lists and related data stored on a computer network that is part of the deal. While the buyer may plan to migrate the data to new data storage system, until such time the buyer must be comfortable with the stability of the seller's network of computers and data storage system.

[10]During Hurricane Sandy, many companies were confronted with the unfortunate fact that the companies providing electronic information backup were equally devastated by the hurricane. Of course, Sandy was an unprecedented weather event, but businesses should consider the need for multiple operational and information backup redundancies.

The damages arising from a violation of medical records privacy laws or the failure to safeguard medical records can destroy a business. Insurance may be too expensive, may not be sufficient to cover all the losses, or may be an inadequate remedy for the harm to the reputation of the business. The investor in Karly Medical needs to understand what obligations are imposed on companies that store patient records—as does an investor in any business in which customer information is retained by the company. The investor also needs to make sure Karly Medical and its new technology are in compliance with the law, and determine whether proper safeguards are in place to prevent unintentional or intentional access and release of the information.[11] The investor should either walk away from the transaction or condition the investment on the adoption of protocols, systems, and safeguards that protect private customer information in compliance with applicable laws and regulations.

Partnership (Case Study 7)

Even a small business like the music store (Case Study 7) can require a multifaceted disaster recovery plan. The owners need to have contingency plans in the event a natural or other disaster damages the store, including a back up of electronic records, financial data, and customer information; a means to access their computer network off-site in the event the store is inaccessible; and clear protocols safeguarding company and customer information. The business can also be affected by less obvious but equally serious disruptions of the company's operations. If the company orders its musical instruments from a supplier that is having a labor issue, had a fire, or went bankrupt, for example, the store may not have inventory to sell. Thus, despite the fact it is a small business with operations that do not seem to have the complexity of a high-tech company, it still requires a disaster recovery plan addressing a broad spectrum of business issues. If the company does not have protocols and procedures to prevent business disruption or to recover quickly from such a disruption, the new partner should demand the implementation of the plan as a condition of joining the business.

Personnel Issues

During the course of the due diligence investigation, the examining party may discover issues relating to company personnel that can be rectified and should be addressed as a pre- or postclosing condition. The list of possible

---

[11]Accidental release, or the access and eventual release of customer information resulting from hacking, poses a major concern for all companies that store customer information electronically. Credit card companies, financial institutions, and merchants face substantial damages (which can put a company out of business) when safeguards protecting customer information are not implemented and followed properly.

personnel-related issues that the due diligence process might uncover is long, and this is evidenced by the number of questions relating to personnel matters in the sample Due Diligence Questionnaire for the Franchise Transaction (Appendix B). Rather than detail every potential issue, this section looks at several common personnel issues examined as part of the due diligence process.

Noncompete Agreement

There are two possible concerns relating to noncompete agreements. First, a buyer should be concerned whether any current employees are subject to a noncompete and confidentiality obligations at the time of hiring that is still enforceable. At the time of the hiring, the employee may have been subject to a non-compete that, at the very least, prohibits her from soliciting customers of a prior employer or, on the other extreme, precludes her from working for the new employer for a defined period of time. Companies also have to be concerned that employee does not disclose or utilize confidential information of the prior employer in connection with the performance of their employment duties. If a current employee is bound by a noncompete or confidentiality agreement, the purchaser should confirm that the employee is not in violation of their legal obligations under these agreements. Any violation of a noncompete or confidentiality agreement certainly exposes the employee—and quite possibly the new employer—to substantial damages, and perhaps an injunction against employment for the term of the noncompete. Imagine discovering that the newly hired chief executive officer (CEO) or salesperson for Karly Medical (Case Study 4), who previously worked for another medical device company, is bound by a noncompete. Equally problematic is a discovery that an employee has incorporated proprietary information or technology into any products or services being developed or offered by the company that is the target of the due diligence. When a key employee is in violation of a noncompete or confidentiality agreement entered into with a previous employer, the effect on the new employer can be devastating in terms of potential monetary liability as well as creating uncertainty regarding the employee's status with the company.

Second, a buyer needs to consider whether key personnel, including founders and majority shareholders, should be bound by a noncompete. It is important to recognize that a decision by a company not to require employees to sign a noncompete agreement is not always a problem; these restrictions on employment are not appropriate for every employee or every company. This means the buyer has to assess whether a noncompete is appropriate in light of the nature of the business and of each employee's particular job responsibilities. Enforcing a noncompete clause in an employment agreement can be tricky, because most courts are reticent to restrict the ability of a person to obtain a job. As a result, these agreements are construed narrowly, and enforceability depends on a number of factors, including the nature of the employee's job, his or her access to proprietary information and trade secrets, the amount of consideration received by the employee, the geographic scope, and the time period of the restriction.

A separate concern is whether a founder or a shareholder is bound by the terms of a reasonable noncompete. The noncompete for founders and shareholders is generally set forth in one of the entity's governing documents, such as the operating agreement or shareholder's agreement, or in the investment documents. Often, an investor with a noncontrolling, passive interest in the company will not agree to be bound by a noncompete clause; however, a new investor should be concerned if a founder or a controlling shareholder refuses to execute a noncompete with reasonable restrictions.

If, during the course of the due diligence investigation, it is determined that there may be employees in violation of a noncompete with a former employer, or that certain personnel or shareholders should have entered into a noncompete, the buyer should address these issues in the definitive transaction documents.

Possible solutions include the following:

- Require the seller to obtain a waiver of an existing noncompete from the prior employer, which obviously may be very difficult to obtain.

- Include an indemnification in the purchase contract that requires the seller to indemnify the purchaser for any claims arising under the noncompete.

- Escrow a portion of the purchase price (a concept that is discussed in Chapter 8).

- If the purchaser or investor determines that certain key employees should be bound by a noncompete, execute a reasonable noncompete by these key employees as a condition to closing the transaction.

Invention Assignment Agreement and Confidentiality Agreement

An invention assignment and confidentiality agreement should be signed by all employees of a company. The invention assignment agreement ensures that any intellectual property, inventions, or ideas created during the course of employment belong to the employer and not the employee. Without the invention assignment agreement, a question can arise regarding whether a particular invention or other intellectual property is owned by the employee or the company. For example, an employee who develops a software application may argue that she developed the application and was simply allowing the company to use it. Although the company may be able to argue and ultimately show the application was created on company time, during the course of the employment and with company resources, clearly a business does not want the issue to become a lawsuit with an uncertain outcome. Lawsuits concerning intellectual property can be costly and scare off potential buyers or investors, especially if they involve an important aspect of the company's business. Employees who are bound by an invention assignment agreement are much less likely to assert ownership of key intellectual property absent substantial evidence that the invention was created outside the scope of employment.

A confidentiality agreement confirms the obligation of employees and equity holders to preserve the confidential information of a business. The agreement proscribes the disclosure of confidential information and trade secrets, except under limited circumstances.[12] The existence of a confidentiality agreement also serves another very significant purpose relating to the protection of a company's proprietary information. It demonstrates that the company, in fact, deems certain information to be confidential or proprietary, and requires a confidentiality agreement as a measure to safeguard the information. Even in the absence of a confidentiality agreement, employees, shareholders, directors, and professional advisors have a duty not to disclose secrets of the business because of the relationship of trust and confidence arising from their position with the company. However, it can be harder to seek redress for the release of confidential information, if the company has not taken adequate measures to safeguard the information in the first place. Moreover, if the release of the information has harmed a third party, such as a customer whose private data has been disclosed, the absence of a confidentiality agreement or a policy of seeking to protect confidential information can have a bearing on any damages awarded the aggrieved customer. Confidentiality agreements and the imposition of and adherence to safeguards to protect confidential information of a business and its customers are essential.

As a possible solution, in light of the potential exposure to the business in the absence of invention assignment and confidentiality agreements, the buyer should demand the following as part of the deal conditions:

- Require all current and new employees and consultants to sign an invention assignment agreement and a confidentiality agreement.[13]

---

[12]Exceptions include disclosure to professional advisors, with consent or as required by law.
[13]It, admittedly, can be difficult to get existing employees to sign invention assignment agreements. They will be concerned about giving up rights, and some may even refuse. The buyer then needs to decide whether to make this a nonnegotiable deal condition.

- If there is a concern that an employee (or founder) may have a claim with respect to any of the company's intellectual property, require that the person execute an assignment of his or her right in the particular intellectual property to the company.

- Require new hires to list all inventions they claim to have created prior to joining the company.

- If an employee, consultant, or founder is contributing or licensing the invention to the company, execute a technology assignment or licensing agreement (as applicable) – which would have prevented the material due diligence issue in the ABB transaction where a former partner is claiming rights to ABB's proprietary technology

- Establish procedures for safeguarding company, client, and third-party confidential information.

Misclassification of Employees as Consultants

Ask any accountant and he or she will likely tell you one of the biggest red flags for the Internal Revenue Service (IRS) is a company's misclassification of employees as consultants. The advantage for a company in classifying employees as independent contractors is the company is not responsible for paying state and federal employment taxes or offering any benefits required by state or federal laws. Businesses may operate under the false assumption that engaging a person under a "consulting agreement" and identifying her as an "independent contractor" or "consultant" avoids the obligations associated with regular employment. If the IRS discovers the person does not qualify for independent contractor status, the company is responsible for either a percentage or all of the unpaid employment taxes, withholdings, interest, and penalties, depending on whether the misclassification was an honest mistake as opposed to intentional. The tax liability can be substantial, and the employer is the one held responsible, especially when the employee's share of the withholding cannot be collected from the employee.

As a possible solution, the due diligence investigation should include a careful vetting of how personnel are classified to make sure those identified as consultants are truly independent contractors. If there is a concern, a closing condition for the sale of a business should include an indemnification to cover any exposure and even an escrow of a portion of the purchase price. An investor may want to require that the company provide an opinion from the company's tax advisor or consider whether the company should approach the IRS about settling potential tax liabilities arising from the (hopefully) honest misclassification of certain company personnel.

Policies Governing Employees

Privately held, small companies often do not put into place any formal employment policies for a number of reasons, including the misperception that formal policies are unnecessary because common sense should prevail, the growth of the business has outpaced the focus on internal compliance matters, or there is a lack of available resources to formulate and implement personnel policies.[14]

First, companies should implement policies governing hiring procedures. These policies should include:

- A clear statement of nondiscriminatory hiring practices

- Performing background checks of potential hirees[15]

- Completion of employee eligibility verification forms (U.S. Citizenship and Immigration Services Form I-9)

Second, companies need clear statements of workplace policies, preferably in a well-drafted employee manual, addressing the following matters, to name just a few:

- An explanation that the company makes required deductions for federal and state taxes, as well as voluntary deductions for the company's benefits programs

- Explanation of work hours and schedules, and any attendance or punctuality policies, and any dress code

- An outline of overtime pay, pay schedules, performance reviews, time-keeping record obligations, and any salary increases or bonus policies

- An explanation of company policies for creating a safe and secure workplace

- An explanation of policies required for a safe working environment that are mandated by law, such as compliance with OSHA regulations that require employees to report all accidents, injuries, potential safety hazards, safety suggestions, and health and safety related issues to management

---

[14]In the dotcom era, it was shocking what some companies called *employment manuals* and yet were able to raise tens of millions of dollars. Some manuals featured funny pictures of employees, the right to bring dogs and cats to work, statements about the importance of a fun working environment, and very little (if anything) about important workplace policies.
[15]Companies need to follow state and federal laws regulating employment background checks, and potential hires should be informed of their rights and must provide consent, in writing, to these checks.

Third, companies should document and implement rules defining the appropriate behavior of employees in the workplace. Employee issues can arise if the company has not adopted policies and educated its employees regarding a variety of issues, including the following:

- Sexual harassment
- Discrimination (race, sex, age, sexual orientation)
- Procedures for employees to report workplace issues
- Work schedules; vacation, personal, and sick days; lunch and break times
- Use of company e-mail and other means of electronic communication
- Use of company cell phones, computers, software, Internet, and other technology
- Record-keeping obligations
- Requirements with respect to safeguarding proprietary or confidential company information as well as private customer data

Admittedly, for a startup, small, or emerging company, writing a full-fledged employee manual can be too costly or consume too much of its limited resources. If employment policies and rules have not been implemented, the buyer needs to consider the measures the buyer wants to demand the company adopt as a condition to the deal.

Concerns Related to Corporate Structure

The due diligence investigation can also uncover a variety of issues regarding governance of the business and the rights of its owners. These issues can either create restrictions on an investor's rights or impose obligations on the investor once it becomes a minority or noncontrolling owner of a business. Matters of corporate governance and the rights of shareholders/members are usually found in the following documents and agreements:

- For a partnership, the partnership agreement.
- For a corporation, the certificate of incorporation (or similar document), corporate bylaws, director or shareholder minutes, resolutions and consents, a shareholders agreement, co-sale/right of first refusal agreement, and an investor rights agreement.

- For an LLC, the articles of formation (or similar document), operating agreement, and management/member resolutions.

- There also can be various agreements between the company and a founder or investor granting particular rights vis-à-vis the company or other shareholders/members.

Issues relating to corporate governance and shareholder/member rights can arise because of specific provisions in corporate governance documents or shareholder/member agreements. However, often it is not what the corporate documents state—but what they *don't* state—that can be an issue for a potential partner in a business. The following are just a few examples relating to governance and ownership rights that can arise during the course of a due diligence review.

No Buy–Sell Provisions

It is important that the governing documents of a closely held business include buy–sell provisions or a separate buy–sell agreement. The buy–sell gives the company or the owners the right to purchase the interests of a member on the occurrence of triggering events that cause the termination of his or her rights in the business. Typical triggering events essentially relate to occurrence that could result in a transfer of the shares to a third party, including death, disability, bankruptcy, and voluntary withdrawal of a member, and may also include "for-cause" events that give the company the right to purchase the rights of a defaulting partner. The provisions of a buy–sell are found in the operating agreement of an LLC, the partnership agreement, or the shareholder agreement of a corporation.

Why is this important in a closely held business? These companies tend to have an ownership base built on relationships among or contributions made to the business by the owners. Consider how unsettling it would be for the partners in a small business to learn the membership interests of a deceased partner have been transferred to a drug-addicted ex-spouse or that a bankrupt member's interests are being auctioned off to satisfy her debts. Buy–sell provisions are necessary to prevent the equity ownership (e.g., membership interests, partnership share or stock) of a departing owner from being transferred to a third person without consent.

A possible solution would be to require amendments in the operating or shareholder agreement to include a buy–sell or enter into a separate buy–sell agreement. A properly drafted buy–sell includes a method for calculating the fair market value of the interests to be purchased and the terms of payment upon occurrence of the triggering event. The purchase right may be vested in the company or the members, and often an insurance policy will be obtained to covering the buy-out price upon the occurrence of certain events, such as death or disability.

The LLC Is Member-Managed Instead of Manager-Managed

The management of an LLC can be vested in an appointed manager or board of managers (manager managed) or in each member of the LLC (member managed). In many states, the failure to make a selection on formation of the LLC means the entity is automatically member managed. The problem with a member-managed LLC is that every member has full management rights and can bind the entity; a member who owns 1% has the same management rights as a member who owns 99% of the membership interests. The risk of giving every member equal authority to bind and manage the LLC is self-evident and, although members with a small ownership interest may initially like the idea that they have management rights, their view may be substantially different view when they realize all the other members have the same rights. A manager-managed LLC, in which one member or a board of managers is elected by the members, is therefore preferred in most circumstances.

A possible solution would be to require the LLC to amend its governing documents to create a manager-managed entity. If there is an objection to the change, a fallback position is to amend the operating agreement to require that specific types of transactions or undertakings require the approval of a certain number of members or percentage of the total membership interests.

No Right of First Refusal

The right of first refusal gives members and shareholders the right to purchase any equity offered by the company before any third parties can purchase shares.[16] Existing shareholders can purchase pro rata based on their percentage of ownership in the company. The right of first refusal gives existing owners the opportunity to prevent the dilution of all or part of the ownership interest percentage. If the operating agreement of an LLC or a shareholder agreement of a corporation does not include a right of first refusal, the company can offer interests to third parties and dilute existing shareholders.

---

[16]Other parties can also have rights of first refusal, including lenders and convertible note holders, which demonstrates the importance of reviewing all the material contracts, agreements, and undertakings during due diligence.

A possible solution would be to require an amendment to the governing agreements to add a right of first refusal. The right can also give shareholders the right to purchase all or a pro rata portion of the offered shares that are not purchased by the other shareholders.

No Tag-Along (Co-Sale) Right

Commonly referred to as a *tag-along* or *co-sale right*, this provision gives equity holders the right to participate in the sale of shares by another member of the company. Although the obligation often is imposed on company founders, it can also apply to all members, regardless of whether they are a founder. The tag-along is important because often an investment is made on the presumption the founders will stay with the business; this provision prevents founders from selling without the other members being given the same opportunity.

A possible solution would be to require that the company amend the governing documents so that all owners have a right to participate pro rata in the sale of ownership interests by another equity holder. If the founders or majority shareholders are unwilling to agree to a co-sale right, a compromise would allow them to sell a portion of their interests exempt from the co-sale obligation.

Too Much Control Vested in Management

Investors in a closely-held company can have different approaches to their desire to be involved in the management of the company; some investors are purely passive and do not have any desire to be involved in the management or direction of the business whereas others want to have the right to participate in at least material business decisions. The investor who wants to participate actively in management may decide to demand a seat on the board of directors or appointment as a managing member as a condition of the investment. Whether the company acquiesces to the request depends largely on factors such as the size of the investment, the particular expertise the investor brings, the breadth of the investor's contacts, and the ability of the investor to assist the company in achieving business goals. Even if an investor does not desire or have the negotiation power to demand a seat in management, ensuring there are controls on the otherwise unfettered authority of management should be important to potential investors.

Let's assume the investor reviews the bylaws, governing corporate documents, and the capitalization table of Karly Medical (Case Study 4) and discovers the board of directors consists of three members, with the board chairman also holding 30% of the stock in the company. Of the remaining two directors, one was nominated by the chairman and they are partners in several other ventures. The investor is concerned the board essentially "rubber-stamps" decisions of the chairman, and there is no collar on the authority of the chairman. On the one hand, the investor has a strong belief in the management and, in particular, the ability of the chairman to steer the right course for the company. The investor does not want to be actively involved in management of the business but does want some restrictions in place to limit the unfettered control of the chairman.

A possible solution would be to ask the company to amend its operating agreement (for an LLC) or bylaws (for a corporation), or to execute an investor rights/shareholder agreement to add restrictions on the scope of the authority of directors or managing members of a company. The provision may require that certain actions must be submitted to the members/shareholders for approval, including issuance of additional shares/membership interests, sale of all or substantially all the assets or equity of the company, borrowing money, reorganization, merger or other restructuring of the company, and changing the business purpose substantially. Sometimes investors want the right to review and approve business plans and budgets, or want informational rights that require the company to provide investors periodic updates on the business and its financial situation. Even if the company is willing to submit certain material decisions to its shareholders, the structure of the approval right needs to take into account the capitalization table of the company. For example, in the Karly Medical scenario, if the chairman and his partners make up the majority of the ownership of the company, the submission of certain transactions to shareholder vote has no practical value. The investor, therefore, may need to demand that a favorable vote of a supermajority (e.g., 66% or even 75%) be required for approval of material transactions or business decisions.[17]

Additional Issues Relating to Governance

A review of the governing corporate documents is necessary to understand the fundamental aspects regarding how the business is governed. The additional agreements, such as shareholder and investor rights agreements, can create additional rights and privileges for one or more corporate shareholders or LLC members. It is beyond the scope of this discussion to list all of the rights and obligations that may be set forth in the governing corporate documents, but below are several points to consider.

---

[17]The investor has to understand the capitalization table and which shareholders are aligned or will likely vote in a block before determining the vote percentage that makes sense. In the Karly Medical situation, the chairman owns 30% and the investor owns 33%, leaving 37% representing other shareholders. If the investor is concerned that at least 33% of the other shareholders are controlled by the chairman, the only meaningful approach may be to demand all votes on material transactions be approved by a supermajority consisting of 75% of the outstanding shares.

First, an investor may be concerned about the size and composition of the board of directors (or that the LLC has one managing member). If the board is comprised of one director who is also the president and controlling shareholder, the investor might want to push for an expansion of the board and increased delegation of authority. In some circumstances, the investor may suggest formation of an advisory board that can provide non-binding advice on important business matters. For example, advisory boards comprised of scientists, physicians or financial advisors are often established by emerging technology and healthcare companies because of the technical or financial guidance they can provide on the development of products and services.

Second, there may be different classes of equity (ownership) and, if so, these classes will have different (and likely unequal) economic and voting rights. There may be, for example a class of common stock (or membership units, in the case of an LLC) and one or more classes of preferred stock (or preferred units). In addition to different economic rights, the preferred classes may not only have the right to vote for all directors, but also the right to elect or remove one or more directors (or LLC managers). An investor must consider the ramifications of owning common stock in a business capitalized with both common and preferred equity. It can refuse to proceed unless offered preferred (instead of common) shares or try to negotiate an investor's rights agreement that includes additional rights that the investors deems particularly important.

Third, the governing corporate documents will define the authority of the board of directors (or managers). As previously discussed, an investor may want to demand a revision to the governing documents that requires shareholder/member approval (or even supermajority approval) before the corporation proceeds with a defined list of actions. The list can be wide-ranging, but typical restrictions relate to borrowing, sale of material assets, issuance of additional equity, expenses, compensation of officers, and material changes to scope, structure and nature of the business. Investor's often also demand adoption of budgets and business plans, approval of any material deviation from such, and periodic financial and business updates.

Fourth, aside from the annual shareholder meeting, an investor needs to pay attention to the scope of its voting rights and any procedures for holding special meetings of the equity owners. For example, how much notice is required before a special meeting can take place? Can equity holders vote at a special meeting to remove a director and if so on what grounds?

Fifth, there are usually restrictions precluding the transfer of shares to a third party, whether by death, withdrawal, sale of the shares, or a pledge in connection with a financial undertaking. An investor needs to demand changes to the governing documents if these limitations on the transfer of shares or membership interests are absent from the governing corporate documents.

Sixth, the governing documents may contain "drag-along rights," enabling the majority shareholders or LLC members to force the minority to join in the sale of the company. The fact that all equity holders are subject to a drag-along might not be an issue for a particular investor as it ensures that a minority shareholder cannot unreasonably prevent a favorable opportunity to sell the business, but she should be aware if the obligation exists.

Seventh, a new investor or partner should review and have a clear understanding of the rights and privileges granted to a current shareholder or group of shareholders (or LLC members) through a stock purchase, investor rights, or shareholder agreement. The rights can be wide ranging (including liquidation preferences, dividend preference, antidilution protections, right of first refusal, and protective covenants), but the shareholders with those rights may only be a small subset of the total capital structure of the business. When a new investor learns about the privileges and preferences granted to some of the existing owners, he or she should demand the same rights as a condition of the investment.

Conclusion

This chapter demonstrated that there are circumstances when the due diligence investigation improves bargaining power, creating an opportunity for the buyer to demand more favorable deal terms than anticipated at the outset of the deal negotiations. We looked at examples of issues that can arise during the course of a due diligence investigation and how they can lead to a renegotiation of the deal terms. We have seen that due diligence issues can do the following:

- Affect assumptions about the appropriate valuation for the transaction
- Reveal issues about the structure and operations of the business
- Raise questions about how well the company is managed
- Uncover issues arising from the absence of or failure to enforce employment policies
- Raise issues relating to corporate governance and shareholder rights.

These issues can lead a lender, buyer, investor, or potential partner to reconsider the structure of the transaction and deal terms. If the issues undermine the presumed valuation of the business, the solution may be to renegotiate the financial deal terms so the consideration is in line with the appropriate valuation. Other issues, however, cannot be resolved by reducing the purchase price or changing the payment terms, and instead may result in the addition of preclosing conditions, postclosing obligations, indemnifications, or an escrow of a portion of the purchase price or investment.[18]

---

[18]Pre-closing conditions and post-closing covenants, as well as the mechanisms for enforcement of any post-closing rights are addressed in Chapter 8.

Applying Due Diligence Principles: The Franchise Purchase

As reiterated throughout this book, the guiding principle of due diligence is seeking to confirm the story about the business as told by the company that is the target of the investigation. Each of the chapters has shown a progression of steps during the course of preparing and conducting the due diligence questionnaire, and then using the information learned from the due diligence investigation to prove or disprove elements of the company's story. To review, the progression has been:

1. A recognition that due diligence focuses on the four business cornerstones: the company, its business operations, its valuation, and its personnel

2. An introduction to the importance of a due diligence plan, which seeks to test the story touted by the company as

the reason for entering into the proposed transaction. The story the business is promoting is usually found in the business plan, investment decks, financial statements, and in discussions with key members of management. The plan essentially sets out the story as presented by the proposed business transaction, and then it identifies the claims that need to be verified by you and your professional advisors before proceeding with the business deal. The framework for the due diligence plan is series of broad questions about the four business cornerstones, and those broad questions are formulated based on the facts and components of the transaction under review. In sum, the due diligence plan is the strategy to be followed for conducting the due diligence review.

3. The preparation of the due diligence based on the strategy defined in the due diligence plan. An understanding of the importance of a well-crafted due diligence questionnaire—not a "one-size-fits-all" questionnaire, but one that is designed to elicit information relevant to the nature and terms of the specific transaction

4. A dissection of the due diligence questionnaire to identify the different groups of questions: those that are almost universal to all transactions (standard questions), those that are almost universally important to ask based on the type of the transaction (deal-type questions), and those that are designed to address unique aspects of the deal (deal-specific questions)

5. A determination of what should be done with the information learned about the business through the due diligence process. In certain circumstances, it became evident that an issue discovered or the deviation from the story told by the company was so fundamental that the transaction could not proceed. In other circumstances, the examination provided an opportunity to try to renegotiate financial terms or rectify operational issues as a condition of the transaction.

6. Possible solutions to due diligence issues, such as including pre- and postclosing conditions and covenants along with mechanisms for enforcement, escrow, purchase price adjustment, indemnification, transition, and post-closing cooperation.

The culmination of this work is the application of these concepts to a transaction. In this chapter, we examine the transaction as it revolves around the purchase of a franchise.

The Franchise Purchase (Case Study 8)

Ellen Kay has entered a memorandum of understanding for the purchase of 33% of the LLC membership interests in KMF Franchisee, LLC—a franchisee that owns four franchises of Rocky Robbins Ice Cream Bar, Inc.—for $225,000. KMF Franchisee owes $100,000 to Mishy Enterprises, which represents the purchase price for an earlier buyout of its equity interest in KMF. Mishy, the principal owner, has complained that she was underpaid for her 33% interest and is considering opening a competing ice cream restaurant across the street. There are two members of the LLC, and they never executed an operating agreement, but there is a draft that has been proposed. KMF has many full- and part-time employees. The four stores are managed by Lara Melanie, the manager of operations, who is in the past year of her four-year contract. Two of the franchise locations are in strip malls and are leased from the mall owner; one location is leased through a sublease that is expiring, and there are rumors about the financial condition of the sublessor; and the fourth location is a stand-alone store that is currently leased, but KMF has exercised an option to purchase the property.

Creating the Due Diligence Plan for This Transaction

An important theme has been that the due diligence investigation should not be approached with the mind-set that "one size fits all." Too often, parties or their advisors simply use the same due diligence questionnaire used for other transactions without giving proper consideration to the nature and terms of the deal, and the particular business that is the focus of the transaction. An uneducated approach to the due diligence process can mean important issues are missed or the process is useless, with the possibility of unforeseen financial or legal liabilities for a lender, buyer, or investor. This is why, in Chapter 2, we examined the importance of first preparing a due diligence plan that incorporates the key aspects of the transaction and thereby serves as a road map for the investigation.

The framework for the due diligence plan is the four business cornerstones: the company, its business operations, its valuations, and the personnel. The facts that need to be verified and the issues that need to be examined regarding the particular business all fall into one of the four business cornerstones. The transaction first must be dissected to identify the material facts relating to the target company and the terms of the transaction. Once the key components of the business and the deal are identified, the process of fitting the material aspects of the business into one of the four business cornerstones, and thus creating the due diligence plan, can begin. The due diligence plan sets forth the strategy for the entire investigation. Therefore, a well-conceived plan greatly improves the value of the due diligence investigation.

What Is the Underlying Business Story of the Transaction?

As explained throughout, due diligence is really a process by which a party to a potential business transaction seeks to verify the story told about the business that is the target of the deal. Whether the party conducting the due diligence is contemplating making a loan to, buying all or part of, or becoming a partner in, the business, the due diligence investigation asks whether the business story can be corroborated. The due diligence plan identifies the material facts about the business and the transaction that a party is seeking to confirm through the due diligence examination. What, then, are the key facts of the transaction involving Ellen Kay's potential purchase of 33% of the multiple franchisee, KMF Franchisee, LLC?

The facts are as follows: purchase of a 33% interest in an LLC that owns four Rocky Robbins Ice Cream Bar franchises for $225,000; the former partner may be opening a competitive store and holds a $100,000 loan; the existing partners never executed an operating agreement; the person managing all four stores is in last year of her contract; all four locations are leased, with one lease expiring; and the LLC has exercised an option to purchase the building where one of the stores is located.

Based on this information, the initial page of the due diligence plan may be structured similar to that shown in Figure 7-1.

DUE DILIGENCE PLAN
KMF FRANCHISEE INVESTMENT

I. Transaction overview

- *Nature of the transaction*: acquisition of an ownership interest in an LLC (KMF Franchisee LLC), which currently has two partners

- *Asset to be acquired*: 33% of the membership interest in an LLC

- *Nature of the business*: four Rocky Robbins Ice Cream Bar franchises

- *Consideration*: $225,000 (all cash)

- *Personnel*: Multiple full- and part-time employees; manager of all four stores in past year of contract

- *Initial deal issues*

  ❖ Terms of the franchise agreements for the stores

  ❖ Potential competition from former partner

  ❖ $100,000 loan held by former business partner

  ❖ An operating agreement that was never executed by the partners

  ❖ One of the locations leased through a sublease, which is expiring; sublessor is having financial difficulties

  ❖ Company exercised option to purchase the property where one of the stores is located

Figure 7-1. KMF due diligence plan: Key Transaction Facts

▨ **Tip** An example of a complete due diligence plan for the purchase of an ownership interest in KMF Franchisee is included in Appendix A.

The first page of the Due Diligence Plan for the purchase of the 33% interest in KMF Franchisee LLC is structured in terms of the four business cornerstones. It also identifies specific issues that are apparent before the actual legal, financial, and operational due diligence investigation is undertaken by the potential investor. As set forth below, the remainder of the due diligence plan identifies on what the investigation should focus for each of the four business cornerstones as well as for each of the material issues identified prior to commencement of the examination.

What Needs to Be Examined Regarding the Company?

As mentioned, the due diligence plan is a road map of the major topics to be explored in detail using the due diligence questionnaire. Having first defined the major aspects of KMF Franchisee investment transaction in Figure 7-1, the next step is to identify the key issues under each of the business cornerstones, starting with the company itself. Here we ask, in light of the facts of the transaction, what the main areas to be examined are and what facts need to be verified with respect to the formation and existence of the company. Of course, there are many issues that need to be confirmed about the financial and operational aspects of the business, but when considering the business cornerstones, the focus on the *company* is in terms of the legal structure and the rights and obligations of its owners. Figure 7-2 presents the main areas to be addressed via the due diligence process for the first business cornerstone: the company.

■ **Tip** The due diligence plan does not include the questions that will be posed to the target business, that is the purpose of the due diligence questionnaire, but rather outlines the main topics from which the questionnaire is developed.

DUE DILIGENCE PLAN
KMF FRANCHISEE INVESTMENT

II. The company

1. Verify the proper formation and good standing of the company, and ascertain what organizational documents exist.

2. Review the unsigned draft of the operating agreement. The investor will become a member of the LLC, so it is essential to understand the terms of the proposed operating agreement—whether it is sufficient in addressing the rights and obligations among the members.

    a. Determine who are the members and what is each member's percentage of interest in the LLC;

    b. Consider how the LLC managed?

    c. Understand what management/voting rights the members have in the LLC;

    d. Review specific financial rights of members;

    e. Determine if there are specific tax provisions affecting members;

    f. Consider whether there are restrictions on ownership and transfer of the membership interests in the LLC; and

    g. Determine if the proposed operating agreement needs to be revised to protect the rights of the members.

3. Review any additional agreements affecting the structure or organization of the company.

4. Determine if there are any agreements in addition to the operating agreement that affect member rights (for example, voting agreements, investor rights agreements, rights of first refusal, joint venture)?

5. Ensure that there are no unusual provisions in any of the corporate documents?

Figure 7-2. The due diligence plan: structure of the company

What Needs to Be Confirmed about the Business Operations of KMF Franchisee LLC?

The due diligence plan next needs to identify the major aspects about the company's business operations that have to be examined before proceeding with the transaction. Tying the discussion back to the four business cornerstones, the plan should define the material issues to be confirmed about the company's products/services and its operations—the business operation. The key here is that the due diligence plan should highlight the material topics to be examined in the context of the particular transaction. The goal of the plan is to facilitate the drafting of (rather than serving as) the substantially more detailed due diligence questionnaire. Figure 7-3 sets forth the main topics that the potential investor in KMF Franchisee LLC would want to examine regarding the products and operations of the target business.

DUE DILIGENCE PLAN
KMF FRANCHISEE INVESTMENT

III. The business operation

1. Understand the nature of the KMF Franchisee business.

2. Determine if there are issues arising from the sale of ice cream and related items.

3. Identify the key assets necessary to operate the business, if they are owned, leased, or licensed; and the due diligence required regarding those assets.

4. Examine the particular issues arising from the fact that the company operates franchises.

    a. Identify the structure of the ownership of the franchise rights.

    b. Understand the rights under the franchise agreements, including any issues relating to termination of the rights.

    c.   Define the obligations of the company under the franchise agreements and whether they change over the course of the franchise.

    d.   Determine if the franchise rights be transferred or are they affected by a change of ownership of KMF Franchisee LLC.

5.   Review and understand what IP the business depends on to operate the business, and if it is owned or licensed from a third party.

6.   Determine if there are clearly defined and documented policies and procedures for operation of the business in place and whether the company and its employees comply with these policies.

7.   Identify the material contracts/agreements and business relationships that are essential to operation of the business (in addition to the franchise agreements):

    a.   Supplier agreements

    b.   Equipment leases/software licenses

    c.   Noncompete or restrictions on scope of business

    d.   Sales/marketing agreements

    e.   Insurance

    f.   Any undocumented arrangements that are material to the operation of the business

8.   Review the material terms of the leases for each franchise location.

    a.   Consider the issues raised by the fact one location is subleased.

    b.   Understand the issues raised by the fact the sublease is expiring and the sublessor is rumored to be in poor financial condition.

9.   Obtain a clear picture of the due diligence that needs to be performed in connection with the potential purchase of the stand-alone store location.

10.   Verify the sufficiency of the company's information technology (IT) systems and networks necessary for its operations. The review should also include:

    a.   Back up and disaster recovery

    b.   Appropriate privacy, data security, credit card policies

11. Identify legal compliance issues that are raised by the operation of the business.

    a. Licenses and permits

    b. Compliance under environmental, health, and safety laws

    c. Compliance with franchise agreement

    d. Compliance with local laws

    e. No default under material contracts

12. Confirm that the owners are in compliance with their obligations and that they are good business partners.

Figure 7-3. The due diligence plan: the business operations

Figure 7-3 demonstrates that, with respect to the business operation cornerstone, the due diligence plan should include those fundamental topics that are almost universally important to all operating companies:

- What is the type of business is involved?
- What goods, products, and/or services does it sell?
- What assets are essential to operate the business?
- Does the business operate in compliance with the relevant laws?
- Are the business and operational policies defined and documented?
- What contracts are necessary to operate?
- What undocumented agreements and business relationships are material to the operation of the business?

Separately, there are topics that are not universal but are important in light of the particular nature of the business and its operations. The due diligence plan thus also needs to identify those additional topics that arise from the nature or unique features of the company's operations. In this case, additional issues about the company's business operations emanate from two significant facts:

1. The business is not simply an ice cream restaurant, but a franchise with multiple franchise locations.

2. Simultaneous to the investor's potential transaction to purchase an ownership interest, the company is buying the real estate where one of the stores is located.

These facts regarding the KMF Franchisee transaction create additional layers of due diligence that would not otherwise exist if the investor was simply purchasing an interest in a restaurant business with multiple locations. Drawing out the material aspects of the business operations in the due diligence plan facilitates the drafting of a thorough due diligence questionnaire that hones in on the issues specific to the business operation of the company being examined.

What Are the Key Areas to Explore to Confirm the Purported Valuation of the Company?

The due diligence plan should also serve as a road map for determining whether the purported valuation of the business is justified. In terms of the KMF Franchisee transaction, the question is whether $225,000 is a reasonable purchase price for a 33% ownership interest. Figure 7-4 sets forth a due diligence plan as it might be used in connection with the valuation of the KMF Franchisee transaction.

DUE DILIGENCE PLAN
KMF FRANCHISEE INVESTMENT

IV. Business valuation

    1. Evaluate the assets

        a. Identify the material assets used in the operation of the business and how revenues are generated.

        b. Determine if the company owns the material assets and, if not, what the terms of any lease or license are.

        c. Determine if the assets are subject to any liens, encumbrances, or security interests.

        d. Identify any other issues affecting the value of the assets, including the condition of physical assets.

        e. If the assets include IP decide what additional due diligence is required.

    2. Review company liabilities

        a. Long- and short-term financing or other debt obligations.

        b. Lease obligations.

        c. Obligations created by contract or other agreements.

      d.   Outstanding financial obligations to members of the LLC.

      e.   Outstanding judgments, awards, or fines.

      f.   Pending or threatened audits, claims, lawsuits, or legal proceedings by any person, agency, or regulatory body.

3. Review tax matters.

4. Understand the terms of the franchise agreement:

      a.   Financial and nonfinancial obligations to franchisor.

      b.   Financial and nonfinancial rights of franchisee.

5. Review the financial statements, books, and records to understand what they show with regard to the financial status of the business.

6. Identify the potential business risks relating to the franchise.

      a.   Competition, including from disgruntled former partner.

      b.   Financial condition of the franchisor.

      c.   Demand for franchisor's products or services.

7. Confirm that the pending purchase of the stand-alone location makes financial sense.

8. Identify the potential financial risks arising from the upcoming expiration of one of the leases.

9. Consider the financial issues relating to the expiration of the manager's contract?

Figure 7-4. The due diligence plan: Business valuation

The due diligence plan for confirming the valuation of KMF Franchisee demonstrates that a review of the financials is only a part of the valuation story. A company's financial records are a piece of the puzzle, but do not, alone, provide the complete picture of the value of the business. The plan not only identifies the standard topics regarding valuation, such as the assets, liabilities, and the strength of the financials, but raises questions about business growth, the status of the market for the company's products, and potential competition. Plus, the due diligence plan for KMF Franchisee includes additional areas that require focus based on the specific deal facts, including that this transaction involves a franchise, the company is purchasing the real estate for one of the locations, a lease is expiring, a former partner is threatening to compete, and the manager's contract is expiring. Having identified what needs to be examined regarding the financial aspects of KMF Franchisee, the foundation exists for preparing the due diligence questions that aid in verifying the valuation of the business.

What Are the Key Personnel/Management Concerns?

The last of the four business cornerstones to be addressed by the due diligence plan is personnel. The goal here is to identify the key personnel, ascertain whether they are capable of operating the business and executing the business plan, and to ensure there are no existing or potential legal or business issues relating to such personnel. When drafting the due diligence plan, keep in mind that key personnel may be not only employee–owners or management-level personnel, but also can include a wide range of employees depending on the nature of the business. Figure 7-5 provides an example of the due diligence plan relating to personnel matters for the KMF Franchisee investment.

DUE DILIGENCE PLAN
KMF FRANCHISEE INVESTMENT

V. Personnel

1. Organizational chart

   a. Identify key personnel at the management level

   b. Identify key owner/nonowner employees

2. Understand if there are owner–employees that serve a significant role in the business and the likelihood of their continued participation in the business.

3. Employment terms

   a. Financial

   b. Nonfinancial terms and benefits

4. Liabilities relating to personnel

   a. Pending claims and lawsuits

   b. Threatened claims and lawsuits

   c. Compliance with payroll and other obligations relating to employment

5. Legal documentation relating to personnel

    a. Ensure the company requires and properly retains all documentation relating to personnel

    b. Confirm there are no undocumented workers

    c. Confirm that employees and members have signed confidentiality, invention assignment, and noncompete agreements, as appropriate

6. Consider if there is sufficient staffing given the fact this a restaurant business, an industry known for having employee retention issues.

7. Confirm that the company has well-defined, written policies and procedures regarding employees and that they are followed.

8. Review whether the company complies with employment laws.

9. Retention of manager of the four franchise locations

    a. Employee who manages all four stores in past year of contract.

    b. Determine if the manager can be retained on reasonable employment terms.

    c. Decide if there is a reasonable backup plan if manager leaves.

Figure 7-5. The due diligence plan: personnel

The topic areas set forth in Figure 7-5 regarding the personnel aspects of a business can be applied almost universally to transactions involving the purchase of a business. The fact that the KMF deal involves an ice cream restaurant franchise raises additional issues because of the likelihood there are multiple seasonal and young employees, in addition to the usual staffing concerns. An investor would want to make sure the company complies with employment laws, which can create material liabilities for the business. The plan also highlights the upcoming expiration of the manager's contract, which the investor needs the company to resolve as a condition of the investment.

▩ **Tip** Employee retention can be an issue in many deals involving the purchase of, or investment in, a business. For the purchaser, ensuring key personnel remain after closing the deal is of paramount importance. For the business, retaining personnel is also very important, but the investor should be mindful and not allow the deal to become leverage for employees in their contract negotiations.

Putting time into considering and then drafting the due diligence plan pays off in the preparation of the due diligence questionnaire. The plan is the strategy for conducting the due diligence, providing a road map of the most significant topics under each of the four business cornerstones, emphasizing issues that are common across various types of deals, and highlighting other issues that arise because of facts that are particular to the target business and the actual transaction. Legal and financial advisors may resist the notion of preparing a due diligence plan, skipping this step in the due diligence process and instead opting to tweak one of the many precedents in their library of due diligence questionnaires. For the inexperienced, skipping the planning stage and relying instead on a generic questionnaire or one from another transaction is dangerous because it will not be based on the facts of the particular transaction. An entrepreneur or inexperienced practitioner who is not as well versed in the due diligence process will benefit immensely from creating the due diligence plan as a precursor to drafting the due diligence questionnaire. Although the advisor who is experienced at conducting due diligence may not prepare a formal plan prior to preparing the questionnaire, practitioners still canvass the unique aspects of the deal or facts about the business operations to ensure the questionnaire is thorough.

Creating the Due Diligence Questionnaire

Having first prepared the due diligence plan, the entrepreneur who is investing in, purchasing, or considering becoming a partner in a business is in a much easier position to take the next step of drafting the questionnaire. The plan identifies the key topics for due diligence and the due diligence questionnaire drills down on those topics. The questionnaire is used to ask the company owners and other employees a series of questions designed to test the veracity of story the owners have presented regarding their business. Drafted with due consideration to the actual nature and terms of the transaction and the particular facts regarding the business being scrutinized, the due diligence questionnaire is an essential tool to the investigative process.

Not All Due Diligence Questionnaires Are Equal

Crafting a due diligence questionnaire around the facts of the transaction (rather than trying to fit the transaction into a form questionnaire) is the difference between a well-conceived approach to a due diligence investigation and one that is likely to miss potentially significant business issues. The average questionnaire asks a number of cookie cutter questions, seeking information about standard legal and financial matters without demonstrating an understanding of the transaction, the potential pitfalls, or the business being examined. In contrast, the useful due diligence questionnaire not only includes the basic requests for information, but also homes in on questions raised by the factual underpinnings of the company's story. Consider, for example, the excerpts from two different due diligence questionnaires in Figure 7-6 and the markedly different approaches to the request for information about the subject company's revenues.

EXAMPLE 1. DUE DILIGENCE QUESTIONNAIRE

Financial information

1. Provide all financial statements for past six years.

2. Provide all financial books and records, including but not limited to balance sheets, P&L statements, and financial ledgers.

3. Provide an aging schedule for accounts receivables.

EXAMPLE 2. DUE DILIGENCE QUESTIONNAIRE

Financial information

1. Provide all financial statements for past six years.

2. Provide all financial books and records, including but not limited to balance sheets, P&L statements, and financial ledgers.

3. Provide an aging schedule for accounts receivables.

4. Detail monthly revenues by store location.

5. Provide a list of the company's ten biggest customers by revenue for each of the past five years.

6. Provide any notices (including any bankruptcy petitions) or other information regarding the financial solvency of any of the company's ten largest customers by revenue.

7. List the top five products, goods, services, or other sources of revenues for the company for each of the past five years.

Figure 7-6. Questionnaire excerpts regarding financials

The two examples are not different merely because Example 2 asks more questions than Example 1. The information Example 2 aims to elicit will provide a substantially more useful picture regarding the nature of the company's revenues. Example 2 seeks the standard financial documents, but also requires the company to detail information about its most important customers and sources of revenues. The information requested in Example 2 will reveal

- Who the company's most significant customers are

- Whether the revenues are generated primarily from one or a few customers and, if so, does that create any risk (of too many eggs in one basket)

- How the revenues compare by location

- Whether there has been a change throughout the past five years regarding who are the most important customers (do we need to consider why this change has occurred?)

- Whether there is a concern that any of these significant customers are in financial trouble, and how this would affect the financial status of the company

- The main revenue sources in terms of products, goods, services, or other sources

- Whether the balance of revenue sources has changed and, if so, what (if anything) this means with respect to the financials, management focus, or business operation

Clearly, just asking for financial records, as in Example 1, does not provide the insight about the company's revenues, trends, and financial stability that the more pointed questions in Example 2 provide.

The Due Diligence Questionnaire for the KMF Franchise Transaction

As mentioned, the previous chapters in this book have set forth important principles about preparing for and conducting due diligence. This chapter has been about applying those principles to a particular transaction—namely, the purchase of an ownership interest in a franchise. The franchise transaction was chosen because the multifaceted nature of operating a franchise provides a good basis to examine how the due diligence questionnaire elicits the information needed to verify legal, financial, operational, and personnel aspects of a business. Thus far, the following stages of the due diligence process have been considered:

1. The franchise deal was dissected and broken out into its key facts and the potential issues were highlighted.

2. The importance of the four business cornerstones was highlighted because every aspect of the due diligence investigation examination relates back to one or more of these pillars.

3. The due diligence plan was created, further indentifying the key areas on which to focus during the due diligence process, and providing a road map for the questionnaire.

The next step is to create a due diligence questionnaire for the KMF Franchisee deal. To facilitate the discussion, the following pages contain a due diligence questionnaire for the KMF Franchisee transaction broken out into separate topics, with commentary detailing the purpose of the questions.

Note Appendix B includes the comprehensive version of the due diligence questionnaire that could be used for the KMF Franchisee transaction.

Corporate Organization and Ownership Structure

Ensuring the target company is structured properly is usually the focus of the first set of standard questions in the due diligence questionnaire. The KMF Franchisee transaction is no exception; thus the questionnaire begins with a series of requests delving into the corporate structure of the LLC. The goal is to determine whether the LLC was formed correctly as well as to elucidate the rights that are granted to, and the obligations and restrictions imposed on, owners of the business based on the structure of the LLC. This goal ties back directly to part II of the due diligence plan (Figure 7-2), which identified the need to review various issues related to the corporate organization of the business. Figure 7-7 contains a list of questions addressing fundamental issues about the organization and ownership structure of the LLC.

CORPORATE ORGANIZATION

1. Provide all documents relating to the formation of the LLC,[1] including, without limitation, the articles of organization and operating agreement (and all amendments thereof).

   Comment: The legal existence of the company needs to be confirmed and the formation documents reviewed to understand fully the rights and obligations of its members. An issue highlighted in the due diligence plan is that the original partners of KMF never executed an operating agreement, raising concerns about the structure of the LLC and the rights and obligations of its members. The investor should require execution of an operating agreement as a condition of the investment and include, for example, provisions regarding management of the LLC, financial rights of members, restrictions on transfer of membership interests, and buy–sell obligations relating to the withdrawal or termination of a member.

2. Provide all corporate record books (including minutes of meetings of members, managing members, or directors and committees thereof).

   Comment: Members (shareholders) and managers (directors) can adopt resolutions that affect the company, its operations, and the rights of the members/shareholders materially that are not contained in the initial formation documents.

3. List all officers and managers (directors) of the LLC.

4. List

   a. All jurisdictions where the LLC, its subsidiaries, and affiliates (the "Company" or "Companies") is incorporated or qualified to do business

   b. The address of the chief executive office, any other jurisdiction, and the address where the Company owns, stores, leases, or licenses properties or assets; has employees, agents, or customers; or keeps books and records relating to the Company.

5. Provide all certificates of authority, existence or good standing, and tax status certificates for each Company for their respective jurisdictions.

---

[1] The questionnaire includes instructions that would define the LLC to mean both KMF Franchisee and any subsidiaries and affiliates.

6. Provide a list of all assumed names, division names, or other names under which any of the Companies is conducting or has conducted business.

7. Has the Company changed its identity or corporate structure? If so, indicate the nature of such change, give the names of each company that was incorporated, merged, or consolidated with or acquired by the Company and provide the address of each place of business prior to such incorporation, merger, consolidation, or acquisition.

8. Provide a list of any corporations, partnerships, limited liability companies, joint ventures, or other entities in which any of the Companies has an interest or is affiliated, and a description of the interest or affiliation.

   Comment: Questions 4 through 8 seek information regarding the LLC and any affiliated companies to obtain a complete understanding of the corporate organization; to ensure the investigation covers not just the LLC, but also any related companies (especially if the potential investor will be an owner in the parent company); to confirm the authority of the company to do business in all jurisdictions where it operates; and to have the correct current name, any prior names, and trade names and d/b/a names so that lien, judgment, and other searches can be done for the LLC and its related entities, under all assumed names.

Corporate Ownership Structure

1. List the number of authorized and outstanding membership interests/units of each class of ownership interests in the Company.

2. List the names of each member of the LLC and the number and class or type of membership interest held.

3. List the holders of any options, warrants, rights, subscriptions to acquire, or securities granting rights to acquire, exercisable for, or convertible into, membership interests in the LLC, the terms of such right to acquire, exercise or right of conversion (and all agreements relating thereto) and the number of membership interests/units issuable in connection therewith.

4. Provide all documents relating to any employee options, bonuses, or other similar plans.

5. Provide all membership agreements, investor rights agreements, buy–sell agreements, redemption agreements, revocable and irrevocable proxies, voting agreements, and similar agreements with or among the members of any of the Companies.

6. Provide all documents relating to the buyout of Mishy, including any purchase agreement and loans made in connection with the buyout.

   Comment: The corporate ownership structure section asks the target company to provide information regarding the capitalization (i.e., ownership) of the company, the existence of any rights in any person (including current members, employees, or third parties) to acquire ownership interests in the company that would result in a dilution of the ownership of the current members, and the rights and obligations as agreed to among the members separate from the operating agreement (including, among other possible agreements, voting agreements, restrictions on transfer, and buy–sell obligations).

Figure 7-7. Corporate organization structure section of the questionnaire, with comments

Financial Information

A significant aspect of due diligence in most transactions is a review of the company's financial status as a component of determining the appropriate valuation of the business and the proposed transaction. Questions relating to the company's financials, financing obligations, and taxes therefore will comprise a major portion of the due diligence questionnaire (Figure 7-8). As a point of reference, these financial questions are aimed at addressing the issues in part IV of the due diligence plan (Figure 7-4).

FINANCING OBLIGATIONS

1. Provide promissory notes, commercial paper, loan or credit agreements, indentures, and other agreements or instruments relating to borrowing of money or a commitment to borrow money involving the Company.

2. Provide guarantees, repurchase obligations, surety contracts, and other arrangements whereby the credit of the Company is obligated for the indebtedness of a person.

3.   Provide documents purporting to create liens, mortgages, security agreements, pledges, charges, or other encumbrances on the membership interests of the Company, or on any assets, real or personal property of the Company, or in favor of the Company.

4.   Provide letters of credit, financial surety bonds, or similar credit support devices outstanding for the benefit of the Company and related reimbursement or indemnification agreements.

5.   Provide agreements pursuant to which the Company is or will be subject to any obligation to provide funds to or to make investments in any other person (in the form of a loan, capital contribution, or otherwise).

6.   Provide material correspondence with any creditor of the Company.

7.   List any existing defaults under credit arrangements of the Company and any events that have occurred that, with the giving of notice or the passage of time, will become such a default.

8.   Provide all notes payable to or notes receivable from any employee, manager, affiliate, agent, or member of the Company.

9.   Provide all other financing agreements relating, directly or indirectly, to the Company.

10. Has the Company granted any security interests in its assets, property or rights? Has it pledged any of its assets, property, or rights as collateral or security in connection with any obligation or for any other reason? Does there exist any encumbrance, lien, or security interest in the assets, property, or rights of the Company? If so, provide all documents and information relating thereto.

     Comment: These inquiries seek information regarding any loans and other financing obligations of the LLC, and any liens or encumbrances on the LLC's assets, property, or rights as a result of such obligations. When a loan is secured by company assets, an additional layer of risk is created, which is part of the valuation calculus.

Financial Information

1.   Provide all monthly, quarterly, and annual financial statements and balance sheets for the past six years and the current year to date, and all supporting schedules to such financial statements.

2.   Provide all quarterly projected income statements and cash flows for the next three years.

3. Provide a schedule of any contingent liabilities.

4. Detail any liabilities not reflected in the financial statements.

5. Detail all aged accounts receivables and payables as of each quarter for the past three years and for each quarter of the current year to date.

6. List all accrued expenses as of each year end for the past three years.

7. Set forth all net operating loss carry-forwards.

8. Provide all capital expenditure schedules (current and projected).

9. Provide all information concerning the number of customers, average purchase size/amount per transaction, and highest grossing products, highest margin products, broken out by location of each store/restaurant and by season.

10. Provide all agreements and detail all arrangements with merchant processors and credit card companies.

11. Detail all monthly charge-backs and issued credits for the past 24 months.

12. Provide all business plans, market surveys, and reports, and any report or summary regarding the financial condition of the Company.

    Comment: The crux of the questions here is to probe the financials and determine the appropriate valuation of the business. As a side note, questions 9 through 11 are examples of financial questions geared to the actual type of business that is the subject of the due diligence review, rather than generic financial questions.

Tax Matters

Provide all:

1. Federal, state, and local tax returns (for income, gross receipts, sales or use, property, employment, or other taxes) for past six years

2. Federal, state, and local audit and revenue agent reports, settlement documents, and correspondence relating to the Company

3. Agreements that waive statutes of limitations or extend time in connection with federal, state, and local tax matters

4. Deficiency assessments filed against any of the Companies by federal, state, or local tax authorities and the resolution of such deficiency (if any)

5. Copies of all documentation concerning any elections made under the Internal Revenue Code or other tax laws that could have a material effect on any of the Companies

   Comment: The tax documents are important to verifying information on a company's financial statements with respect to profits, losses, assets, and liabilities. However, requests relating to tax information are also important to make sure the company does not have outstanding tax disputes or unsettled obligations that already are, or could eventually become, liens on the assets. Another major concern, as addressed in question 1, is compliance with tax filing and payment obligations, especially for companies selling goods or services subject to state or local taxes. In New York, for example, the purchaser of assets in a company is responsible for any unpaid state sales taxes of the Seller, regardless of how liability is allocated in the purchase agreement between the seller and purchaser.

Figure 7-8. Financing obligations section of the questionnaire, with comments

Contracts and Agreements

Contracts and agreements entered into by a business can result in material (financial and nonfinancial) obligations or confer substantial benefits on a company. A clear picture of a business cannot be obtained without a comprehensive understanding of the contractual rights and obligations of the company that is the subject of the due diligence investigation (Figure 7-9). The importance of obtaining a complete understanding of the obligations and rights of the business is a substantial component of the due diligence plan (Figure 7-3, part III and Figure 7-4, part IV).

CONTRACTS, AGREEMENTS, AND COMMITMENTS

1. List each of Company's major suppliers and dollar volume of purchases from each for each fiscal year. (A "major supplier" means the top ten suppliers [by purchase volume]).

2. List any supplier for which practical alternative sources of supply are not available.

Provide all:

3. License, sublicense, royalty, and franchise agreements, including, without limitation, the franchise agreement with Rocky Robbins Ice Cream (the "Franchise") and all agreements, contracts, undertakings, and documents relating to the Franchise

4. Distribution, agency, manufacturer, and similar contracts

5. Joint venture or partnership agreements

6. Management, services, and marketing agreements

7. Hold-harmless, indemnification, or similar agreements

8. Leases and the status of negotiations to renew any of the leases

9. Agreements relating to the sale or lease of the company's assets

10. Warranty and service agreements

11. Agreements out of the ordinary course of business to which the Company is a party or by which it or its properties are bound

12. Standard form agreements used by the Company

13. Brokers or finders agreements

14. Confidentiality and nondisclosure agreements binding the Company

15. Agreements relating to any merger, acquisition, divestiture, consolidation, reorganization, spinoff, or disposition of assets and any documentation relating to any previous or proposed transaction

16. Agreements affected in any manner by a change in control of any of the Companies or that require consent of a third party to assignment

17. Insurance agreements and policies held for the benefit of the Company (e.g., fire or casualty insurance, loss of business, "key man") or its directors, officers, or employees

18. List and provide copies of all agreements and arrangements among any of the Companies and any officer, manager, or member, or any of their respective families or affiliates currently existing

19. Agreements that prohibit or restrict the Company's ability to compete in any business anywhere in any geographic area, or the customers with whom the Company may do business or the prices the Company may charge for its services

20. Material correspondence relating to any of the foregoing, including, but not limited to, notices of default in the performance or observance of any term thereof

   Comment: A significant aspect of a due diligence investigation is the review of the material contracts. An understanding of the contracts entered into by a business is necessary to have a complete picture of the financial as well as nonmonetary obligations undertaken by and rights granted to the company.

   Question 3 focuses on the Franchise agreements pursuant to which the KMF Franchisee has a right to operate the four Rocky Robbins Ice Cream bar locations. The investor would want to vet the Franchise agreements to understand the rights of the franchisee and obligations to the franchisor.

   Question 8 relating to the leases is especially important in this transaction because the lease for one of the locations is expiring.

   Question 20 is one that is often overlooked in due diligence. It is quite important to make sure the company is not in breach of any of the material agreements, including the Franchise agreements.

Figure 7-9. Contracts, agreements, and commitments section of the questionnaire, with comments

Intellectual Property and Technology

IP and technology are vital to the operations of large technology companies and small businesses as well. Servers at restaurants use mobile devices to take food orders, doctors store patient information in electronic records, and the local dry cleaner locates your clothes among the hundreds of items on the rack through a software application. Technology has become the backbone of taking and processing orders for goods and services, order fulfillment, manufacturing, distribution, customer service, and record keeping. The role that technology and IP plays in businesses has elevated its importance in due diligence. Part III of the due diligence plan highlights the importance of conducting a copious review of the company's IP rights as well as a technical review of its computer systems, software programs, and applications (used in the operation of the business, or constituting a product or service, of the business), and data storage systems and protocols (Figure 7-3, part III). With this in mind, see the questionnaire for the KMF scenario in Figure 7-10.

INTELLECTUAL PROPERTY AND TECHNOLOGY

1. List all patents, trademarks, service marks, logos, copyrights, and licenses worldwide, including all issued, registered, or pending applications ("Intellectual Property"). Provide details regarding the status of all patents, trademarks, copyright issuances, registrations, or applications.

2. Provide all contracts and proposed contracts concerning Intellectual Property owned, used or licensed by or licensed to the Company, including, but not limited to, license and royalty agreements.

3. List all domain names owned or used by the Company and to whom they are registered.

4. List all technology and computer software owned, held for use by, or being developed by or for the Company.

5. List all:

   a. Material third-party computer software used by the Company or incorporated into any software or product of the Company

   b. Open-source, freeware, or other software having similar licensing or distribution models used by the Company or incorporated into any software or product of the Company

6. List all trade secrets and other proprietary know-how or processes owned or held for use by the Company.

7. Provide all agreements and proposed agreements pursuant to which any Intellectual Property is assigned, sold, or otherwise transferred, or licensed by the Company to any party or subject to a covenant not to sue.

8. Provide all documents concerning any liens, pledges, or encumbrances against the Intellectual Property of the Company.

9. Set forth all claims, causes of actions, disputes, or threatened claims against the Company or brought or contemplated by the Company concerning the Intellectual Property or claims or threatened claims of infringement and the like.

10. List all technology and software owned, leased, or licensed to the Company and provide copies of any related agreements.

11. List all software programs and applications sold, distributed, or licensed to third parties by the Company.

12. Provide a description of procedural safeguards with respect to the trade secrets/confidential information and internal policy statements or manuals for procedures relating to the trade secrets and confidential information.

     Comment: Most franchises will include all the IP and technology needed to operate the franchise. However, the due diligence investigation should still include a review of the IP and technology, because the LLC could develop IP and technology for use in its operations separate from the technology provided to franchisees.

IT Systems and Networks

1. Provide copies of all agreements related to the provision of IT, data, or Internet-related products or services to or by the Company.

2. Describe all computer systems, software packages, networks, and computer services ("Computer Systems") in use by the Company, by location.

3. Provide copies of all policies, procedures, and plans for the Company's Computer Systems.

4. Describe any backup and disaster recovery arrangements, facilities management, and ongoing support arrangements, including details of service levels and charges.

5. Describe and provide copies of all documents related to whether the Company has access, or rights of access, to the source code of material licensed software to ensure adequate maintenance and updating of that software.

6. Describe any Company procedures to monitor compliance with the terms of software licenses, including whether these procedures monitor the use of software by the Company to ensure that multiple copies of any software are not used in breach of the relevant license terms.

7. Describe and provide copies of the Company's website security policies and procedures.

8. Confirm whether the Company owns all IP in the design and content of its web sites.

9. Describe any insurance coverage for business losses related to the Company's Computer Systems.

10. Describe any material interruptions of the Company's Computer Systems during the past three years.

Comment: The existence of the appropriate computer system for the nature of the business is an issue, but of equal concern is backup and disaster recovery, arrangements given the importance of IT to most businesses.

Figure 7-10. Intellectual property and technology section of the questionnaire, with comments

Privacy and Data Security

Businesses may have access to, and collect and store private information relating to customers and employees. Customer information may be used for marketing purposes and to process credit card payments. Health care providers maintain electronic health records. Computer networking services have access to and may store customer files. A loss of the data or a system breach allowing access by third parties can mean the ruin of a company. Due diligence regarding privacy and data security policies has become a crucial part of the process of buying or investing in a business (Figure 7-11 and, for reference, Figure 7-3, part III).

PRIVACY AND DATA SECURITY

Provide all:

1. Copies of all current and historical privacy and data security policies and practice manuals of the Company, including, without limitation, all privacy policies and procedures for the Company's use and disclosure of customer or personal information

2. Copies of all policies, procedures, and written information security programs for compliance with data protection and privacy legislation

3. Copies of all reports or audits (internal or external) that have been performed on the Company's information security programs or any other reports prepared by or for the Company concerning the implementation of information security programs

4. Copies of any other documentation and information regarding the Company's collection, use, storage, or disposal of customer or personal information (whether the Company's or a third party's).

5. Copies of all agreements the Company has with any third parties that act as the Company's agents or contractors and that receive customer or personal information subject to any statutory or regulatory data privacy or security requirements from or on behalf of the Company

6. Details regarding any actual or potential data and information security breaches, unauthorized use or access of the Company's computer systems or data, or data and information security issues affecting the Company that have been identified during the past three years.

    Comment: Any company that collects or has access to private information of customers or employees must comply with various privacy laws, a breach of which can carry substantial penalties and destroy the reputation of a business. Buyers and investors should also recognize the necessity of protecting and maintaining backups of customer data as well as the Company's own books and records. Furthermore, the existence of sufficient redundancies with respect to the computer network and data storage systems is crucial in response to a natural or other disaster.

Figure 7-11. Privacy and data security section of the questionnaire, with comments

Real Property

If a buyer is purchasing all the stock or assets of a business or considering becoming a partner in a business, the due diligence questionnaire should inquire about ownership, and the right to use and acquire any real property (Figure 7-12 and, for reference, Figures 7-3 and 7-4).

REAL PROPERTY

1. List real property owned by the Company, including size, location, and use of each parcel. Provide documents of title, title insurance, mortgages, deeds of trust, leases, and security agreements for these properties.

2. List all real property under contract for purchase by the Company. Provide any title report or title search in connection with any real property under contract to purchase.

3. Provide any appraisals or surveys of real property owned or being purchased by the Company.

4. Provide copies of all outstanding leases for real property to which the Company is either a lessor or lessee, including ground leases and subleases, estoppel certificates, and related subordination or nondisturbance agreements.

5. Provide any option or development agreements involving real property to which the Company is a party.

6. Provide all certificates of occupancy related to any real property owned or leased by the Company.

7. List all material encroachments, liens, easements, or other encumbrances on any real property owned or leased by the Company.

8. Provide any building, structural, engineering, and other inspection reports related to any property owned or leased by the Company.

   Comment: The fact that a lease is expiring is an important concern in the context of the Rocky Robbins transaction. Equally important is the pending purchase of one of the locations. An investor in the LLC would want to review the purchase contract and appraisal, and be provided a report of any issues arising from a title search, an environmental assessment, or inspection of the property.

Figure 7-12. Real property section of the questionnaire, with comments

Personnel and Employment

Personnel matters is one of the four business cornerstones and therefore its importance in the due diligence process cannot be overemphasized (Figure 7-4, part IV). The questions directed to the target business should be drafted with the goal of obtaining a clear understanding of the corporate organizational chart, the employees/consultants engaged by the company, employee compensation and benefits, labor relations, whether confidentiality and invention assignment agreements have been executed, and whether the company is in compliance with employment laws (Figure 7-13).

PERSONNEL AND EMPLOYMENT

Provide:

1. An organizational chart that lists directors, officers, and key personnel, and their title and job responsibilities

2. All employment, consulting, or management agreements with any current or former (if any term thereof is still in effect) employee or consultant of any of the Companies

3. All confidentiality, nondisclosure, invention assignment, and noncompete agreements with any current or former director, officer, partner, employee, or consultant of the Company

4. All termination or release agreements with any current or former employee or consultant of the Company

5. Descriptions (and plan documents, if any) of all significant fringe benefits, including holiday, vacation, personal leave, insurance policies or plans (medical, disability, life, travel, accident, dental, vision, or other), deferred compensation, salary continuation, and severance plans of the Company

6. All documents relating to any pension and retirement plans, including defined benefits plans, defined contribution plans, and simplified employee pension plans of the Company

7. Descriptions of any other benefits offered or provided to employees on retirement or current retirees of the Company

8. All plan documents relating to any bonus, profit sharing, stock option, stock bonus, phantom stock, stock appreciation right, or other incentive plan of the Company

9. Descriptions of material labor disputes, requests for arbitration and grievances, and union or labor organizational activities of the Company

10. A list of all officers, directors, management personnel, and any other employee or consultant of the Company who earns more than $30,000, together with such person's total compensation and all contracts

11. A list of all current personnel (including directors, officers, employees, and consultants) that delineates function, years of service, and compensation (base, bonus, granted options, vested options, or other compensation rights)

12. A list of the total number of employees by category, location, union/ nonunion status, starting date, and current compensation

13. All employee manuals for each Company

14. All notices and election forms provided to qualified beneficiaries advising of Consolidated Budget Reconciliation Act of 1985 (COBRA) coverage, initial notice advising participants of COBRA rights, documentation showing such notices have been provided, list of individuals covered by COBRA and date eligibility will terminate, and list of qualified beneficiaries who are eligible to elect COBRA but who have not yet done so, and the date the COBRA election period will end

15. A description of all loans or advances to or from directors/managers, employees, or consultants of the Company, including the amount of such loan or advance, its purpose, repayment terms, and, if applicable, a copy of any promissory notes or agreements related thereto

16. All filings with and material correspondence to or from the Department of Labor, the IRS, or any other government agency related to employment or labor issues

17. A description of any union organizations or membership drives that are threatened or pending, or that have occurred

18. All Equal Employment Opportunity Commission (EEOC) compliance files and notices of violations under any laws related to the EEOC or other employment related or antidiscrimination laws

19. A description of worker compensation policies, procedures, and claims (pending or concluded)

20. A detailed status of negotiations with the operations manager (Lara Melanie) and a list any other key personnel positions that remain to be filled or eliminated

21. All material correspondence and documents relating to the foregoing not otherwise provided hereunder

    Comment: Question 1 (organization chart) and question 15 (list of employees and functions) are important to understand the key employees of the Company and their responsibilities. Question 3 focuses on the important concern of whether key personnel have executed confidentiality and invention assignment agreements. A number of the questions address compensation and benefit rights as well as any right to acquire an interest in the LLC. Question 20 puts the pending contract expiration of the operations manager in the spotlight.

Figure 7-13. Personnel and employment section of the Questionnaire, with comments

Litigation and Claims/Legal Compliance

The existence of any judgments or pending lawsuits can have a substantial impact on the company. A large monetary judgment or pending claim can affect the financials of the business. A nonmonetary judgment or potential claim can be even more of an issue, such as one that enjoins an aspect of the business operations, determines a company does not own or have a right to use key IP, claims the company engages in employment discrimination, or declares that a noncompete is unenforceable. Figure 7-14 sets forth questions seeking information regarding civil, criminal, administrative, or similar claims or causes of action involving the company.

LITIGATION AND CLAIMS/LEGAL COMPLIANCE

Provide:

1. A list and summary of any insurance claims outstanding

2. A list and summary of all actual or threatened civil or criminal actions, litigations, proceedings, arbitrations, claims, or investigations by any person, entity, third party, or government, administrative, or regulatory authority involving the Company during the past ten years

3. In addition to the preceding items, details and all documents concerning any criminal or civil claims, causes of action, proceedings, litigations, or investigations involving any executive officers, directors, employees, directors/managers (e.g., bankruptcy, criminal, securities, taxation, employment)

4. All orders, injunctions, judgments, or decrees of any court or regulatory body applicable to any of the Companies or any of its properties or assets

5. A description of settlements of litigation, arbitration, and other criminal or civil proceedings, and copies of settlement agreements, releases, and waivers related thereto

6. All documents and a description of any litigation or threatened litigation concerning any IP owned or used by the Company

7. All documents and a description of any litigation, claims, or causes of action or threatened litigation, or claims or causes of action concerning environmental matters

8. All documents and a description of any litigation or threatened litigation against or by any employees or relating to any employment matters

9. All copies of any notices, citations, reports, letters, or other communications from federal and state government agencies

10. A description of all bankruptcy proceedings in which any of the Companies is a creditor or otherwise interested

11. A description of any contingent liability of any of the Companies not referenced herein or in the financial statements provided hereunder

12. All government permits, licenses, and other approvals

13. A list of all material claims and proceedings that have been settled, stating the amounts claimed, the amounts ultimately paid, and any equitable relief

14. A list and summary of all suits, actions, or claims pending or that existed during the past ten years

15. Any criminal actions, convictions, settlements, awards, judgments, fines, and the like pertaining to the Company, directors/managers, management, and the shareholders/members

16. Provide documents, if any, related to any bankruptcy filings, assignment for the benefit of creditors, dissolution, reorganization, appointment of a receiver or trustee, merger, or consolidation of the Company.

Comment: From the due diligence plan, the potential investor already knows there is a potential dispute involving a former partner of the LLC. In addition, an investor or potential purchaser of the business would be concerned about any existing or threatened claims arising from various aspects of the business, including employment issues, claims by or against existing or former partners, contract disputes, pending or threatened lawsuits, and criminal or civil actions or investigations commenced by any government body.

Figure 7-14. Litigation and claims/legal compliance section of the questionnaire, with comments

Environmental Matters/Health Compliance

Companies that fail to comply with environmental laws and regulations can face tremendous liabilities. In many cases, the liability and costs to remedy the issues will bankrupt the business. Environmental compliance affects a variety of businesses—not just those handling hazardous substances or pollutants. Even an ice cream restaurant such as Rocky Robbins needs to be mindful of environmental regulations. For example, restaurants use cleaning solvents, need to dispose of waste, and must maintain health code standards (Figure 7-15, and, for reference, Figure 7-3, part III).

ENVIRONMENTAL MATTERS

Provide:

1. A list of all real estate now or previously owned, operated, or leased by the Company, including a description of current and past uses thereof

2. A list of all hazardous substances used, generated, treated, stored, and/or disposed of by the Company

3. A list of (and copies of) all licenses and permits (including conditions) issued to the Company related to environmental or health code laws

4. A list of (and copies of) all pending or threatened claims, investigations, administrative proceedings, litigation, regulations, arbitrations, mediations, judgments, settlements, and demands for remedial action or for compensation alleging noncompliance with or violation of environmental laws, health code or permit conditions, or seeking relief under any environmental law or health code

5. A description of any contingent liability arising from or out of any environmental matter or health code violation

6. Any environmental reports, including Phase 1 and Phase 2 assessments in connection with any real property owned or to be purchased by the Company

   Comment: Question 1 is important because the company can be liable for environmental claims arising from real property it owns or leases, or previously owned or leased. Restaurants are heavily regulated by health codes. Multiple health code violations could result in fines and could pose a risk of loss of the right to the franchise, depending on the terms of the Franchise agreement.

Figure 7-15. Environmental health code matters section of the questionnaire, with comments

Personal Due Diligence

It is common to direct due diligence questions to directors and key equity holders. Investors want to make sure the key players in the business do not have personal, financial, or other issues that could create concerns about their involvement in the company. The questions in Figure 7-16 should be a separate questionnaire provided to directors and founders/key shareholders, who would be asked to submit personal responses to the questions and even agree to a background check.

DIRECTOR/MAJOR SHAREHOLDER QUESTIONS

1. Have you ever been found or pleaded guilty (including a plea of *nolo contendere*) to a felony or misdemeanor, or has there been any criminal investigation against you during the past five years?

2. Have you ever filed for bankruptcy?

3. Are there any lawsuits pending against you or your spouse, or have you or your spouse received any notice of a potential lawsuit? If so, please describe.

4. Have you ever been the subject of a criminal or civil proceeding or investigation by any government, regulatory, or administrative agency or body (including, without limitation, the Securities Exchange Commission)?

5. Do you have any tax liabilities other than those relating to the current tax year?

6. Have you been audited during the past six years?

7. Do you have any material disputes with a potential liability in excess of $10,000?

8. Do you or your spouse hold equity of 5% or more in any company? If yes, please list all companies.

9. Are you currently bound by a personal guarantee of a third party's obligations?

10. Are you currently bound by a noncompete or nonsolicitation agreement?

11. Will you agree to a personal background check regarding issues such as any pending criminal indictments or investigations, and any civil lawsuits, bankruptcy filings, and the like; as well as agree to a credit check?

    Comment. Obtaining responses to a personal due diligence questionnaire can be challenging, because directors and equity holders are reticent to provide personal information, arguing it is irrelevant to the business. However, investors need to be comfortable with their potential partners, recognizing that personal issues can, at a minimum, be a distraction, and, at an extreme, be a huge red flag counseling against the investment. As an aside, the company may similarly ask the new partner to submit to a background check because, once a new partner joins the company, it is legally very difficult to terminate his or her ownership rights.[2]

Figure 7-16. Stand-alone personal due diligence questionnaire, with comments

[2]The importance of conducting background checks is discussed more fully in Chapter 9.

Where Do You Go from Here?

After you submit the due diligence questionnaire to the target business, the question then is: Where do you go from here? The company will—hopefully, in a timely manner and without complaint—provide you with their response in the form of both written answers and corresponding documentation. A thorough review of these materials should be conducted to ensure the company has duly provided the information requested in the questionnaire. It is not unusual for companies to provide incomplete information or simply to skip questions altogether, necessitating follow-up from the requesting party. Any professionals engaged to assist with the due diligence process, including legal counsel, accountants, financial advisors, technology experts, or other advisors should review the information provided by the company and identify any issues of concern. As discussed in Chapter 6, if the issues cannot be resolved, or the party refuses to negotiate a resolution, the transaction should be terminated. On the other hand, as discussed in Chapter 8, in most transactions the parties will at least attempt to arrive at a solution to problems discovered during due diligence, including establishing an escrow, requiring indemnification, adding postclosing transition and cooperation clauses, and even restructuring the deal terms.

Resolving the Issues

When the responses to the due diligence questionnaire are received from the target company, the party conducting due diligence needs to determine how to address any issues that have been uncovered as a result of the investigation. Assuming the issues do not lead to a termination of the deal, the parties can then try to negotiate solutions to the problems that have been discovered. As discussed in this chapter, possible solutions include preclosing conditions, an adjustment of the company valuation (and thus the purchase price), and postclosing covenants and agreements. The contract should also include enforcement mechanisms that can be invoked in the event of a breach of a preclosing condition or covenant, including establishing an escrow, granting a right of repurchase, postclosing price adjustments, and indemnification.

Before considering possible solutions to various due diligence issues, however, we examine the importance of obtaining a period of exclusivity from the seller as well as a clear agreement on the right to conduct the due diligence examination. The benefits of a no-shop clause are discussed, which prohibits the company from seeking other bidders while providing the potential purchaser an opportunity to conduct due diligence and negotiate a binding agreement. In addition, even if the parties do not enter into a precontract letter of intent, they should consider entering into an agreement outlining the right of the purchaser to conduct due diligence.

At What Point during the Transaction Should Due Diligence Commence?

Due diligence can occur at different points during the life of a transaction. In some deals, the parties will agree that the investigation should be conducted before execution of the definitive deal documents whereas others may require that due diligence be a condition contained in the executed contract. A major aspect of a transaction is, therefore, determining at what point the due diligence process should begin in earnest. The parties may not always initially be on the same page regarding whether the definitive documents (for example the asset purchase agreement or subscription agreement) should be executed (or even negotiated) before completion of the due diligence investigation. Eventually, the parties need to agree on the appropriate timeline of the transaction. The following factors will likely influence a party's preference for when the due diligence should start.

Conducting the due diligence examination can be expensive. Given the cost of conducting the due diligence, the purchaser may want to enter into a binding agreement to prevent the seller from walking from the deal. The party conducting the due diligence will incur substantial costs, including preparation of the questionnaire; review of documents and information related to the legal issues by counsel; review of financial-related information by an accountant or other financial advisor; possible engagement of other professionals, such as computer/networking or IT experts, attorneys with knowledge of a specialized area of the law, possibly foreign counsel, and other consultants; lien, judgment, litigation, and similar searches; and the subsequent legal and accounting fees that can be incurred to negotiate a resolution of issues that may be discovered during the investigation. From the perspective of the party conducting the investigation, he or she may not want to commence due diligence without an agreement obligating the other party to proceed with the transaction. A company selling its assets, for example, can continue to shop the deal and, in the absence of a binding deal agreement or right of exclusivity, walk away from the transaction, leaving the other party with a large due diligence bill and no recourse against the company.

Responding to the due diligence questionnaire can be expensive. The company that is the subject of the transaction can also incur substantial costs during the process of responding to due diligence requests. The company has to respond to the due diligence questionnaire and marshal together the requested documents, which can be a substantial distraction for management and staff who are otherwise focused on business operations. Smaller businesses may not have an accountant or legal counsel on staff, requiring them to engage outside professionals. As with the potential buyer or investor, the company will be concerned about expending resources in response to due diligence requests without first entering into a binding agreement.

Disclosing confidential and proprietary information. The risks of disclosing confidential information without a binding agreement can be substantial. As part of the deal discussions and due diligence process, the parties will necessarily disclose confidential and proprietary information. Of course, before doing so, they should execute a nondisclosure agreement ostensibly designed to prevent the receiving party from disclosing or using the other party's confidential information. Nondisclosure agreements are commonplace in the deal process, but the actual protection they provide the disclosing party can be less than ideal. When a company discloses information to its competitor, can it ever be certain the nondisclosure agreement will completely prevent misuse of the information? For example, information about how a competitor prices goods or services, employees are compensated, and marketing strategies and business plans cannot be wiped easily from the mind of the receiving party if the deal fails to close. Nondisclosure agreements include remedies in the event of a breach, but enforcement can be costly, a considerable amount of time can pass before a final resolution is obtained, and, after the proverbial barn door has been opened, any eventual remedy may be too late to rectify the damage already done. Before agreeing to respond to any diligence requests, a party may therefore insist on a binding deal agreement that is subject to revisions based on the material due diligence uncovers.

A binding agreement is too risky until due diligence has been completed. If it is anticipated that the scope of diligence review will be fairly broad, the party conducting the examination may sense that entering into a binding agreement—even one with rights to adjust the terms based on the due diligence findings—would be premature. He or she may feel there are too many potential issues to be concerned about before getting a handle on how to negotiate the definitive deal agreements. The negotiation of a binding agreement would, therefore, await completion of the due diligence investigation, when all the issues are on the table and can be addressed at once—as opposed to using resources to draft an agreement that has to be renegotiated and then revised. The company often takes a similar view that it does not want to enter into a binding agreement that, in reality, can be revised substantially based on the rights granted the purchaser under the due diligence provisions of the contract. One approach to the issue regarding the timing of the due diligence investigation is for the parties to agree to deal exclusivity for a limited period of time or a due diligence clause that sets forth the timing, rights, and any limitations regarding the due diligence investigation.

Exclusivity

The party conducting the due diligence may be concerned about incurring substantial costs only to have the target company use the proposed deal to shop the transaction and obtain more favorable terms from a third party.

He or she may therefore demand a right of exclusivity that prevents the company from shopping the deal for a defined period. The exclusivity or no-shop clause can be a separate binding agreement or a binding provision in an otherwise nonbinding letter of intent.[1] The intent of the no-shop is to allow time for the due diligence investigation, negotiation, and drafting of a binding deal agreement. The following are examples of exclusivity provisions that can be included in a letter of intent or deal term sheet for different types of deals.

■ **Note** The sample contract provisions are intended for reference only. The provisions of a contract should be drafted in light of the underlying facts of the transaction. It is very important to obtain the advice of an experienced corporate/business attorney before entering into any agreement.

NO-SHOP CLAUSE: EXAMPLE I

The Company agrees that during a period of sixty (60) days from the date of the signing of this letter of intent, the Company, its shareholders, board members, employees, affiliates, or any agents thereof shall not, directly or indirectly, take any action to solicit or support any inquiry, proposal, or offer from, furnish any information to, or participate in any negotiations or discussions with, any third party, or enter into any agreement or arrangement regarding any equity/debt funding or sale. Notwithstanding the forgoing, if neither the Company nor the Investors give written notice of its wish to terminate this letter of intent at least five (5) days before the end of the exclusivity period, the letter of intent shall remain in full force and effect, and the Company shall continue to negotiate exclusively with the Investors until the Company or the Investors give written notice of termination.

Companies trying to raise money can be caught between an interested investor who insists on a no-shop clause and the risk associated with shutting down efforts to raise financing if the initial investor decides not to proceed. Due diligence and the negotiation of private-equity financing terms can take

---

[1]A letter of intent may be entered into during the initial stage of the deal and will contain the material terms the parties have negotiated and expect to be included in the definitive transactional documents. The letter of intent is generally nonbinding because and is not intended to include all the provisions of the final transaction documents. However, the letter will often include several provisions that the parties expressly agree are binding: confidentiality, exclusivity, the right to conduct due diligence (especially where there is an exclusivity clause), and a dispute resolution clause in the event of a breach of the binding terms of the letter of intent. The pros and cons of entering letter of intent are discussed in Chapter 9.

longer than anticipated, and if the deal is never concluded, the company may have lost an opportunity to raise money at a crucial juncture in its business. Having said this, most potential investors will not consider undertaking due diligence until a no-shop is in place, and thus the company may have little choice but to agree to exclusivity.

NO-SHOP CLAUSE: EXAMPLE 2

The Company agrees to negotiate in good faith and work expeditiously toward a closing. The Company, its members, directors, managers, employees, relatives, affiliates, or any agents thereof agree that for a period of ninety (90) days from the date of this letter of intent they will not, directly or indirectly, (1) take any action to solicit, initiate, encourage, or assist the submission of any proposal, negotiation, or offer from any person or entity related to the sale or issuance of any of the stock of the Company or the acquisition, sale, lease, license, or other disposition of the Company or any part of the stock of the Company or any part of the assets of the Company (except during the ordinary course of business); or (2) enter into any discussions or negotiations, or execute any agreement related to any of the forgoing, and shall notify the Investors promptly of any inquiries by any third parties in regard to the forgoing.

In contrast to Example 1, the no-shop clause in example 2 includes an obligation to negotiate in "good faith." The meaning of good faith in the context of negotiations and the obligations the phrase imposes on the parties are not easy to define and are beyond the scope of our discussion. However, if you choose to include some form of a good-faith obligation in the no-shop, recognize that its meaning and effect can be open to interpretation, is fact specific, and may end up being the dominant issue in any action seeking to enforce the exclusivity provisions.

NO-SHOP CLAUSE: EXAMPLE 3

The Company agrees to work in good faith and expeditiously toward a closing. The Company and its shareholders, directors, employees, affiliates, or any agents thereof agree they will not, for a period of ninety (90) days from the date of execution of this Term Sheet by all parties, take any action to solicit, initiate, encourage, or assist in the submission of any proposal, negotiation, or offer from any person or entity other than the Purchaser related to the sale or transfer of all or part of the shares of the Company or all or part of the assets of the Company. In the event of a breach of this exclusivity obligation, the Company shall pay the Purchaser $[xxx] as liquidated damages. The Company will not disclose the terms of this Term Sheet to any person other than officers, members of the board of directors, and the Company's accountants and attorneys, without the written consent of the Investors.

Example 3 includes a liquidated damages clause in the event of a breach of the no-shop by the company, requiring the seller to pay a defined amount as damages. Determining the appropriate (and mutually agreeable) amount will be the subject of negotiations between the parties. However, if a liquidated damages amount can be agreed to, it will save the purchaser the expense of litigation.

NO-SHOP CLAUSE: EXAMPLE 4

The Company, management, or any of their respective advisors, officers, directors, affiliates, employees, or agents will not initiate, encourage, solicit, or continue any negotiations or discussions with any third party, other than Buyer, for the purpose of soliciting any proposals related to the purchase of any assets or equity of the Buyer for a period of sixty (60) days after the signing of this Letter of Intent. In the event of a breach of this provision, the Company shall reimburse the Buyer for all costs and expenses incurred by the Buyer in connection with the contemplated transaction, including but not limited to all legal fees, due diligence costs, professional and advisor fees, and other related expenses. Furthermore, the Buyer may seek any form of equitable relief, including, without limitation, a restraining order or injunction to enforce Buyer's rights under this provision.

In Example 4, the buyer does not define a damages amount, but has the right to hold the company liable for all transaction costs. The example also specifically includes a right to enjoin any breach of the no-shop by the Company.

NO-SHOP CLAUSE: EXAMPLE 5

The parties agree to extend every effort (1) to negotiate, execute, and deliver by the date that is forty-five (45) days following the date of this letter of intent, a definitive asset purchase agreement and (2) to close the acquisition as soon as practicable but no later than forty-five (45) days from the date of signing the definitive agreements after the last of any required approvals shall have been received. Therefore, the Company agrees to negotiate in good faith an exclusively with the Buyer, and not to negotiate directly or indirectly with, offer to sell any or all of its assets, or solicit any offer or any interest in any or all of assets, or accept any offer to purchase its assets for a period that is forty-five (45) days from the date of this letter of intent ("Exclusivity Period"). Further, the Company shall, immediately halt any discussions with (including persons with whom the Company may have had discussions before the date hereof) any other party during the Exclusivity Period. In the event the Company, its shareholders, directors, officers, employees, affiliates, or agents in any manner breaches the terms of this No-Shop Clause, at a minimum, the Company shall reimburse the Buyer all of its reasonable costs of due diligence related to the proposed transaction. It is also understood and agreed that monetary damages would not be a sufficient remedy for any breach of this No-Shop Clause and that the Buyer shall be entitled to seek equitable relief, including injunction and specific performance, as a remedy for any such breach. Such remedies shall not be deemed to be the exclusive remedies for a breach of this No-Shop Clause but shall be in addition to all other remedies available at law or equity.

NO-SHOP CLAUSE: EXAMPLE 6

No Solicitation of Other Bids

1.   For a period of sixty (60) days from the date of this Term Sheet, the Company shall not, and shall not authorize or permit any of its affiliates or any of its or their representatives to, directly or indirectly, (a) encourage, solicit, initiate, facilitate, or continue inquiries regarding an acquisition; (b) enter into discussions or negotiations with, or provide any information to any person concerning a possible acquisition; or (c) enter into any agreements or other instruments regarding an acquisition. The Company shall immediately cease and cause to be terminated, and shall cause its affiliates and all of its and their representatives to cease immediately and cause to be terminated all existing discussions or negotiations with any persons conducted heretofore with respect to, or that could lead to, an acquisition. Acquisition shall mean (a) a merger, consolidation, liquidation, recapitalization, share exchange, or other business combination transaction involving the Company; (b) the issuance or acquisition of shares of capital stock or other equity securities of the Company or loans convertible into equity; (c) the sale, lease, exchange, or other disposition of any significant portion of the Company's properties or assets; or (d) a pledge of all or a significant portion of its assets as collateral for any loan or financing agreement.

2.   In addition to the other obligations under this section, the Company shall promptly (and in any event within three [3] business days after receipt thereof by the Company or its representatives) advise the buyer orally and in writing of any inquiry or solicitation regarding an acquisition, any request for information with respect to an acquisition, or any inquiry with respect to or that could reasonably be expected to result in a proposal for an acquisition, the material terms and conditions of such request, an acquisition proposal or inquiry, and the identity of the person making the same.

> 3. The Company agrees that the rights and remedies for noncompliance with this section shall include, without limitation, having such provision specifically enforced by any court having equity jurisdiction, it being acknowledged and agreed that any such breach or threatened breach shall cause irreparable injury to the Buyer and that monetary damages would not provide an adequate remedy to the Buyer.

Examples 5 and 6 incorporate many of the concepts found in the previous examples. Moreover, Example 5 permits the buyer to pursue different non-exclusive remedies, including a right to reasonable due diligence expenses, specific performance, and other equitable remedies.

Understand that there is no "standard" form of an exclusivity clause. Although the main goal is to prevent deal shopping during the defined no-shop time period, these clauses can differ in terms of issues such as the period of exclusivity, the responsibility of the parties to negotiate during the exclusivity period, and the availability of damages and other remedies in the event of a breach.

Due Diligence Provisions

The deal term sheet (or the letter of intent) should include a provision that outlines specifically the right of the buyer/investor/lender to conduct due diligence. The binding purchase or investment agreement should similarly include a due diligence clause giving the buyer or investor the right to terminate the agreement in the event issues are discovered during the course of the due diligence investigation. Several examples of due diligence provisions are presented next.

DUE DILIGENCE CLAUSE: EXAMPLE I

As a condition of the transaction, the Buyer shall have the right to conduct due diligence concerning the Company and its business for a period of thirty (30) days ("Due Diligence Period"). The Buyer shall have the right to terminate this Letter of Intent for any reason based on the due diligence findings at any time during the Due Diligence Period. Notwithstanding anything to the contrary, this due diligence provision shall be binding on the parties to this Letter of Intent.

DUE DILIGENCE CLAUSE: EXAMPLE 2

Section [X], Due Diligence and No Material Adverse Change. The Company shall have provided the Buyer access to such information as the Buyer shall have reasonably requested in connection with its due diligence investigation, and the Buyer shall have concluded its due diligence investigation of the Company to Buyer's complete satisfaction and shall be reasonably satisfied that there has been no material adverse change in the business, operations, financial condition, or prospects of the Company.

Example 1 is a simple due diligence clause that may be included in a letter of intent or similar document. It provides the buyer complete discretion to terminate the transaction for any reason based on its due diligence investigation. Example 2 is a similar provision in a stock purchase agreement.

DUE DILIGENCE CLAUSE: EXAMPLE 3

Section [X], Access to Information. From the date hereof until the closing, the Company shall (1) provide the Buyer and Buyer's representatives full and free access to and the right to inspect all of the assets, real property (including, without limitation, conducting any environmental assessments), properties, premises, books and records, contracts and other documents, and data related to the Company and the business (as defined above); (2) furnish the Buyer with such financial, operating, and other data and information related to the Company and the business as the Buyer or any of the Buyer's representatives may reasonably request; and (3) cooperate with the buyer and Buyer's representatives in the investigation of the Company and the business. Any investigation pursuant to this Section shall be conducted in such manner as not to interfere unreasonably with the conduct of the business of the Company. No investigation by the Buyer or other information received by the buyer shall operate as a waiver or otherwise affect any representation, warranty, or agreement given or made by the Company in this agreement.

. . .

Section [XX], Termination. This Agreement may be terminated at any time before closing as follows:

By the Buyer, provided the Buyer is not then in material breach of any provision of this Purchase Agreement and there has been a breach, inaccuracy in, or failure to perform any representation, warranty, covenant, or agreement made by the Company pursuant to this a Purchase Agreement, and such breach, inaccuracy, or failure has not been cured by the Company within ten (10) business days of the Company's receipt of written notice of such breach from the Buyer.

Example 3 is a due diligence clause that could be included in a purchase agreement. The provision gives the buyer the right to conduct the due diligence investigation and requires the company to cooperate with the buyer's investigation of the company and its business. If the assets of the seller include real property, an environmental assessment should be conducted, and therefore the due diligence clause also should specifically include the right to conduct an environmental assessment. An important aspect of the provision is that it expressly precludes the company from trying to limit the scope of the representations or warranties under the purchase agreement by arguing that the buyer had an opportunity to conduct due diligence. Although there is nothing in the due diligence provision itself that gives the buyer the right to walk away from the deal based on the due diligence results, in a separate provision the buyer has a right to terminate the deal for a breach of any of the representations, warranties, or covenants given by the company under the purchase agreement.

DUE DILIGENCE CLAUSE: EXAMPLE 4

Section [X], Due Diligence. (1) The Buyer and Buyer's representatives shall have the right to, and the Company shall afford the Buyer and Buyer's representatives, reasonable access and the right to inspect all the assets and the business of the Company, including, without limitation, the real property, properties, assets, premises, books and records, contracts and other documents, and data related to the business; (2) The Company shall furnish the Buyer and Buyer's representatives with such financial, operating, and other data and information related to the business as the Buyer or any of Buyer's representatives may reasonably request; and (3) the Company and its representatives shall cooperate with the Buyer in its investigation of the business; provided, however, that any such investigation shall be conducted during normal business hours on reasonable advance notice to the Company, under the supervision of the Company's personnel, and in such a manner as not to interfere with the conduct of the business. All requests by the Buyer for access pursuant to this Section shall be submitted or directed exclusively to [named Company representative] or such other individuals as the Company may designate in writing from time to time. Notwithstanding anything to the contrary herein, the Company shall not be required to disclose any information to the Buyer if such disclosure would, in the Company's sole discretion (1) cause significant competitive harm to the Company and its businesses, including the business, if the transactions contemplated by this agreement are not consummated; (2) jeopardize any attorney–client or other privilege; or (3) contravene any applicable law, fiduciary duty, or binding agreement entered into before the date of this agreement. Prior to the closing, without the prior written consent of the Company, which may be withheld for any reason, the Buyer shall not contact any suppliers to, or customers of, the business, and the Buyer shall have no right to perform invasive or subsurface investigations of the real property. The Buyer shall, and shall cause Buyer's representatives to, abide by the terms of the confidentiality agreement with respect to any access or information provided pursuant to this Section.

. . .

Section [XX], Termination. This agreement may be terminated at any time before closing as follows:

By the Buyer, provided the Buyer is not then in material breach of any provision of this agreement and there has been a breach, inaccuracy in, or failure to perform any representation, warranty, covenant, or agreement made by the Company pursuant to this agreement and such breach, inaccuracy, or failure has not been cured by the Company within ten (10) business days of the Company's receipt of written notice of such breach from the Buyer.

The right of the buyer to conduct due diligence is similar to Example 3 in many respects, but it also deviates in other respects by prohibiting unfettered access to information regarding the seller's business. In particular, the company may refuse to disclose any information it deems would cause competitive harm if the deal is not consummated. A buyer may not want to agree to the limitation on disclosure, arguing that the very purpose of the confidentiality agreement is to prevent misuse of proprietary information by the receiving party. The company's likely response is that an nondisclosure agreement is insufficient to prevent competitive harm because after the information is disclosed, it cannot be wiped from the memory of the receiving party. Furthermore, the buyer is protected by the representations and warranties made by the seller in the purchase agreement. If the buyer is willing to accept the provision in principle, it might counter with a modification that changes the right to one that can be exercised in the company's "reasonable discretion" rather than its "sole discretion."

The question associated with all these due diligence clauses is: what is the obligation of either party, if any, to negotiate to resolve issues that arise as a result of the due diligence investigation? A seller that does not commit to negotiate before entering into the definitive deal agreements will have complete latitude to make a decision whether to engage on an issue or simply approach the deal as "take it or leave it." A seller or a company issuing stock who believes there are other potential bidders or investors in the wings, or who is suddenly no longer interested in proceeding with the transaction can then simply ride out any exclusivity period.

In contrast, the party conducting the due diligence investigation will want the right to terminate the deal if the results of the investigation are unsatisfactory, but it also wants the right to force the company to negotiate if it still wants to proceed with the transaction. The buyer does not want to be used by the company to attract other buyers (and potentially drive up the valuation of the business) in the event the deal does not close. The buyer may try to push the company to agree to the inclusion of a due diligence clause in the purchase agreement pursuant to which the company must take all reasonable measures to resolve any issues that undermine the validity of the representations and warranties within a defined period following notice from the buyer. If due diligence is to occur before execution of the deal documents, the buyer should require the seller to negotiate in good faith to address any material issues discovered by the due diligence investigation. However, as noted previously, the meaning and scope of what constitutes good faith can be hard to determine and should be viewed in terms of the law governing the transaction. Furthermore, the company's willingness to accept an obligation to rectify or negotiate any due diligence issues depends primarily on the bargaining power of the buyer/investor seeking to include the obligation in the due diligence clause.

Resolving Due Diligence Issues

The remainder of the chapter focuses on how to resolve issues discovered during the course of the due diligence investigation through preclosing conditions and postclosing covenants, and how to enforce the seller to abide by these contractual obligations. Let's revisit the proposed investment in the KMF Franchisee business because it is helpful in illustrating various mechanisms for resolving deal issues.

Let's assume the lawyer for the investor has received the responses to the due diligence questionnaire from the company and has reviewed the responses and documentation provided by the company as well as information obtained from his own investigation and inspection of the company, its assets, and business operations. The lawyer, Jay Warren, has called his client, Ellen Kay, to discuss the major issues revealed through the due diligence investigation. There are occasional breaks from the dialogue to interject comments that explain the solution the attorney is proposing for the particular due diligence issue.

Attorney: Good afternoon! It's Jay Warren. We received the due diligence materials from KMF and I want to go over some of the more important issues. Is this a good time?

Investor: Thanks for the call. This is definitely a good time because I am anxious to move forward. Did you find anything particularly troublesome?

Attorney: There are few significant issues, but I believe that if the company is willing to work with us, they can be resolved. Also, earlier today I spoke with your accountant, who reviewed KMF's financials, and she gave me her comments. Let me walk you through all the concerns, with suggestions on how to handle them.

Investor: Perfect.

Attorney: First, both your accountant and I noticed that one of the KMF staff is being treated as a consultant/independent contractor. The benefit of the classification is it saves the company from paying any employment-related taxes and offering healthcare benefits. However, if the person should have been treated as an employee, the company can be subject to payment of the payroll taxes (including the employee's share if the employee fails to pay it) as well as penalties and interest. Classifying employees as consultants is a glowing red flag that can attract an audit. If a worker or workers are actually employees, even after rectifying the past violations, KMF will likely be subject to increased IRS scrutiny going forward. I can tell you, this is a big no-no. Both your accountant and I believe that the nature and manner of the services the staff member provides require reclassification of the worker before the IRS notices. Further, since KMF is required by law to offer healthcare benefits to its employees, it will face substantial penalties from misclassification of staff as independent contractors or part-time employees.

Investor: Makes sense. What do you recommend we tell KMF?

Attorney: There are procedures for voluntarily correcting the misclassification of an employee as an independent contractor. In fact, being proactive can reduce the penalties, and so I suggest we propose a condition that requires the company rectify the issue before closing.

■ **Comment** A common method of addressing issues discovered during due diligence is through closing conditions. The purchase agreement can be amended (if it has already been executed) or can include (if due diligence was conducted before the contract was drawn up) that a party take certain actions or resolve a defined issue as a condition to closing. The inclusion of *preclosing conditions* in the deal agreements is one of the solutions discussed later in this chapter for addressing due diligence issues.

Investor: Agreed. What's the next issue?

Attorney: The company still has not entered into a new contract with Lara Melanie, the manager of operations. Her current contract expires in two months. She has managed all four stores for the past three years and is obviously crucial to the business.

Investor: I've thought a lot about this since the issue first came to light. I do not feel comfortable proceeding unless the company either extends Lara Melanie's contract or finds an acceptable replacement.

Attorney: Then I suggest that we require a satisfactory resolution as a condition of closing. We need to have the right to approve the employment terms of any contract extension or of any replacement for Lara Melanie. In addition, we should have a right to terminate the deal if the matter is not resolved in a defined time frame; otherwise, the deal could drag out forever.

▓ **Comment** The lawyer has again identified an issue that needs to be resolved as a condition to closing the transaction. The investor is unwilling to proceed with the transaction unless the company has entered into a contract with either Lara Melanie or a suitable replacement for the manager of operations position. The attorney has astutely added the right to approve the terms of any contract for the manager of operations to avoid a scenario in which the company agrees to unfavorable financial terms to be able to close the transaction. The ability to terminate the deal (*right of termination*) is also important, because otherwise the investor could be bound by the contract indefinitely while the matter remains unresolved. The company may balk at accepting the closing condition, arguing that it gives Lara Melanie too much leverage in her contract negotiations. In essence, Lara Melanie may realize that she can extract substantially better contract terms if the deal is dependent on the company entering into a new employment agreement with her. However, the investor can compromise by agreeing that any approval by the investor cannot be withheld unreasonably whereas the company can use this right of approval as leverage in negotiations with the manager if she insists on unreasonable contract demands. The investor will want the unilateral right to terminate rather than give the company an excuse for walking away from the deal if, for example, more advantageous investment terms are offered by a third party.

Attorney: The expiring lease also is an issue, and similar to the situation with Lara Melanie. We should demand execution of a new lease with acceptable terms as a closing condition.

Investor: Makes sense. Separately, I heard there may be an environmental issue with the property the company is buying.

Attorney: Yes, and if there are any environmental issues and the company decides to proceed, the purchase agreement for the property must include indemnifications and a sufficient escrow of the purchase price. However, I'm also going see if the company will give us the right to approve the terms related to the environmental issues.

▧ Comment   Environmental issues can create liabilities for any subsequent owner of the property. It may be that the potential liability is too great to proceed with the purchase of the property. If this issue can be addressed, the purchaser of the property (here, KMF) wants an indemnification from the seller of the property. KMF also wants a sufficient portion of the purchase price held in escrow to ensure there are funds to address any indemnification obligations. These contract rights may be included in the membership purchase agreement between Ellen Kay and KMF and are examples of obligations that will survive the closing.

Attorney: The next issue is a big one. You are aware that a former partner, Mishy, is threatening to open an ice cream bar that is very similar to Rocky Robbins, correct? Mishy was very involved with the operations of the LLC, and therefore could easily replicate the Rocky Robbins model. Any competition from Mishy could seriously affect the company's financials and the value of your investment.

Investor: Is Mishy bound by any noncompete?

Attorney: Amazingly, the LLC never had Mishy execute a noncompete, either as a partner in the business or as a condition of the buyout of her membership units. She did, however, sign a confidentiality agreement.

Investor: What do we do here? I'm not interested in the investment if we can't obtain assurances that Mishy won't open a competitive ice cream bar nearby our stores.

Attorney: There are a couple of potential ways to address the matter. First, Mishy signed a confidentiality agreement. If she uses confidential information or proprietary information to start a competitive business, the company should have a claim. However, assuming the LLC has a claim, the legal costs could be substantial and preventing harm to the business would depend on whether the LLC obtained a temporary injunction against Mishy opening the restaurant during the pendency of the lawsuit. Second, the franchisor separately may have claims against Mishy. Of course, we have no assurances that Rocky Robbins would take any action or that it could obtain a favorable outcome in a timely manner to avoid a devastating hit to the LLC's business.

Investor: Well, neither of those solutions gives me much comfort. I'm not sure I want to buy into a business knowing its success may depend on the outcome of various potential lawsuits. The competitive risk substantially affects the valuation of the business, but I don't think it's possible at this point to determine with any certainty how much the business would be impacted if Mishy tried to open a new ice cream bar.

Attorney: Your points are absolutely justified. We could demand a revision of the purchase price for the membership units, and even if the company agrees, which I doubt, measuring the possible effect of Mishy opening a similar ice cream restaurant has too many variables. You could walk from the deal now without any exposure.

Investor: Is that the only option?

■ Comment   The due diligence investigation can take place before or after execution of a binding agreement. If there is no binding agreement, a party can terminate the transaction at any time. If a contract to purchase was executed before completion of due diligence, the contract should grant the purchaser/investor the right to terminate the contract based on the discovery of (material) due diligence issues. However, as previously mentioned, deal negotiations, contract drafting, and responding to due diligence can run up substantial costs for a seller, which will weigh on its decision about negotiating and executing a contract before the due diligence is completed.

Attorney: I've talked to the company's counsel about one other approach to the matter. They propose giving you a right whereby you could sell back the units for the full price paid in the event that during the next year Mishy opens a competitive ice cream bar and that business substantially impacts the LLC's business. However, they also want each partner (including you) to put in additional funds to pay off the Mishy loan.

Investor: Let me think about the proposal. One concern I have is if the business is not doing well, then how could it afford to repurchase my units?

Attorney: I've been considering the very point, and if you agree, I would suggest the partners give personal guarantees and the company give you a security interest in its assets. We'll have to see if KMF will agree. I have no doubt the partners will seriously push back as far as the personal guarantees, but it doesn't make sense to proceed without some form of enforcement mechanism related to the repurchase right.

■ **Comment** There is quite of bit going on in the previous exchange regarding the proposed repurchase right. It is a fairly draconian measure to allow an investor to redeem its interests after the closing if an issue discovered during the due diligence process cannot be resolved satisfactorily. It requires a business to pay back an investor and unwind the entire deal. Moreover, the existing partners may object to a redemption right because the investor would essentially reduce her investment risk at the expense of the other partners. From the investor's perspective, the main concern is ensuring the company can, in fact, honor the redemption commitment.

Investor: Are there any other major issues we need to talk about?

Attorney: There are some less important financial and legal issues, but we are already addressing those with KMF. I'll discuss the various points with KMF's counsel and get back to you.

Investor: Thanks.

The conversation between the potential investor and her attorney detailing the results of the due diligence investigation is instructive because it highlights issues and solutions that could arise realistically in a deal. With the conversation in mind, we can examine in more detail solutions for resolving due diligence issues, including those raised by the attorney in the KMF transaction.

Preclosing Conditions

When the due diligence investigation leads to a discovery of one or more material issues, one method to address the concerns is to include preclosing conditions in the definitive agreement. These conditions give the buyer the right to delay the closing until the conditions have been satisfied. Preclosing conditions address issues that are so important that the party conducting the due diligence can refuse to close if the matter is not addressed. Revisiting some of the legal, operational, financial, and personnel issues highlighted in the case studies illustrates some examples when inclusion of a preclosing condition would be advisable to ensure proper execution of the transaction.

Case Study 1: The Loan Transaction

Overlook, Inc., a computer repair company, wants to expand its business. It has negotiated with the landlord to lease the additional space next door. Private lender Lucy is prepared to loan Overlook $100,000 for the expansion. The loan will have five-year term and an annual interest rate of 9% payable monthly. It will be secured by all the assets, including the receivables, of Overlook, Inc.

During the course of due diligence, it is discovered that there is currently a judgment against Overlook in the amount of $20,000. In addition, the key man insurance of the sole owner of Overlook will expire during the term of the loan.[2] Table 8-1 contains an overview of the key issues and suggested preclosing conditions that could be applied.

Table 8-1. Preclosing Conditions for the Loan Transaction

Due Diligence Issue	Preclosing Condition
A judgment against the borrower in the amount of $20,000 remains unsatisfied.	Require the borrower to settle the judgment as a condition of the loan.
The owner's key man insurance policy is expiring.	Require evidence of a policy renewal before closing as well as the lender's right to the proceeds in the event of death or disability.

Case Study 2: Purchase of the Assets of ABB

Jack Enterprises has offered to purchase certain assets of ABB, which sells gift cards offered by a variety of major chain stores. The assets include ABB's software, customers, and contracts with retail chains.

During the course of due diligence, several issues are uncovered that could potentially kill the deal, including (1) a former partner has claimed ownership of the software application that is the crown jewel of the business, (2) the seller has outstanding state sales tax obligations, (3) a third party has a right of first refusal to the assets, and (4) the key contracts require consent before assignment to the purchaser. Table 8-2 contains an overview of the key issues and suggested preclosing conditions that could be applied.

---

[2] Key man insurance provides insurance proceeds to a business in the event of disability or death of a person vital to the ongoing existence of the business. Here, the owner is the "key man" and, in the event of his death or disability, the survival of the business may be in question. Therefore, the lender (who assumes the business cannot survive without the owner) wants a key man policy in place and an assignment of the proceeds as necessary to satisfy the loan.

Table 8-2. Preclosing Conditions for ABB Asset Purchase

Due Diligence Issue	Preclosing Condition
The former partner has filed a lawsuit seeking declaratory judgment that she owns the key software application.	Obtain a release and assignment of all rights to the software from the former partner as a condition of closing.
ABB has failed to submit state sales taxes for the first and second quarters of the year, and will eventually owe sales taxes for that portion of the third quarter up to the closing date.	Require the company to submit all state sales taxes owed before closing.[3]
ABB granted a right of first refusal to a third party in the event of a sale of the business.	Obtain a waiver of the right of first refusal before closing.
Several of the contracts with the retail chains require the consent of the retailer before reassignment.	Condition the closing on obtaining the necessary consents, because the contracts are a significant aspect of the ABB business.

Case Study 3: Purchase of SamGar Technology, LLC

SamGar Technology, LLC, wishes to sell its business to Kobe Zander, a software developer. Zander has offered to purchase all the membership interests in SamGar for $175,000. SamGar wants to structure the transaction as a sale of the equity, rather than the assets, because its accountant has determined that sale of the membership interests is preferable from a tax standpoint. Zander is willing to purchase the equity in the company because he believes the value of the enterprise is closer to $300,000, less an outstanding loan that is, according to SamGar, $65,000. Due diligence has uncovered the following issues: (1) a minority shareholder is refusing to sell, (2) the employees have not executed confidentiality or invention assignment agreements, and (3) the company is not in good standing under the laws of the state where it was incorporated. Table 8-3 contains an overview of the key issues discovered during due diligence and suggested preclosing conditions that could be applied.

---

[3]Under bulk sales laws, a buyer in an asset sale can be on the hook for unpaid sales tax amounts owed by the seller; therefore, the buyer needs to make sure the seller pays its obligations before closing or that money is held in escrow to pay any outstanding sales tax obligations. A portion of the sales price should be held in escrow after the amount of the seller's share of the third-quarter payment is known.

Table 8-3. Preclosing Conditions for the SamGar Stock Purchase Transaction

Due Diligence Issue	Preclosing Condition
A shareholder who holds a minority interest thinks the purchase price is too low and refuses to sell at the deal price. Furthermore, there is no drag-along provision that requires the shareholder to tender her shares.	Refuse to close unless 100% of the shares are delivered at closing.
None of the employees have signed an invention assignment and confidentiality agreement, which raises potential issues regarding ownership of company IP.	Require all personnel to sign invention assignment and confidentiality agreements before closing.
The company failed to pay annual state fees and has been dissolved administratively.	Require the company to pay all outstanding fees and provide proof of revival of the entity as a condition of closing.

Case Study 4: Purchase of Series A Preferred Stock in Karly Medical Device Co.

Hannah Nicole is the majority shareholder and managing director of Venture Medical, LLC, a fund investing in new medical technologies and health care businesses. Venture Medical has signed a nonbinding letter of intent to purchase Series A Preferred Shares in Karly Medical Device Co., a developer of a potentially groundbreaking medical devices for conducting colonoscopies. Venture Medical will invest $500,000 for 33% of Karly Medical, at a post-transaction valuation of $1.5 million. During the course of due diligence, the investor learns that (1) the company has not authorized the preferred shares, (2) the company lacks sufficient policies for protecting medical patient data, (3) the founders are not bound by any cosale or other restrictions on the transfer of their shares, and (4) the corporation has elected S-Corp tax status, but the investor is not a U.S. citizen. Table 8-4 contains an overview of the key issues discovered during due diligence and suggested preclosing conditions that could be applied.

Table 8-4. Preclosing Conditions for Purchase of Series A Stock in Karly Medical

Due Diligence Issue	Preclosing Condition
The corporation has not authorized Series A Stock.	Obtain the necessary authorizations for issuance of Series A shares.
The investor is concerned about the adequacy of the company's protocols regarding protection of patent information.	Require the implementation of policies that comply with applicable laws regarding data storage as well as sufficient system redundancies.

(continued)

Table 8-4. (*continued*)

Due Diligence Issue	Preclosing Condition
There are no founder cosale obligations giving other shareholders right to sell *pro rata* if founders wish to sell shares in the corporation.	Amend the shareholders' agreement to include cosale rights.
The corporation has elected S-Corp status but the investor is not a U.S. citizen and therefore cannot invest in an S-Corp.	Demand a restructure of the company to eliminate S-Corp status or walk from the transaction if the restructuring creates an unfavorable tax structure.

Case Study 5: Purchase of a Strip Mall

Debra Lynne has signed a nonbinding letter of intent to purchase from Mr. G Development Corp. a strip mall that consists of five stores. Of the five stores, four are occupied. The vacant store was leased previously by a dry cleaner. The purchaser wants to expand the strip mall by adding four more stores on a portion of the undeveloped property. The buyer also wants to put in a fast-food franchise with a drive-thru. The purchase price is $1.2 million. During the course of due diligence, the buyer discovers that (1) there is a title defect with respect to the real property, (2) the lease for the largest store is expiring and that store generates a substantial portion of the income from the property, (3) the building inspection has uncovered issues, (4) there is an open lien, (5) the adjacent land owner has a right of first refusal to purchase the property, and (6) the local zoning board has indicated it opposes allowing a drive-thru, which affects the economics of the transaction if approval cannot be obtained. Table 8-5 contains an overview of the key issues discovered during due diligence and suggested preclosing conditions that could be applied.

Table 8-5. Preclosing Conditions for the Strip Mall Deal

Due Diligence Issue	Preclosing Condition
There is a break in the chain of title to the property as a result of a failure to file a document in connection with a decade-old probate matter.	Demand that the title issues be resolved.
The anchor tenant's lease is expiring and an extension is still under negotiation.	Require a new lease to be executed on terms approved by purchaser.
The heating, ventilation, and air-conditioning system is not working and roof is leaking.	Require that the heating, ventilation, and air-conditioning system and roof be repaired to the satisfaction of the buyer.

(*continued*)

Table 8-5. (*continued*)

Due Diligence Issue	Preclosing Condition
A lien is in place for unpaid real estate taxes.	Required satisfaction and release of the lien.
The seller granted a right of first refusal to the adjacent landowner, who has since died.	Obtain the necessary waiver of the right of first refusal from the representative of the decedent's estate.
The zoning board opposes a drive-thru.	Require the seller to assist with obtaining the necessary approvals, and condition the sale on acquiring such approvals.

Case Study 6: Exclusive License of Patents from Jordan Creatives, Ltd.

Kilbourn Pet Toys wishes to enter into an exclusive license of three patents covering designs for indestructible doggy chew toys and teeth cleaners. The licensor, Jordan Creatives, Ltd., owns the patents but has not actually developed any pet toys. Furthermore, the licensor has its offices in Hong Kong, and the actual company is a British Virgin Islands entity. The licensee is concerned about proceeding with the transaction having learned that (1) the patent maintenance fees are due and failure of the licensor to pay these fees will result in cancelation of the patent, (2) a creditor is seeking to enforce a judgment by foreclosing on the patents, (3) an existing licensee has a right to renew its current license covering several foreign markets, and (4) the licensor is incorporated abroad and the potential licensee is concerned about being able to enforce of the license. Table 8-6 contains an overview of the key issues discovered during due diligence and suggested preclosing conditions that could be applied.

Table 8-6. Conditions to an Exclusive License Deal with Jordan Creatives

Due Diligence Issue	Preclosing Condition
Maintenance fees are due and must be paid to retain the patents.	Require payment of all maintenance fees.
There is a pending foreclosure action by a judgment creditor in connection with a $20,000 judgment.	Require the licensor to obtain a settlement and release; otherwise, the licensor could lose the patents.
A third party was granted a license to certain foreign markets. The license is expiring in 30 days if the licensee does not renew.	Require the licensor to provide a waiver from the foreign licensee.
The licensor is based in Hong Kong and incorporated under the laws of the British Virgin Islands.	Require the licensor to provide a legal opinion from qualified counsel regarding the ability to enforce the license.

Case Study 7: Purchase of 50% of a Music Store Owned by Your Friend

Adrian has negotiated to purchase 50% of the membership interests in an LLC for a music store now owned by his friend, Rowland. Rowland, who has been successfully operating the store for 10 years, is an expert at repairing stringed instruments, especially electric guitars. He recently invested in a restaurant/bar and wants to spend about half his time growing the restaurant, including promoting it as a venue for bands. One of the employees also has been building an excellent reputation for repairing string instruments. Adrian is well-known for repairing electric and traditional pianos, but knows nothing about repairing guitars and has never operated a retail store. Rowland has offered to sell 50% of the company to Adrian for $35,000, plus an agreement to replace Rowland as the personal guarantor on a $50,000 line of credit, of which $20,000 is outstanding. The company has not filed tax returns for the previous fiscal year.

Due diligence has disclosed several areas of concern for the incoming partner: (1) The LLC does not have an operating agreement (which is a minor issue for a single-member LLC, but is a major concern now that there will be two members); (2) a buy–sell agreement needs to be entered into between the partners addressing disability, death, or withdrawal of a member; (3) the business and the property where the music store is located are owned by the LLC; (4) the company does not have policies to cover important aspects of the business operation, resulting in, among other issues, employees applying inconsistent pricing and refund policies; and (5) the company's employee record keeping is a mess, and the absence of I-9 employment eligibility verification forms for any of the staff exposes the LLC to penalties. The incoming partner has refused to move forward unless these matters are addressed through the conditions to closing presented in Table 8-7.

Table 8-7. Preclosing Conditions to Purchase 50% Interest in a Music Store

Due Diligence Issue	Preclosing Condition
No LLC operating agreement exists.	Negotiate and prepare a multimember LLC operating agreement.
There is no buy–sell agreement that addresses disability, death, or withdrawal of a member.	Include buy-sell provisions in the revised LLC operating agreement or prepare a separate buy–sell agreement. Purchase key man insurance as well as insurance to fund a buyout in the event of death or disability of one of the partners.
Both the business and the property where the music store is located are owned by the same LLC.	Transfer the real estate to a new entity to eliminate potential exposure to the liabilities of the distinct assets, then enter into a lease between the entities to improve the financial structure of the business.

(continued)

Table 8-7. (continued)

Due Diligence Issue	Preclosing Condition
The absence of written policies has resulted in employees applying inconsistent pricing and refund policies.	Implement written business policies for employees to follow.
The company does not maintain employment records properly. No I-9 employment eligibility verification forms for any of the staff exposes the LLC to penalties.	Require institution of record-keeping procedures related to employees, and obtain I-9s from all employees.

Case Study 8: Purchase of an Ownership Interest in a Fast-Food Franchisee

Ellen Kay has entered a memorandum of understanding for the purchase of 33% of the LLC membership interests (a total of $225,000) in KMF Franchisee, LLC, a franchisee that owns four franchises of Rocky Robbins Ice Cream Bar, Inc. KMF Franchisee owes $100,000 to Mishy Enterprises, which is the purchase price for an earlier buyout of Mishy's equity interest in KMF. Mishy, the principal owner, has complained that she was underpaid for her 33% interest and is considering opening a competing ice cream restaurant across the street. There are two members of the LLC, and they never executed an operating agreement. KMF has many full- and part-time employees. The four stores are managed by Lara Melanie, the manager of operations, who is in the last year of her four-year contract. Two of the locations are in strip malls and are leased from the mall owner; one location is leased through a sublease that is expiring, and there are rumors about the financial condition of the sublessor; and the fourth location is a stand-alone store that is currently leased, but KMF has exercised an option to purchase the property.

Several areas of concern have come to light during the course the due diligence, including (1) the misclassification of one of the employees as a consultant, (2) ongoing contract negotiations with the manager of operations, (3) the upcoming expiration of the sublease for one of the locations and the rumored financial issues with respect to the sublessor, (4) the absence of an operating agreement for the LLC, (5) a fired bookkeeper continues to have signatory authority on the LLC bank accounts, (6) the Rocky Robbins franchise agreement requires approval for change of ownership of the franchisee, and (7) there are outstanding (although relatively minor) health code violations. Table 8-8 outlines the deal issues and preclosing conditions suggested by the attorney for the potential new LLC member.

Table 8-8. Preclosing Conditions for the KMF Franchisee Deal

Due Diligence Issue	Preclosing Condition
One of the employees is misclassified as a consultant.	Require the company determine the tax liability and file the necessary documentation with the IRS to rectify the misclassification.
There are unresolved contract issues with the manager of operations.	Enter into a new contract or hire a new manager, subject to terms acceptable to investor.
A sublease for one of the store locations is expiring and the sublessor may be having financial issues.	Require that the company enter into a new lease on terms reasonably acceptable to the investor. Require the company obtain a nondisturbance agreement from the master lessor.[4]
There is no operating agreement for the LLC.	Execute an operating agreement for a multimember LLC and include restrictions on transfer of units, buy–sell terms, and protective provisions requiring supermajority approval for certain transactions.
A fired bookkeeper still has signatory authority on bank accounts.	Require that the company adopt a new resolution to remove the signatory authority of the fired employee.
The franchise agreement requires approval for change of ownership of the franchisee.	Demand the company obtain approval from the franchisor to the change in the ownership structure of KMF Franchisee.
There are outstanding (although relatively minor) health code violations.	Require the company address these code violations to avoid continued issues with the state health department as well as prevent a possible breach of the franchise agreement.

These tables are just a few examples of issues that may arise during the due diligence investigation and should be addressed before or at the time of the closing of the transaction. In addition to including any preclosing conditions in the definitive agreements, one must consider how to address the timing and the target company's noncompliance with the closing conditions. How much time should the company have to satisfy the closing terms? What if the company does not meet the terms? Can they (and should they) be waived by the purchaser? What if the company is purposefully dragging its feet? Can the investor/purchaser force the company to address the issues uncovered by due diligence? Can the buyer require the company to meet a good-faith effort or higher standard in the contract? What if the standard is not met? Should there be financial penalties or a right of specific enforcement?

---

[4]The investor is concerned about the financial condition of the sublessor. If the sublessor defaults on his lease with the master lessor (i.e., the owner of the property), Rocky Robbins could be joined in an eviction proceeding. Rocky Robbins should obtain a nondisturbance agreement allowing it to continue its lease, provided it is not in default under its sublease.

At this juncture in the transaction, the purchaser likely has incurred substantial costs trying to move the deal forward. The purchaser should consider not only which preclosing conditions to incorporate in the binding contract, but also what rights the purchaser should have if the company is uncooperative or trying to kill the deal. In contrast, the company may believe it undervalued the business, commenced discussions regarding an extremely beneficial business opportunity, heard rumors that there are other interested purchasers, or simply have seller's remorse. The purchaser, therefore, needs to consider incorporating into the purchase agreement mechanisms to enforce the obligation of the company to rectify any due diligence issues or satisfy preclosing conditions.

Postclosing Covenants

Often there can be issues discovered during due diligence that can only be resolved, or the parties prefer to resolve, after the deal has closed. Reasons for needing to await until after closing to resolve one or more issues include, among many others, the pressure to get the deal done by a certain date as a result of extraneous factors, incomplete (financial or other) information that will only be available after closing, or the fact that issue may be relatively minor and cannot be resolved until after the closing. Issues that can or must be resolved after closing should be incorporated into the deal agreements as covenants or postclosing agreements. The covenants are express undertakings by a party to complete an action or resolve an issue after the closing of the transaction.

Examples

The parties to a transaction can agree to a wide variety of postclosing obligations as part of the transaction. These undertakings are significant because they often salvage a deal that would otherwise not be able to close, in many cases, because of problems that arose during the course of the due diligence investigation. The postclosing obligations that the parties might agree to in the context of the various case studies illustrate the breadth of the commitments that a company or selling shareholder may be willing to assume to complete the deal.

Case Study 1: Postclosing Covenants for the Loan Transaction

On completion of due diligence for the proposed loan to the computer repair shop, Overlook, Inc., the lender advises the borrower that here is an outstanding judgment for $20,000 and she is concerned about the level of the borrower's expenses and the owner's poor health. The lender is willing to proceed with the loan subject to the borrower's undertakings regarding these issues (Table 8-9).

Table 8-9. Postclosing Covenants for the Loan Transaction

Due Diligence Issue	Postclosing Covenant
There is an outstanding judgment for $20,000. The borrower has agreed to settle before entire loan principal is advanced by lender. The borrower may not be able to obtain dismissal of the claim from the court before closing.	The borrower shall obtain notice of dismissal of the action from the court, and the lender shall hold back $20,000 until she receives the notice of dismissal, which she can use to pay off the judgment if it remains unpaid.
The lender is concerned about level of the borrower's expenses.	Lender approval is required for expenses in excess of a defined amount, the breach of which can constitute a loan default.
The owner of business has health issues and the lender is concerned about possible business disruption.	The borrower must provide ongoing proof of payment of key man insurance, commercial liability, flood, and other insurance premiums.

Case Study 2: Postclosing Covenants for Purchase of the Assets of ABB

Jack Enterprises, the purchaser of the assets of ABB (including a key software application, customers, and contracts with chain stores), is concerned that an important cross-marketing agreement with one of the retail chains has not been finalized because there are a few minor contract points that need to be resolved. In addition, he has concerns about the software updates since they are due to be completed by a third-party vendor several weeks after closing. Because of deal time constraints, these issues cannot be resolved before closing. Instead, the seller has agreed to the following postclosing covenants (Table 8-10).

Table 8-10. Covenants for the ABB Transaction

Due Diligence Issue	Postclosing Covenant
A major cross-marketing agreement is being negotiated, but it likely will not be signed before closing.	The seller must provide assistance to buyer after closing to finalize the new marketing agreement.
A key software update is underway with a third-party vendor, but will not be completed for several weeks after closing.	The seller must pay all developer fees and cooperate with the buyer as reasonably necessary to ensure the software developer completes the update properly and in a timely manner.

Case Study 3: Purchase of SamGar Technology, LLC

In the proposed buyout of all the membership interests of SamGar Technology, LLC, due diligence has raised the following concerns: (1) the company is changing the service provider that handles its computer networking requirements and is moving large amounts of data to the Cloud; (2) an invention assignment is needed for a patent application, but the shareholder/inventor is traveling for three months in a remote part of the world; (3) the valuation of the business incorporates assumptions about net working capital that cannot be confirmed until after the closing; (4) there is a pending infringement claim against a competitor, and one of the partners is integral to the lawsuit; and (5) two key employees may want to leave after the sale because they will receive a substantial payout in connection with the sale of SamGar. SamGar does not want to hold up the closing because the funds are needed for a new venture. The purchaser is willing to proceed subject to the seller's commitment to comply with the following postclosing covenants (Table 8-11).

Table 8-11. Covenants for SamGar Stock Buyout

Due Diligence Issue	Postclosing Covenant
The company is in the process of changing its network provider and is moving large amounts of data to the Cloud.	The majority shareholder/chief technology officer (CTO) who has spearheaded the project must personally commit to provide assistance during the transition of the project to a new CTO.
Invention assignments are lacking for a patent application from one of the partners who is traveling for three months in a remote part of the world.	The company must obtain the invention assignments within two weeks of closing. A portion of the purchase price will be held in escrow to ensure compliance.
The valuation of the business incorporates assumptions about net working capital that cannot be confirmed until after closing.	The Buyer will escrow a portion of the purchase price and then adjust the purchase price after the closing based on the final determination of the net working capital as of the closing date.
The company has a pending infringement claim against a competitor and one of the partners is integral to the lawsuit.	The partner must continue to assist with prosecution of the lawsuit.
The purchaser is concerned about the possible departure of two key employees, who will receive a substantial payout in connection with the sale of SamGar.	Incorporate in the purchase agreement a hold-back of the purchase price that will be released to buyer in the event that the two key employees leave before a set date.

Case Study 4: Purchase of Series A Preferred Stock in Karly Medical Device, Co.

An investor considering the purchase of stock in Karly Medical, the developer of a potentially groundbreaking medical device, is concerned about whether the company will finalize a pending agreement that could mean a substantial new revenue source. In addition, due diligence has discovered weaknesses in the operation related to budgeting and financial planning. The investor is also concerned about the absence of written protocols, policies, and procedures related to workflow matters. She is demanding the incorporation of the post-closing covenants presented in Table 8-12.

Table 8-12. Covenants for Karly Medical Series A Transaction

Due Diligence Issue	Postclosing Covenant
The investor is concerned about the ability of the company to finalize a new contract since the failure to do so will affect revenues negatively.	Either the contract must be finalized by a certain date or the investor's ownership interest will be increased based on a postclosing adjustment.
The company has weak budgeting and financial planning processes.	The company must prepare financial plans and budgets on a set schedule for review by the investor.
There is an absence of written protocols, policies, and procedures related to workflow.	The company must prepare written policies and procedures, and if timing constraints limit the ability to complete before closing, these policies must be finished by a set date workflow.

Case Study 5: Purchase of a Strip Mall

Due diligence in connection with the purchase of the strip mall has uncovered issues that cannot be resolved before closing: (1) the undeveloped portion of the property has a buried oil tank, (2) a tenant is in default under his lease and is being evicted, and (3) one of the partners is using a store rent free. The seller has committed to the postclosing covenants in Table 8-13.

Table 8-13. Covenants for Strip Mall Transaction

Due Diligence Issue	Postclosing Covenant
An oil tank is buried in the undeveloped portion of the property.	The seller shall pay the costs for removing the oil tank and for any remediation. The seller shall agree to indemnify purchaser for any environmental claims and a portion of the purchase price shall be escrowed to cover any potential environmental liabilities.
A tenant is in default of his lease and is being evicted.	The seller's attorney must handle the eviction. Any related fees must be paid by the seller. The purchase price will be adjusted if the tenant is not evicted by a defined date.
A partner is using a store rent free.	The seller must ask the partner to vacate the premises within five days of closing or pay market rent for the location.

Case Study 8: Purchase of an Ownership Interest in a Fast-Food Franchisee

KMF Franchisee has negotiated the sale of a stake in the LLC, which is the owner and operator of several ice cream franchise locations. However, the purchaser does not want to proceed unless the following due diligence issues are resolved after closing: (1) a former partner is threatening to open a competing restaurant, (2) there is no financing mechanism to support the buy–sell rights on the death or disability of a partner, (3) the company guaranteed one of the partner's personal loans, and (4) the business is suffering from the absence of financial controls. Table 8-14 contains postclosing covenants that the new partner requires as a condition to proceeding with the transaction.

Table 8-14. Postclosing Covenants for the KMF Franchisee Transaction

Due Diligence Issue	Postclosing Covenant
There is possible competition from former partner.	The company must give the investor the right to repurchase her units if the competition causes a material decline in gross revenues.[5]
There is no financing in place to support a buy–sell on the death or disability of a partner.	The company must obtain an insurance policy to finance a buy–sell.
The company guaranteed one of the partner's personal loans.	The company shall arrange for a release from guaranty or the partner shall pay off loan. Failure to do so will result in a pledge of the partner's units to the company until the loan is satisfied.
There is an absence of financial controls.	Investor approval is required for expenses in excess of a set amount.

[5]The meaning of "a material decline" would have to be well-defined in the agreement.

These examples demonstrate that postclosing obligations can be relatively simple, such as requiring a document to be filed or payment of a judgment that could not be completed before closing the transaction. On the other hand, the obligations may involve a significant commitment, such as assistance with pending litigation, cooperation with the transition of an aspect of the business, implementation of financial controls or new operating procedures, or resolution of a difficult business issue. Typically, postclosing obligations are chock-a-block with phrases such as "meaningful," "reasonably necessary," "substantial," or "good-faith efforts" when referring to the level of assistance or cooperation a party must provide. Furthermore, the postclosing undertaking will often include completion within a defined time period; otherwise, it can be difficult to determine whether or when a breach of the obligation has occurred. The lesson here is that parties need to define clearly the terms of the postclosing obligations to avoid the otherwise inevitable disputes about the scope of the postclosing commitment.

Enforcement of Postclosing Obligations: Escrow

If the definitive agreements include postclosing obligations (regardless of whether they are intended to address issues discovered in due diligence), the beneficiary of the covenant needs to be concerned about mechanisms for enforcement. Of course, there is always a right to file a lawsuit for breach of contract or for specific performance issues, but this act may be impractical because of the costs and time that may be required to obtain a court judgment. Enforcement can be especially tricky when the deal involves a buyout, because the seller could be "judgment proof"—meaning, the seller cannot be located, the seller no longer has the funds required, or the seller's assets are well shielded from potential claims. Accordingly, the parties typically agree to a holdback, or escrow, of a portion of the purchase price as security for breach of a postclosing obligation. Agreeing to escrow some portion of the purchase price to ensure satisfaction of an undertaking by the company, founders, or selling shareholders is usually not a big issue. Instead, there is most likely disagreement about the amount of the escrow, which then turns to wrangling over the terms under which funds will be released in the event of a purported breach of the covenant.

The amount to be held in escrow usually is not a major issue when the holdback relates to an obligation that can be quantified reasonably, such as unpaid invoices, a monetary judgment, unpaid sales tax, a lawsuit in which the size of the potential claim can be determined, or a federal tax liability. Using our case studies, examples of when the parties can derive a reasonable amount to hold in escrow to ensure compliance with postclosing commitments include the following:

- The $20,000 judgment owed by the borrower in the loan transaction in Case Study 1 (Table 8-9)

- Depending on the results of an environmental assessment, the possible reasonable assessment of the costs of oil tank removal and remediation in the strip mall transaction in Case Study 5 (Table 8-13)

- The loss of rental income from the failure to evict the tenant in the strip mall transaction in Case Study 5 (Table 8-13)

- Release from the guaranty given by KMF Franchisee in connection with the personal bank loan owed by one of the LLC's partners in Case Study 8 (Table 8-14)

However, in other situations, it can be difficult to assign a dollar amount to the potential financial risk from the breach of a postclosing obligation. If the scope of liability from a claim is unknown, or the effect on the business from a delay or complete failure to fulfill a term of the contract cannot be calculated in advance, how are the parties to arrive at a fair amount to hold in escrow? If the party conducting due diligence is still willing to proceed with the transaction,[6] his or her only option may be to rely on an educated guesstimate regarding a sufficient amount to hold in escrow in the event of a breach of a postclosing contractual obligation. The following are examples from the case studies when the portion of the purchase price to hold in escrow cannot be determined with any degree of certainty:

- The impact on the business from the failure of the seller to assist with finalizing the cross-marketing agreement in the ABB asset sale (Case Study 2; Table 8-10).

- The negative effect on revenues from the refusal of the seller in the ABB deal to cooperate with the developer handling the software updates (Case Study 2; Table 8-10).

- The harm to SamGar's business from the former CTO's lack of meaningful assistance with the transition, the extensive delay or inability to obtain the invention assignment

---

[6]As discussed in Chapter 5, if the buyer or investor believes the liability associated with one or more due diligence issues is too great or a dollar figure cannot be assigned to the business risk, he or she may condition the closing on resolution of the issue or may walk away from the deal altogether.

agreement from the inventor–partner, or the refusal of the partner to cooperate with the buyer's lawyer in the prosecution of the infringement litigation (Case Study 3; Table 8-11).

- The effect, if any, on net income from the company's continued failure to adhere to the obligation to prepare periodic budgets in the Karly Medical transaction (Case Study 4; Table 8-12) or to implement the required financial controls in the KMF Franchisee buy-in (Case Study 8; Table 8-14).

The purchaser or investor may engage in a sophisticated calculation of the impact from a breach of a contract covenant. The calculation may involve the projected value of a contract that was delayed or never finalized, the potential loss of customer orders, the harm to the reputation of the business from a delay in the release of a software update, or the effect on the business from the absence of financial controls. For example, the following provision sets forth the terms of a holdback that might be used to address the purchaser's concern in the SamGar buyout regarding the departure of key employees:

If, on or before the first (1st) anniversary of the closing, any of the key personnel (as listed in Schedule C) shall have (1) resigned voluntarily from his or her employment with or voluntarily terminated his or her engagement from the Buyer, except when such individual has resigned because of serious illness or disability, or in circumstances when the Buyer has breached materially the applicable employment agreement between such individual and the Buyer, or in the event when the Buyer has violated materially applicable law to the detriment of the employment relationship between the Buyer and such individual; or (2) had his or her employment terminated validly for cause (as defined in his or her employment agreement), the Buyer shall have the right to a payment from escrow of the amount set forth next to the name of such key personnel in Schedule C.

Assigning an exact dollar amount may not be possible, but the purchaser or investor may be able to arrive at an escrow proposal sufficient to give him or her comfort in the event of a delay or total breach of a postclosing covenant.

Enforcement of Postclosing Obligations: Purchase Price Adjustment

Another mechanism to enforce compliance with a postclosing agreement is an adjustment of the purchase price. The adjustment protects the purchaser or investor by effectively reducing the amount of consideration paid by the purchaser/investor in the event of a breach of the contract. In essence, the adjustment of the purchase price is a recognition by the parties that the valuation of the business is too high if certain postclosing terms are not satisfied. The adjustment can occur through (1) a (nonescrow) holdback by the purchaser of a portion of the total purchase price or an installment payment structure; (2) the placement of a portion of the purchase price in escrow, which is released back to the investor or purchaser upon a breach; or (3) an increase in the number of shares or membership interests originally purchased by the investor in the company. Examples of an adjustment of the purchase price as compensation for a breach of a postclosing obligations include the following:

- The termination of negotiations related to the new cross-marketing agreement in the ABB asset sale because of the seller's failure to cooperate with the purchaser (Table 8-10)

- Refusal of former a shareholder to assist with the infringement lawsuit in the SamGar buyout, requiring dismissal of a claim valued at $25,000 (Table 8-11)

- Failure of the company to finalize the material contract that would have generated substantial revenues (Table 8-12)

- Delay in the eviction of a holdover tenant in the strip mall transaction (Table 8-13)

By way of illustration, assume the parties in the SamGar transaction agreed to adjust the purchase price after closing as necessary to reflect accurately the net working capital of the business at the time of closing (Table 8-11). The following is an example of what the price adjustment section of the SamGar contract might look like:

SECTION 10

A. As soon as practicable, but in no event later than fifteen (15) days after the closing, the Company shall deliver to the Buyer:

    1. An unaudited balance sheet of the Company as of closing ("Closing Balance Sheet"), that shall (i) be prepared on a basis and in a format consistent with the accounting principles applied by the Company in its historical balance sheets and (ii) shall include an attachment containing supporting schedules.

    2. A statement reasonably detailing calculations of the net working capital amount (as defined earlier) as of closing based solely on the Closing Balance Sheet (collectively with the Closing Balance Sheet, the "Adjustment Statement").

B. If the Buyer disagrees with the Company's proposed calculation of the net working capital amount, the Buyer shall promptly, but in no event later than fifteen (15) days after receiving the Adjustment Statement, deliver to the Company a notice reasonably detailing those items or amounts disputed by Buyer and the Buyer's proposed calculations of such items or amounts ("Dispute Notice"). In the absence of a timely Dispute Notice, the net working capital amount set forth in the Adjustment Statement shall be final as of the date of closing. In the event of a Dispute Notice, the Buyer and Seller shall resolve such dispute in accordance with the exclusive dispute resolution procedures set forth in Section 20, provided that any undisputed items or amounts shall be deemed accepted by the parties. The Final Net Working Capital amount shall be the net working capital amount as determined on resolution of all disputes between the Buyer and the Company in accordance with Section 20 of this Agreement.

C. The Final Purchase Price shall be equal to the Initial Purchase Price, minus the amount by which the Final Net Working Capital Amount is less than the Estimated Net Working Capital Amount or (B) plus the amount by which the Final Net Working Capital Amount is greater than the Estimated Net Working Capital Amount.

If the due diligence investigation raises issues that can only be addressed after closing, the purchaser/investor needs to be concerned about enforcement of the other party's postclosing obligations. The adjustment of the purchase price after closing essentially adjusts the valuation of the business to reflect the financial impact of the failure to satisfy postclosing terms. The adjustment can be achieved through a return of a portion of the purchase, which may be held in escrow; a reduction of the amount of an installment payment;[7] or the issuance of additional equity.

Enforcement of Post Closing Obligations: Repurchase

A particularly draconian method for enforcing a postclosing covenant is to give the investor a right to force the company to repurchase its shares or membership interests. The investor may take the position that the covenant is so fundamental, any breach or inability to fulfill the promise renders the transaction untenable. In most circumstances, the company would be opposed to closing the deal rather than making a promise that could result in an obligation to repurchase the equity after closing. From the company's perspective, it wants access to use the proceeds of the transaction for the business and does not want the uncertainty created by the possibility that the proceeds will have to be returned. The ability of the company to attract future investments will be undermined if potential investors or partners learn the company was forced to repurchase shares sold in a prior financing round. The minority shareholders likely will be perturbed that they have not been offered a buyout and will certainly question the ability of management to operate the business.

Even if the company is willing to grant a repurchase right, the investor should be concerned about the company's financial ability to redeem the shares down the road. Recall the context of the KMF Franchisee deal in which the repurchase right was discussed. The potential investor is hedging his investment in the event that the former partner opens a competitive business. If the competition from Mishy results in a material reduction of KMF's revenues, the investor may exercise the repurchase right. However, if the impact is severe enough to trigger the redemption, will the company have the financial ability to repurchase the shares as promised? Again, a postclosing covenant is of little value if the contract does not include a mechanism for enforcement of rights. If the breach of a contractual covenant cannot be remedied with monetary damages, a purchaser should consider including a right to pursue equitable remedies (such as specific performance of a contractual obligation) when practical.

---

[7]The structure of the deal may dictate payment of the consideration in one or more installment payments. In such case, the purchaser/investor does not pay the entire purchase price at closing, but holds back a portion that is then paid in installments. The installments might be conditioned on detailed business milestones or satisfaction of postclosing undertakings.

Indemnification

Part and parcel with enforcement of contractual representations and post-closing commitments is the concept of indemnification. Indemnification in a business transaction gives a party the right to be reimbursed for damages arising from a breach of the various representations and warranties that were made by another party to the contract and that survived the closing of the transaction.[8] If, for example, a purchase agreement included a representation that none of the assets of the company were subject to any encumbrances, and then later it turned out the company had pledged some of its assets as collateral for a previously undisclosed loan, the breach of the representation would give rise to a right under the indemnification clause. A breach of a covenant or postclosing promise is also a basis to invoke the indemnification provisions of a contract. The indemnification clause sets forth the grounds for indemnification, the procedures for invoking the right and, in conjunction with an escrow provisions, the right to a disbursement from any portion of the purchase price that might be held in escrow.

INDEMNIFICATION CLAUSE: EXAMPLE I
(ASSET PURCHASE/PRO PURCHASER)

INDEMNIFICATION

Section 10.01 Survival. All representations, warranties, covenants, and agreements contained herein and all related rights to indemnification shall survive the closing.

Section 10.02 Indemnification by Seller. The Seller shall defend, indemnify, and hold harmless the Buyer, its affiliates, and its respective stockholders, directors, officers, employees, and agents from and against any and all actual losses, demands, actions, causes of action, assessments, damages, liabilities, costs or expenses, including, without limitation, interest, penalties, fines, fees, deficiencies, claims of damage, court and arbitration costs, and reasonable fees and disbursements of attorneys, accountants, consultants, and other experts as and when incurred, or sustained (a "Claim"), arising from or related to

---

[8]Sometimes, by their terms, certain representations and warranties are not intended to survive the closing, and therefore a breach after closing will not give rise to indemnification.

a. Any inaccuracy in or breach of any of the representations or warranties of the Seller in this Asset Purchase Agreement or any ancillary documents (as defined above)

b. Any breach or nonfulfillment of any covenant, agreement, or obligation to be performed by the Seller pursuant to this Asset Purchase Agreement or any ancillary document.

Section 10.03 Indemnification by Buyer

. . .

Section 10.04 Procedures

a. Whenever any claim for indemnification shall arise under this section, the party entitled to indemnification (the "Indemnified Party") shall promptly provide written notice of such claim to the other party (the "Indemnifying Party").

b. In the event of any claim for indemnification hereunder resulting from or in connection with any claim or legal proceedings by a third party, the Indemnifying Party, at its sole cost and expense, and on written notice to the Indemnified Party, may assume the defense of any such claim with counsel reasonably satisfactory to the Indemnified Party. The Indemnified Party shall be entitled to participate in the defense of any such claim, with its counsel and at its own cost and expense. If the Indemnifying Party does not assume the defense of any such claim, the Indemnified Party may, but shall not be obligated to, defend against such action in such manner as it may deem appropriate, including, but not limited to, settling such claim, after giving notice of it to the Indemnifying Party. No action taken by the Indemnified Party in accordance with such defense and settlement shall relieve the Indemnifying Party of its indemnification obligations under this section with respect to any damages resulting therefrom. The Indemnifying Party shall not settle any claim without the Indemnified Party's prior written consent (which shall not be unreasonably withheld or delayed).

Section 10.05 No Waiver. No investigation by the Buyer or other information received by the Buyer shall operate as a waiver or otherwise affect any representation, warranty, covenant, or agreement given or made by the Seller in this Agreement.

Section 10.06 Cumulative Remedies. The rights and remedies provided in this section are cumulative and are in addition to and not in lieu of any other rights and remedies available at law, in equity or otherwise.

Example 1 is a pro-purchaser indemnification provision. First, it does not place any time limit on the survival period of the indemnification rights. As a result, the buyer could bring a claim several years after the closing. Second, the indemnification obligation applies regardless of the dollar amount of the claim. Third, there is no cap on the total aggregate liability—meaning, the indemnifying party will have unlimited liability for claims arising from a breach of the representations, warranties, and covenants in the asset purchase agreement.

INDEMNIFICATION CLAUSE: EXAMPLE 2 (STOCK PURCHASE AGREEMENT)

INDEMNIFICATION

Section 9.01 Indemnification by the Company. The Company agrees to indemnify, defend, and hold harmless the Investor and its affiliates and controlling persons and their respective officers, managers, members, partners, directors, stockholders, employees, attorneys, representatives, and agents (all such persons and entities being referred to collectively as the "Investor Indemnified Parties") from and against any and all actual losses, demands, actions, causes of action, assessments, damages, liabilities, costs, or expenses, including, without limitation, interest, penalties, fines, fees, deficiencies, claims of damage, court and arbitration costs, and reasonable fees and disbursements of attorneys, accountants, consultants, and other experts as and when incurred, or sustained by any Investor Indemnified Party as a result of or arising from or in connection with

a. Any inaccuracy or breach of any representation or warranty made by the Company in this Agreement prior to the termination of such representation or warranty pursuant to Section 5.01.

b. Any breach of any covenant or agreement made by the Company in this Agreement.

c. Notwithstanding the foregoing, the Company shall have no liability for indemnification pursuant to clause 9.01(a) unless the aggregate amounts for which indemnification may be sought exceed $xx,000 (after which the Company shall be obligated to indemnify the Investor Indemnified Parties for all such amounts, including the first $xx,000).

Section 9.02   Indemnification by Investors.

   . . .

Section 9.03   Claims for Indemnification. Whenever any claim shall arise for indemnification under this Article 9, the party entitled to indemnification (the "Indemnified Party") shall promptly notify the other party (the "Indemnifying Party") of the claim and, when known, the facts constituting the basis for such claim. The Indemnified Party's failure to notify the Indemnifying Party promptly of any such claim shall not relieve the Indemnifying Party of its indemnity obligations under this Agreement, except to the extent the delay in giving notice of the claim materially prejudices the Indemnifying Party. In the event of any claim for indemnification hereunder resulting from or in connection with any claim or legal proceedings by a third party, the Indemnifying Party shall not, without the prior written consent of the Indemnified Party, settle or compromise any claim by a third party unless such settlement or compromise includes an unconditional release of the Indemnified Party from all liability arising or that may arise out of such claim, action, or proceeding. No Indemnifying Party shall be liable for any settlement of any claim, action, or proceeding effected against an Indemnified Party without its written consent, which shall not be unreasonably withheld.

Section 9.04   Defense by Indemnifying Party. In connection with any claim giving rise to a right of indemnification under this Article 9 resulting from or arising out of any claim or legal proceeding by a person who is not a party to this Agreement, the Indemnifying Party at its sole cost and expense may, on written notice to the Indemnified Party, assume the defense of any such claim or legal proceeding. The Indemnified Party shall be entitled to participate in (but not control) the defense of any such action, with its counsel and at its own expense. If the Indemnifying Party does not assume in a timely manner the defense of any such claim or litigation resulting therefrom, (1) the Indemnified Party may defend against such claim or litigation in such manner as it may deem appropriate, including, but not limited to, settling such claim or litigation with the written consent of the Indemnifying Party, and (2) the Indemnifying Party shall be entitled to participate in (but not control) the defense of such action, with its counsel and at its own expense.

Section 9.05   No Waiver by Investigation. No investigation by the Investor or other information received by the Investor shall operate as a waiver or otherwise affect any representation, warranty, covenant, or agreement given or made by the Company in this Agreement.

Section 9.06   Cumulative Remedies. The rights and remedies provided in this Article 9 are cumulative and are in addition to and not in lieu of any other rights and remedies available at law, in equity or otherwise.

The indemnification provisions in Example 2 are more restrictive than Example 1 because they contain a monetary floor below which the investor cannot assert a claim for indemnification. However, the indemnification is not limited by any cap on the aggregate dollar amount nor does the indemnification right terminate at any time.

INDEMNIFICATION CLAUSE: EXAMPLE 3 (ASSET PURCHASE AGREEMENT/PROSELLER)

INDEMNIFICATION

9.1. Indemnification by the Seller. In the event the Seller (a) breaches or is deemed to have breached any of the representations and warranties contained in Article IX or (b) fails to perform or comply with any of the covenants and agreements set forth in this Agreement, the Seller shall hold harmless, indemnify, and defend the Buyer, and each of its directors, officers, shareholders, attorneys, representatives, and agents from and against any damages incurred or paid by the Buyer to the extent such damages arise or result from a breach by the Seller of any such representations or warranties or a violation of any covenant in this Agreement.

"Damages" shall mean shall mean any and all costs, losses, damages, liabilities, demands, claims, suits, actions, judgments, awards, causes of action, assessments, or expenses, including interest, penalties, fines, and attorneys' fees incident thereto, incurred in connection with any claim for indemnification arising out of this Agreement, and any and all amounts paid in settlement of any such claim.

9.2. Indemnification by Buyer.

...

9.3. Notification of Claims. If any party (the "Indemnified Party") reasonably believes that it is entitled to indemnification hereunder, or otherwise receives notice of the assertion or commencement of any third-party claim, action, or proceeding (a "Third-Party Claim"), with respect to which such other party (the "Indemnifying Party") is obligated to provide indemnification pursuant to Section 9.1 or 9.2, the Indemnified Party shall give the Indemnifying Party prompt written notice of such claim for indemnification (an "Indemnity Claim"). The delivery of such notice of Indemnity Claim ("Claim Notice") shall be a condition precedent to any liability of the Indemnifying Party for indemnification hereunder. The failure to deliver a timely Claim Notice shall result in the waiver of such Indemnity Claim if the delay directly results in any material prejudice to the rights of the Indemnifying Party. Any claim for indemnification under this Section 9 must be brought before the expiration of the survival period for the representation and warranty as set forth in Section 12.1. The Indemnifying Party shall have ten (10) days from the receipt of a Claim Notice (the "Notice Period") to notify the Indemnified Party whether the Indemnifying Party disputes its liability to the Indemnified Party with respect to such Indemnity Claim.

9.4.   Defense of Third-Party Claims by Indemnifying Party. With respect to any Indemnity Claim involving a Third-Party Claim, the Indemnifying Party, at its sole cost and expense, and on written notice to the Indemnified Party, may assume the defense of any such Third-Party Claim with counsel reasonably satisfactory to the Indemnified Party. The Indemnifying Party shall proceed with the defense of such Third-Party Claim. During such defense proceedings, the Indemnifying Party shall keep the Indemnified Party informed of all material developments and events relating to the proceedings. The Indemnified Party shall have a right to be present at the negotiation, defense, and settlement of such Third-Party Claim. No consent of the Indemnified Party is required for any settlement of any claim, action, or proceeding unless such settlement imposes any liability for damages or inequity against the Indemnified Party.

9.5.   Defense of Third-Party Claims by Indemnified Party. If the Indemnifying Party does not assume the defense of any such Third-Party Claim, the Indemnified Party may, but shall not be obligated to, defend against such Third-Party Claim in such manner as it may deem appropriate, including, but not limited to, seeking to settle such Third-Party Claim, after giving notice of it to the Indemnifying Party, on such terms as the Indemnified Party may deem appropriate and no action taken by the Indemnified Party in accordance with such defense and settlement shall relieve the Indemnifying Party of its indemnification obligations under this Section with respect to any Damages. The Indemnified Party shall not settle any Third-Party Claim without the Indemnifying Party's prior written consent. Following entry of judgment or settlement with respect to the Third- Party Claim, any dispute regarding to the liability of the Indemnifying Party with respect to the Indemnity Claim shall be resolved as provided in Section 9.6.

9.6.   Dispute Resolution. With respect to any Indemnity Claim not involving a Third-Party Claim, if the Indemnifying Party disputes its liability within the Notice Period, the liability of the Indemnifying Party shall be resolved in accordance with the alternative dispute resolution procedures set forth in Section 12.5. In the event that an Indemnified Party makes an Indemnity Claim in accordance with Section 9.3 and the Indemnifying Party does not dispute its liability within the Notice Period, the amount of such Indemnity Claim shall be deemed conclusively a liability of the Indemnifying Party.

9.7.   Indemnification Threshold. Notwithstanding anything to the contrary herein, in no event shall any party be liable to any other party under any warranty, representation, indemnity, or covenant made by such party in this Agreement until the aggregate amount of Damages thereunder against such party exceeds [xxx] thousand dollars ($xxx,000) (the "Threshold"), at which point such party shall be liable for the full amount of liability for such claims below and above the Threshold.

. . .

MISCELLANEOUS

12.1.   Survival. Unless otherwise expressly stated elsewhere in this Agreement, the representations, warranties, covenants, and indemnities included or provided for in this Agreement or in any agreement, schedule, or certificate or other document or instrument delivered pursuant to this Agreement will survive the closing date for a period of twenty-four (24) months from the closing date. No claim may be made by any party hereto unless written notice of the claim is given within that twenty-four (24)-month period.

Example 3 is more favorable to the seller than the other example indemnification provisions because (1) it provides detailed procedures for notice of a claim, which must be followed to avoid waiver of the indemnification claim; (2) limits the time period for the survival of the representations, warranties, and covenants (unless the agreement provides that the particular representations, warranties, or covenants are excluded from the limitation on survival); (3) incorporates dispute resolution procedures[9]; and (4) precludes claims that are less than a defined dollar amount (threshold).

Summary

This chapter shifted focus from the preparation of the due diligence to several other significant aspects of the due diligence process. First, we examined the timing of the due diligence. Should the due diligence investigation occur before or after entering into a binding agreement? The answer should

---

[9]The language in the alternative dispute resolution clause will dictate significant aspects of the process, including, without limitation, who will determine the issue, where any hearing will be held, timing for resolution of a dispute, the procedural rules that apply, whether the parties can pursue interim remedies, and who is responsible for the costs. Ultimately, the alternative dispute resolution clause can affect the outcome of the dispute. Therefore, if the parties have agreed to settle claims through alternative dispute resolution, it is advisable to have the provision drafted or reviewed by an attorney experienced in alternative dispute resolution maters.

take into account several factors, including the risk of incurring substantial costs to conduct the investigation in the absence of a binding agreement, timing of the transaction, and the rights of a party to address issues discovered during due diligence.

Second, we examine the exclusivity/no-shop clause. Should there be a period of deal exclusivity and, if so, what should be the terms of the no-shop agreement? The buyer or investor will want a period of exclusivity, but the company will be concerned about losing other opportunities if the deal does not close.

Third, we looked at a due diligence clouse in a letter of intent or binding contract. What issues should be considered when drafting the due diligence clause, including the level of cooperation between the parties, access to information, and limitations on the scope of the examination? The parties will need to balance the buyer or investor's interest in the unfettered right to conduct due diligence with the desire of the company to, among other concerns, close the deal in a timely manner, protect its confidential business information and competitive position, and avoid undue interference with the company's business operations.

Fourth, we looked at preclosing conditions. When should a party condition the closing on the resolution of issues discovered during the due diligence investigation? Due diligence can lead to the discovery of financial, legal, operational, or personnel issues that are so fundamental they need to be resolved before the closing can occur. Incorporating the terms of preclosing conditions in the definitive deal documents is a significant byproduct of due diligence.

Fifth, we examined postclosing conditions. When is it reasonable to agree to resolve due diligence issues after the closing? Sometimes the closing can proceed with the understanding that certain issues need to be resolved after closing the deal. Incorporating the terms of postclosing conditions in the definitive agreements is also a significant result of the due diligence process.

Last, we took a look at enforcement of postclosing conditions. The enforcement mechanisms that can be incorporated into a contract to address the possible failure of a party to meet postclosing obligations include the escrow of a portion of the purchase price, a purchase price adjustment, installment payments, the right of repurchase, and indemnification. The beneficiary of the postclosing conditions must not only have a means to enforce its rights, but the mechanisms for enforcement must be an appropriate measure in light of the postclosing conditions.

The Due Diligence Process and Pragmatic Considerations

The goal of the discussions thus far has been to explain the purpose of, and the process for, conducting a well-conceived due diligence investigation of a closely held business in the context of various types of business transactions. It has been explained that, in a nutshell, the party conducting due diligence is testing the veracity of the story that has been posited about the business that is the subject of the review. Throughout the investigation, the buyer or investor is seeking information about the four business cornerstones: the company, the business operations, the valuation, and the personnel who participate in the operation of the business (Chapter 2). Although the term *due diligence* describes a generic process of review, the level and focus of the scrutiny can vary greatly, depending on the company, type of transaction, and the deal terms. Therefore, it has been recommended that, before launching the due diligence investigation, a due diligence plan should be prepared (Chapter 2). The plan dissects the components of the transaction in light of each of the business cornerstones and thereby provides a bird's-eye view of the most significant topics that the buyer has identified based on the information known at the time. The due diligence plan is an extremely helpful aid in formulating the strategy for the due diligence investigation of the transaction under consideration. After the plan has been fleshed out, the party conducting the due diligence should have a clear vision regarding what he or she wants verified before deciding whether to proceed with the proposed transaction.

The focus that results from preparation of the due diligence plan make the process of drafting an effective due diligence questionnaire, which is the next step in the process, much easier. As I've reiterated, the questionnaire is not a generic document; its value depends primarily on adjusting the nature and scope of the questions to fit the facts and issues being tested by the due diligence investigation (Chapter 4). The information obtained from the questionnaire responses, along with a review of the books and records of the business, research of public information, and consultation with consultants (as discussed in this chapter) is the basis for deciding the following:

1. Should the buyer even proceed with the transaction (Chapter 5)?

2. If so, should be buyer try to renegotiate any of the deal terms (Chapter 6)?

3. Are there conditions that must be satisfied before closing (Chapter 8)?

4. Does the buyer want to require postclosing covenants as a condition to proceeding with the transaction? If so, what remedies should be included to enable enforcement of any such covenants (Chapter 8)?

At this point, the hope is that you now understand the objectives of the due diligence investigation, the process of preparing a due diligence questionnaire, and how the information learned during the course of the investigation can affect the deal terms and the final agreement. It is therefore appropriate to turn to some of the nuts-and-bolts aspects of a due diligence investigation that have not been addressed thus far, as well as consider pragmatic issues that can influence the scope of the review and the overall approach to the due diligence process. The topics covered in this chapter include the following: Should the parties execute a letter of intent before the due diligence process is begun? What factors determine the scope of the review? Who should be part of the due diligence team? What kind of research on the target should be performed separate from the due diligence questionnaire? And what self-imposed due diligence should be conducted before seeking to sell or take on new investors in a business?

Should the Parties Execute a Letter of Intent before Due Diligence?

Conducting due diligence can be a costly and time-consuming process. One of the practical considerations a buyer or investor should ponder before commencing due diligence is whether to negotiate a nonbinding letter of intent with the target company. It is usually unwise to enter into a legally binding letter of intent because, by its nature, the document normally covers the basic terms of the proposed transaction only. The letter does not contain sufficiently detailed language regarding the rights and obligations of the parties or any representations and warranties by the parties. Even if the letter includes conditions to closing, because the due diligence investigation has not yet occurred, any stated conditions are based solely on the information known at the time the letter is negotiated. Although a letter of intent may impose some legal obligations on the parties, these binding terms regulate the behavior of the parties before entering into a definitive agreement (exclusivity, confidentiality, and due diligence rights, as discussed in Chapter 8). The letter of intent does not constitute a final statement of the deal terms and, subject to any exclusivity period, does not prevent a party from walking away from the deal.[1]

Given the arguably limited utility of the letter of intent, should the parties execute one before the due diligence process is begun? One might wonder what the harm of entering into a letter of intent might be because it doesn't bind the parties. Notwithstanding the previous paragraph, the letter of intent can serve a useful role in the transaction. Most significant, it forces the parties to consider the material deal terms and then put them in writing. For example, in a business purchase transaction, the letter of intent would likely include following:

- The nature of the transaction (e.g., asset purchase vs. a stock buyout)
- The parties involved in the deal[2]
- A reference to any excluded assets
- The purchase price/payment terms (and thus the valuation of the business)

---

[1] The parties can include an obligation to negotiate in "good faith"; but, often, drafting these provisions leads to disputes regarding what constitutes good-faith negotiations in the context of the facts surrounding a particular deal (Chapter 8).

[2] For example, the buyer might learn in preparing the letter of intent that the assets are owned by an offshore entity and not the domestic corporation, as originally thought.

- Any conditions, covenants, or special deal terms based on information known at the time of the negotiation of the letter of intent

- A due diligence clause

- A projected closing date

- A reaffirmation of any previously executed nondisclosure agreement

- A possible no-shop clause

- A dispute resolution provision relating to any binding provisions of the letter of intent

If the parties negotiate the material terms at the outset of the transaction, even if adjusted later based on the findings of the due diligence investigation, they have a framework for the deal. With this outline of the deal, even if not binding, parties are less likely to seek a substantial change to the main deal terms absent a justification borne out by the due diligence. If, for expediency's sake, the parties agree that the definitive agreements should be prepared while the due diligence investigation is underway, the letter of intent provides a framework for the initial draft agreements. Moreover, by forcing the parties to address the material deal points in the letter of intent, they may discover their goals are not conducive to continuing with the transaction, which saves both parties from incurring due diligence and other transaction costs only to discover later they were not on the same page with respect to material deal terms.

Sometimes, however, the parties elect to skip drafting a letter of intent, choosing instead to jump into the due diligence process and preparation of the deal documents. The reasoning is that the letter of intent is an unnecessary expense and misuse of each party's time and resources when the terms are clear. Usually, when the deal is simple or a party has made it clear there is very little leeway to alter terms, the letter-of-intent stage of a transaction is skipped. If this is the case, the parties should execute a nondisclosure agreement (if they did not do so at the outset of the their discussions), and the investor or purchaser should strongly consider requiring a no-shop to prevent the target company from terminating the transaction and leaving the buyer with the due diligence expenses. The takeaway here is that there is no correct answer to whether the parties should execute a letter of intent before the due diligence investigation is begun. Rather, the decision should be made on a deal-by-deal basis.

What Factors Determine the Scope of the Due Diligence Investigation?

The scope of the due diligence investigation is determined by several factors. The most common substantive factors have already been discussed: the nature of the transaction, the deal structure, proposed deal terms, and the material aspects of the business and its operations (Chapters 2 and 4). The breadth of the investigation of the target company also depends on several additional substantive and pragmatic considerations. In the following paragraphs, I present several other factors that affect the scope of the due diligence investigation.

First, the industry of the business that is the subject of the investigation contributes to decisions about the scope of the review. For example, due diligence relating to the purchase of a restaurant differs from a medical device manufacturer because the latter requires an understanding of a set of federal regulations that have no bearing on the restaurant business.

Second, the scope of the due diligence investigation is significantly broader when the target company is organized under the laws of another country, or any portion of the business is located in a foreign jurisdiction. Foreign legal counsel, and perhaps accountants, need to be engaged to assist with the investigation of the foreign operations. Even if the business is entirely in the United States, but it may rely on an unaffiliated foreign manufacturer, supplier, or distributor; therefore, issues related to the solvency and legal compliance of this third party may be required.

Third, the target business may be the one seeking to limit the scope of the investigation because of its concerns about protecting confidential information and trade secrets. When the buyer is a competitor, the risks are obvious, and the comfort provided by a nondisclosure agreement may not be sufficient. As discussed in Chapter 8, to the extent the seller restricts the scope of the due diligence, the buyer may have to rely on the representations and warranties in the contract as a substitute for due diligence regarding certain aspects of a business.

Fourth, a seller can be skittish about the effect on employee morale and the operation of the business created by the ongoing due diligence investigation. If the selling company has not informed its employees about the possible transaction, the rumor mill could lead to all sorts of stories that affect employee morale. Even if the staff is made aware of the potential sale, they may still have a number of worries, not the least of which relates to their own status after the deal has closed. The need for management (and perhaps other personnel) to assist with the process of responding to the due diligence investigation can also be disruptive because it draws their attention away from operation of the business. Similarly, the seller will be concerned about the effect on customers, if they learn the business is being sold. The target business may therefore raise these concerns as a basis for imposing limitations on the scope of the due diligence investigation.

Fifth, there is the practical consideration for both parties related to the costs of conducting or responding to the due diligence questionnaire. The expenses related to the due diligence investigation can be substantial, depending on the nature of the transaction. These costs can influence decisions about the breadth of the due diligence investigation and may lead the parties to agree to limit it to the most important issues only, leaving the rest to the representations, warranties, and covenants in the definitive agreements.

Sixth, either party may be concerned about timing issues. The seller or issuer (in an equity financing transaction) may be under financial or other constraints to complete the deal by a set date. A business being sold may, for example, need the purchase price to meet a loan obligation or to complete another deal. A company issuing stock may desperately need the proceeds to finance the company or to fund a new development project. The buyer may need the goods or services of the target business to address a hole in current operations. For some deals, the due diligence investigation could stretch out for a lengthy period of time, and the parties may agree to put a limitation on the scope of the investigation or a stop date for its completion.

Who Should Be Part of the Due Diligence Team?

Part and parcel with the questions about the scope of the due diligence investigation is the consideration of who should be included as a member of the due diligence team. An attorney plays an integral role from the start of the deal, reviewing (or drafting) the letter of intent (if any), preparing the due diligence questionnaire, reviewing the responses, advising his or her client about any issues and possible solutions, reviewing the deal documents, negotiating to resolve due diligence issues, and working with the target company's counsel to finalize the transaction. Most transactions require assistance with the financial review. The buyer might have an on-staff accountant, may engage an outside business accountant to assist, or may add a financial advisor to the team. If there are non-U.S. legal or accounting/tax issues, the assistance of a lawyer or accountant from the relevant foreign jurisdiction might be engaged.

Aside from the legal and financial advisors on a due diligence team, the deal could dictate the need to engage other professional advisors. If there are potential environmental concerns based on the nature of the business or because the purchase of real estate is involved (as in the strip mall purchase in Case Study 5), an environmental consultant (and perhaps an environmental attorney) will need to be part of the due diligence process. In addition, if the business operations include the ownership or use of developed real estate (such as the company's business location, warehouses, or other commercial space), a licensed inspector is necessary to review the structural soundness of the building; the electrical system; the heating, ventilation, and air-conditioning system; and other aspects of the property. If the company has a unionized labor force, a retirement plan, employment issues, or a large staff with complex human resource matters, the due diligence investigation might need to involve an employment/labor attorney, retirement specialist, or human resources consultant. A particular industry expert may be important to identifying potential legal risks (e.g., a lawyer experienced with privacy law, and data security and management issues if the business collects personal information or uses the cloud). Another industry expert may examine the financial risks, such as assessing the seller's market and competition. An IT specialist may be hired to review the company's computer network and data security, and to test any hardware or software goods or services sold by or fundamental to the operation of the business. (This would be appropriate in the ABB asset sale in Case Study 2).

The size of the transaction, nature and complexity of the deal, and the type of business are certainly major determining factors regarding who should participate in the due diligence investigation. For simpler transactions, and depending on the nature of the deal, a business lawyer and business accountant may be sufficient to perform the investigation thoroughly. However, do not let the apparent simplicity or dollar amount of the transaction lead to a misimpression that only a lawyer (or a lawyer and accountant) should comprise the due diligence team. It would be a mistake to let cost dictate a short-term decision about engaging additional assistance when the long-term risks could be potentially catastrophic. For example, the costs of engaging an environmental consultant pale in comparison with the costs of environmental remediation. Having the right team improves the value of the due diligence investigation dramatically and substantially reduces the risk of discovering costly or devastating legal, financial, or operational issues after the deal has closed.

What Kind of Research Should Be Conducted Separate from the Due Diligence Questionnaire?

A major focus of this book has been on the preparation of the due diligence questionnaire and how to address issues discovered from the answers and documents provided by the target company. The company that is the subject of the due diligence investigation should not be the only source of information about the business. Various searches of public records and an analysis of publicly available information can be important to obtaining a complete picture of the target business.

Public Record Searches: Legal Due Diligence

Information regarding the formation of a business entity is publicly available from the secretary of state and is often accessible online. In addition, information can be obtained regarding whether the entity is in good standing (or has been suspended or dissolved), operates under an assumed name (e.g., d/b/a), or has amended its original formation document (e.g., to change its corporate name). Business entities can be formed in one state but may also file to do business in other jurisdictions; therefore, a state's business records include any such authorization. Some state public records also include information regarding the names of directors and officers of the entity. For any transaction in which the target is a business entity, the lender/buyer/investor wants to make sure the corporate entity has, in fact, been formed and is in good standing. If the entity has been suspended or dissolved, it would not have the corporate power to enter into a binding contract. When conducting lien searches, it is important to know whether a business operated previously under another name or operates under an assumed name.

A substantial aspect of due diligence in connection with the purchase of commercial property is the title search. The investigator will review local real property records, seeking to establish that the seller has good and marketable title to the property. In addition, the title search will determine whether there are any third-party rights affecting the title, such as an easement, or whether there are any encumbrances, mortgages, or liens that have been entered against the real property.

A state record search for any liens filed against the target business under the UCC is an essential aspect of the due diligence investigation. A lien filed under the UCC is public record and gives notice that the filing party (e.g., a creditor) has or may have an interest in the personal property (but not the real property) of the named debtor. For example, in a loan transaction, the potential lender can determine whether there are any liens filed against the personal property that are intended to serve as collateral for a loan. If such liens exist, the lender will not want to proceed because (assuming the lien is properly perfected), the creditor has a superior right to the collateral.

A search for judgments, pending lawsuits, and bankruptcy filings needs to be performed. Most court files are public and, therefore, a judgment and litigation search at the state, county, and federal levels can determine whether there are any judgments or pending lawsuits against the target company (or an individual). The party conducting the due diligence investigation obviously would also want to know whether the target company has filed voluntarily for bankruptcy or whether an involuntary petition has been filed against the company.

Federal, state, and county tax liens are filed against the property of a business (or an individual) and should be included in a separate due diligence search. A party purchasing the assets of a business does would not want to proceed with the transaction until any tax lien is removed; otherwise, the transferred assets are still subject to the tax lien.

▨ **Note**   Due diligence involves individuals and not just entities. First, a party to a transaction may require personal due diligence with respect to directors, officers, and majority shareholders. Second, in certain transactions, an individual may be the transferor of the assets or stock. For example, in the music store transaction (Case Study 7), the membership interests to be purchased by Adrian may be transferred from Rowland's total ownership interests rather than from the LLC itself. Another scenario is the buyer in an asset purchase transaction may discover that certain assets are actually still owned by a shareholder, in which case that individual would need to be included in the due diligence investigation.

If a business requires any federal, state, or local permits to operate all or an aspect of a business, often the public record can be searched to determine whether the business has the requisite permits. A variety of business activities are supervised and regulated by state, local, and federal agencies and require licenses or permits to operate. Some licenses are held by the operating entity and are necessary to operate all or particular aspects of the business (e.g., daycare centers, adult care facilities, importers and manufacturers of alcohol, exterminators, a restaurant owner's sidewalk license), and for some businesses the individual must be licensed (e.g., attorneys, doctors, accountants, architects, private investigators and cosmetologists) separate from any license that may (or may not) be required for the business.

Information about registered (and applications for) IP rights is available through public database searches. Issued patents and trademarks can be searched through publicly available information at the U.S. Patent and Trademark Office and is easily accessible via their web site. Similarly, registered copyrights are available at the U.S. Copyright Office. Information about foreign patents, trademarks, and copyright registrations is available through the individual countries where the rights have been registered (or, for example, in the case of a community trademark for the European Union, through the Office For Harmonization in the Internal Market). Confirming ownership of domains, which are often overlooked in the due diligence investigation, can also be accomplished through a public registry search.[3]

---

[3] Be careful about checking ownership of domain names. Usually (but not always) by accident, a founder or even an employee will personally register the domain name and fail to transfer it to the corporate entity. If a sale of the assets or even the business as a whole proceeds, the purchaser would not own the domain and would be forced to chase the owner postclosing to arrange (hopefully) the transfer. Worse yet, the owner would control the domain and the web site until the transfer occurred. The transfer of the domain and web site should, therefore, be part of closing conditions.

An environmental consultant can conduct searches of public records and other information to make an assessment regarding any existing or potential environmental issues pertaining to real property being purchased or a location that is part of a transaction. A search of public files, historical research, and chain-of-title examinations as well as onsite inspections can provide an initial assessment of any potential environmental issues. Depending on the results of the Phase I environmental site assessment, a significantly more intrusive assessment (Phase II) may be performed. The discovery of any environmental issues can have tremendous repercussions, and if any issues were discovered during a Phase I investigation, the party conducting due diligence may decide to terminate the transaction before going any further.

Public record searches are a significant element of the legal due diligence process. These searches cover many of the questions that are also posed to the target business in the due diligence questionnaire. However, it is imprudent to rely solely on the responses to the questionnaire when the information can be confirmed through other sources.

Public Information: Finances, Operations, and Business Intangibles

Publicly available information can also assist with a review of the finances and operations as well as certain business intangibles. An Internet search might reveal positive or critical comments about a business, and its products and services. Although Internet reviews are often questionable, they can still be of value if the information is posted on a generally reliable web site. If repeated criticism of a product is found (perhaps even on several sites), at a minimum it might prompt further inquiry. Consider, for example, if the potential investor in KMF Franchisee reads multiple reviews complaining that the quality of the ice cream at Rocky Robbins has declined (Case Study 8). These comments provide insight about the franchisor and the products chain rather than the franchisee itself.

As another example, Jack, the buyer in the ABB asset sale (Case Study 2), might have heard, during the midst of the transaction, that suddenly there are issues with order processing and, after testing the software again, may find that orders cannot be processed. This information may not lead him to end the deal, but Jack may require technical fixes or updates as a closing condition (Chapter 8).

The party conducting due diligence can even use old-fashioned investigatory methods to ferret out information. The buyer conducting due diligence of the Rocky Robbins Ice Cream restaurant, for example, could send one or more "secret shoppers" to eat there and report back about their experience: quality of the food, wait time, and service. The buyer could sit in Rocky Robbins at various times on several days and observe the foot traffic and customer purchasing behavior. In the commercial real estate transaction in Case Study 5, the buyer can obtain another type of traffic information—motor vehicle traffic volume—which can help determine whether there is sufficient traffic volume to support expansion of the mall. The modern equivalent of foot traffic and motor vehicle volume is web site traffic. Information about visitor traffic to a website, click-through rates for web site advertisements and e-mail, and web site rankings can be a meaningful way of calibrating the value of a company's web site and Internet advertising.

Access to the Business

The importance of obtaining access to the business has been touched on already in terms of the factors than can affect the scope of due diligence. In some deals, such as a loan transaction (Case Study 1), for example, it may be sufficient if the business provides copies of all the requested documents as part of the response to the questionnaire. Technology has influenced aspects of the due diligence investigation, allowing the target business to upload electronic copies of documents for review in a "data room." Depending on the nature of the business and the transaction, the universe of documents for review may be small, and any decision to proceed with the transaction can be based on the financial and legal documents provided by the company and limited public record searches.

In other deals, onsite access to the business is important. The sheer volume of business records may render it impractical to make copies for the purchaser or investor. The business may not have the resources (or the desire) to upload electronic versions of the documents for offsite review. It may be more efficient to conduct the financial review at the company if the documents, books, and records are voluminous and there is a need to review the financial backup, schedules, and reports (much of which is likely stored electronically). For components of the business that cannot be gleaned from company documents, only an onsite review suffices. For example, a review of the company's onsite computer network, phone system, electronic data storage system, manufacturing facilities, machinery, warehouses, and inventory require in-person inspection.

Then, there is the often-sensitive issue of access to management and other key personnel. On one level, the party conducting the due diligence investigation may want a liaison at the company who can coordinate administrative issues, such as access to materials or additional information requests, or responses to substantive questions. The person conducting financial due diligence often needs to speak to the company's accountant or chief financial officer. The technology review likely cannot be performed without assistance from the chief technology officer or someone else knowledgeable about the computer network and related matters. And on the operations side, the buyer will want to be able to communicate with the chief operating officer, the director of operations, or a manager with sufficient knowledge of the business operation.

On another level, separate from the due diligence questionnaire, a buyer or investor will want an opportunity to vet the management, key personnel, and partners who are actively involved with the business.[4] An investor or potential new business partner might be concerned about management's vision for the business and its ability to execute on the company's business plan. In the context of a merger of two businesses, one of the intangible issues directly affecting the success of the transaction down the road is whether the business cultures mesh well. The due diligence process is not only about obtaining confidence in the financial and legal aspects of the business, but also in management, its ability to run the company, and whether there is a common mind-set or a clash of business cultures that could jeopardize the success of the posttransaction business. Incompatible business cultures can be a recipe for a merger disaster.

Notwithstanding all the reasons for a purchaser to insist on access to the management and personnel, the target could decide to reject or limit severely access to personnel for the reasons discussed previously, including business disruption and confidentiality. If this is the decision of the company, the purchaser must then evaluate the findings of the due diligence investigation and decide whether it is comfortable with postclosing contract conditions that perhaps include cooperation assurances, assistance with the transition, and resolution of personnel matters (Chapter 8). The other choice for the purchaser/investor is to walk from the deal on the grounds that purchaser cannot proceed without an opportunity to assess and obtain a meaningful level of comfort regarding management and key personnel.

---

[4] If the parties have entered into a binding purchase agreement, the seller will have a harder time justifying limitations on the buyer's reasonable access. As the deal progresses, the buyer may want to be actively involved in the business so that he or she can learn the ropes and facilitate a smooth postclosing transition. The buyer can consider negotiating a deal term that requires assistance from the seller after the closing. In other circumstance, the buyer may actually engage the seller to assist with the transition or under a "smart hands" technology assistance agreement pursuant to which the seller will provide assistance with transition of technology to the buyer.

Due Diligence by the Seller

As mentioned, the focus of the discussion throughout has been on the importance of preparing and then executing a well-conceived due diligence investigation based on the deal terms, nature of the business, and the facts underpinning the transaction. Armed with the information obtained from the investigation, lenders, purchasers, or investors then consider their options:

- Move forward with the transaction based on the negotiated deal terms.

- Walk away because the risks are too great to overcome.

- Adjust the deal valuation consistent with the results of the review and level of risk.

- Revise the terms and conditions of the transaction to address the legal, financial, and operational issues and risks uncovered by the due diligence investigation.

However, a transaction obviously involves at least two parties, and in certain deals the buyer may not be the only one conducting a due diligence investigation. For example, in a merger in which each company survives in some capacity, both companies will engage in the due diligence process. When the transaction involves the sale of an interest in a partnership or the issuance of stock to new investor, the company and current members/shareholders will want to scrutinize the buyer carefully before admitting the buyer to the partnership. Due diligence with respect to a potential new shareholder or business partner can include the following:

The Personal Due Diligence Questionnaire: The personal questionnaire seeks information about any civil or criminal proceedings involving the investor, bankruptcy filings, and financial liabilities. A material lawsuit against an investor, a bankruptcy, or substantial liabilities raise issues regarding the investor's financial status. The fact that the potential investor has filed a number of lawsuits (especially against partners in other businesses or companies in which he or she is an owner) can be a red flag.

Background check: The investor should be willing to submit to a background and credit check. Regardless of whether the background check or credit check is performed, any hesitancy on the part of a potential new partner can be a concern.

Investment questionnaire: Company's offering securities to "accredited investors" in a private placement in reliance on an exemption from registration pursuant to Rule 506(b) of Regulation D of the Securities Act of 1933, as amended, must form a reasonable belief regarding the "accredited investor" status of an investor. When the offering involves general solicitation and general advertising, Rule 506(c) of the Securities Act requires the company to take "reasonable steps" to verify the status of the purchaser.[5] The scrutiny required under Rule 506(c) is much greater, but in both circumstances the verification process includes an investment questionnaire and, in the case of a 506(c) offering, an investor obligation to share documents and information regarding personal finances.

Get-to-know meetings: If the partners or substantial shareholders have not met the potential new partner, they might ask for an opportunity to do so. A closely held business must be careful about who it takes in as a new partner because, after the person becomes a partner, it is very hard to get rid of him or her. Bringing in a new partner is not only about financial wherewithal but also whether their personality and views about the business gel with the owners and management. One of the biggest nightmares for a closely held business is the inability of one or more partners to get along. Although this risk cannot be avoided completely, it can be reduced if the partners vet the potential new member thoroughly before agreeing to his or her admission as a partner in the business.

What Self-Imposed Due Diligence Should Be Conducted by the Seller?

Companies that are considering a sale of the business, are planning to raise additional capital, or want to take on an additional partner should recognize the value of conducting due diligence of the business before going to market. It is important for a company contemplating a sale of its business or issuing new shares to conduct a meaningful evaluation and due diligence of its legal, financial, and business operations to avoid issues arising after a potential buyer

---

[5]General solicitation and the accompanying heightened responsibility of an issue to take reasonable steps to verify accredited investor status are a result of the 2012 Jumpstart Our Business Startups Act (also known as the *JOBS Act*).

has been found. In the sale of a home, a buyer uses the inspection report and appraisal to try to knock down the negotiated price; as discussed in Chapter 8, in the sale of a company, the buyer tries to do the same with information learned from the due diligence investigation. Therefore, a thorough review of the company's business, legal, and financial operations before seeking to sell or raise capital for your business allows you to address potential obstacles to a sale and to reduce the chances the buyer or investor will try to renegotiate the valuation of the business.

Is the company's legal house in order? By now, the paramount importance of legal due diligence and the potential impact on the transaction from the outcome of that legal review is obvious. There are numerous legal areas the buyer will review, and the scope of due diligence will vary greatly depending on the type of the deal, the terms of the transaction, and the nature of the business operations. Thus, not unlike how a buyer or investor would approach due diligence, a company determining whether its legal house is in order should at least consider the following:

- **Corporate structure**: A company should determine whether its organizational documents and records are in order. It also needs to understand whether there are potential obstacles to the transaction. For example, do any of the shareholders or any other third parties have a right of first refusal, or other rights, that could interfere with the transaction? Is there anything in the bylaws or operating agreement that mandate a supermajority or even unanimous approval of a sale? These kinds of rights are often granted freely when emerging companies are desperate to obtain financing, but the restrictions they impose can come back to haunt the company when trying to sell.

- **Permits/compliance with laws**: A company will need to show it has the necessary permits or licenses required for the business, but it also needs to show that it is in compliance with the laws of any jurisdiction where it operates. The absence of the necessary permits or the fact that a company is not in compliance with applicable laws can result in termination, delay, or significant changes to the transaction.

- **Assets/intellectual property**: Can ownership/title to assets be demonstrated or are there potential issues based on third-party claims? Does the company own or properly license necessary IP? If the business is licensing any key IP or other assets, the company should make sure the license is assignable/assumable in a sale or that the rights do not revert to the licensor on a "change of control" of the business. As witnessed in the Case Study 2, a major concern is whether ABB has an invention assignment agreement or can otherwise establish its rights to the IP developed by Dana.

- **Material contracts**: All material contracts should be reviewed to ensure they are assignable/assumable and they do not terminate in the event of a sale of the business or change of control. The company can explore the possibility of renegotiating the assignment clause with the other party to the contract before any attempt to sell the business. First, the company does not want to go down the road of a transaction only to determine later that a material contract cannot be assigned. The issues might not kill the deal, but it could be costly in terms of the valuation of the business and, ultimately, the purchase price. Second, the contract party may be willing to amend the terms, but if it knows about the pressure of a pending deal, the costs of obtaining consent could rise substantially.

- **Employment/labor matters**: A company needs to make sure all employment records are in order. It may choose to prepare a detailed summary of the staff, including job title and responsibility, and information about employee compensation and benefits (e.g., salary, sick/vacation time, stock options, or bonus rights). If there isn't an employee manual, it may be a good time to prepare one. If there are open employment or labor issues, the company should determine what steps it might take to resolve them before any transaction is pursued. Also, the company needs to address whether employees have signed invention assignment and confidentiality agreements, on which a buyer or investor might insist as a preclosing condition.

- **Litigation**: If there are pending litigation matters, the company should prepare a summary of the claims because the buyer will require the summary as part of due diligence. The company should include the list in the disclosure schedules of the purchase agreement. Also, the company will want to consider how it proposes to address these claims in the purchase agreement (e.g., who will assume responsibility for these claims and related costs, and what indemnifications might be given to the buyer). If the company has been threatened with any lawsuits or other claims, it needs to assess the potential impact of the claim and whether it can be resolved before any attempt to sell the business.

- **Loans/liens/encumbrances:** The existence of any liens or encumbrances on the material assets can affect the valuation of the business, cause a delay in the transaction or even prevent the transaction from proceeding all together. If there are liens arising from judgments or tax issues, then the company should try to resolve them or be prepared to explain these and set aside an escrow amount to cover these liens. On the other hand, encumbrances in connection with secured loans in the ordinary course of business or required for operating capital likely would not be addressed until a deal was in hand.

Are the financial records maintained properly? The company should work with its accountant to make sure all the financial records are organized and financial events recorded accurately. The buyer will ask to see balance sheets, tax returns and audits, P&L statements, loan documents, accounts, ledgers, and all backup information. The company will benefit greatly if the financial records are in order before it is subject to the scrutiny of a buyer or investor.

Are the company books and records well organized? The company should make it part of good corporate practice to maintain orderly books and records from the start. It should not wait until there is a possible exit opportunity to then run around and try to gather the due diligence materials the buyer will certainly request. Disorganized records hinder the due diligence investigation, and failure to record properly all financial transactions, assets, liabilities, expenses, and the like could impact valuation or kill the deal.

Does the company have backups of all files, processes, and key software? Maintaining copies of key documents and backups of electronic files and data is necessary for compliance and is good corporate practice.

Does the company have workflow documentation and written policies? If the company prepares a road map of important business processes, creates a corporate organizational chart, and details workflow, policies, and procedures, the buyer will greatly appreciate the positive effect these efforts have on a smooth transition of the business.

In sum, a company does not want to learn from a potential buyer or investor that a major issue has been discovered, especially if it could have been addressed by the company before the buyer's due diligence. At the very least, due diligence issues discovered by a buyer or investor will raise transaction costs as the parties, accountants, and lawyers try to resolve and then document any agreed solution. In addition, it is generally less expensive for a lawyer to draft definitive agreements and accompanying disclosures and schedules if company records are well maintained and the seller's attorney is aware of the issues (if any) at the outset of the transaction. Last, whether a company is in a position to be sold or raise money is often a function of adopting measures along the way to avoid major issues rather than trying to clean them up in response to due diligence. Retaining professional advisors and service providers (e.g., accountants, lawyers, payroll specialists, computer networking consultants) when the company is established and as it grows is an excellent way to avoid issues or to address them as they arise during the course of everyday business. Companies that are vigilant about enforcing good corporate policies and procedures reduce substantially the chance that the buyer's due diligence will uncover legal, financial, or business issues that either undermine dramatically the value of the company or result in a termination of the sale.

Conclusion

In this chapter, we examined the letter of intent, circumstances in which parties are likely to enter into a letter of intent as a deal stepping-stone, and circumstances in which a letter of intent is not productive. The discussion then turned to a consideration of additional factors affecting the approach to the dual diligence investigation: the industry of the target business, whether the business has foreign business operations, limitations imposed by the target company because of a concern about protecting competitive information, potential disruption of the business operations, the costs of conducting a broad-based investigation, and timing issues. We also looked at who to include as part of the due diligence team. An attorney and accountant are obviously significant players, but advisors with particular industry expertise or knowledge of an aspect of the business operation are also important. We then examined how the due diligence process also includes searches of public records as part of the review of the legal, financial, and business operations of the target company. Another major aspect covered was access to the company to review books and records, engage management and key personnel on significant issues, to review the business operations, and to get a feel for the company's business culture. The scope of the access, however, can be a tricky issue because the target company may seek to restrict access to protect competitive information or to prevent any disruption of the business operations.

The final topic of this chapter approached due diligence from the standpoint of the target business. Due diligence can be a two-way street; the target company or the partners may want to conduct due diligence on the buyer or potential investor. The target company should also preemptively conduct due diligence on its own business. Recall the conversations between Jack and his lawyer regarding the ABB Transaction and the substantial issues that could prevent completion of the transaction. Now consider how different the conversation would have been between Jack and his lawyer, and how the deal would not have been placed in jeopardy, if Leah had conducted a proper due diligence on her business before trying to sell it. This internal review will either save a future transaction or prevent a reduction of the company's valuation by addressing legal, financial, or operational matters before they can become an issue for the potential buyer or investor.

Due Diligence Plan for KMF Franchisee, LLC, Investment

I. Transaction Overview

1. *Nature of the transaction*: acquisition of an ownership interest in an LLC, KMF Franchisee, LLC, which currently has two partners

2. *Asset to be acquired*: 33% of the membership interest in an LLC

3. *Nature of the business*: owns four Rocky Robbins Ice Cream Bar franchises

4. *Consideration*: $225,000 (all cash)

5. *Personnel*: multiple full- and part-time employees; manager of all four stores is in last year of contract.

6. *Initial deal issues:*

    a. Terms of the franchise agreements for the stores

    b. Potential competition from former partner

    c. A $100,000 loan is held by the former business partner.

    d. An operating agreement was never executed by all the partners.

    e. One of the locations is leased through a sublease, which is expiring; the sublessor is having financial difficulties.

    f. The company has exercised an option to acquire the property where one of its restaurants is located.

II. The Company

1. Determine if the LLC was formed properly and is it in good standing and what organizational documents exist.

2. The investor will become a member of the LLC. There is an unexecuted operating agreement that the existing LLC members want to adopt; it is essential that the investor understand the terms and whether it is sufficient to address the rights and obligations among the members.

    a. Determine who the members are and what each member's percentage of interest in the LLC is.

    b. Review all organization documents to determine how the LLC is managed and what management and voting rights the members have in the LLC.

    c. Determine the specific financial rights of members.

    d. Consider if the LLC adopted specific tax provisions that affect members.

    e. Review all restrictions on ownership and transfer of the membership interests in the LLC.

    f. Review the unexecuted draft of the operating agreement and determine what needs to be revised to protect the rights of the members.

3. Review any additional agreements, resolutions, or consents that affect the structure or organization of the company.

4. Determine if there any agreements in addition to the operating agreement that affect member rights, such as voting agreements, investor rights agreements, rights of first refusal, and joint ventures.

5. Consider the effect of any unusual provisions in any of the corporate documents.

III. The Business Operation

1. The LLC operates multiple franchises.

2. Consider whether there are issues arising from the sale of ice cream and related items.

3. Obtain a complete picture as to what are the key assets necessary to operate the business. Review the ownership of the assets, including whether owned outright, leased, or licensed from a third party. Determine what due diligence is required regarding those assets.

4. Understand the particular issues arising from the fact that the company operates franchises.

   a. How the franchise rights are owned.

   b. Obtain a clear picture regarding the scope of the rights and obligations under the franchise agreements, including how long they last. Determine what are the obligations of the company under the franchise agreements as well as whether they change during the course of the franchise.

   c. Verify whether the franchise rights can be transferred and if they would be affected by a change of ownership of KMF Franchisee, LLC.

5. If the business depends on the use of intellectual property (IP), determine whether it is owned or licensed from a third party and, if so, what needs to be examined regarding the IP.

6. Establish whether there are clearly defined, documented, and followed policies and procedures for operation of the business.

7. Obtain a clear picture regarding the material contracts/ agreements and business relationships essential to operation of the business (in addition to the franchise agreements), including:

   a. Supplier agreements

   b. Equipment leases/software licenses

   c. Noncompete or restrictions on scope of business

   d. Sales/marketing agreements

   e. Insurance

8. Review the leases and understand the material terms for each franchise location.

   a. Consider what issues are raised by the fact that one location is subleased.

   b. Consider what issues are raised by the fact that the sublease is expiring and the sublessor is rumored to be in poor financial condition.

9. Determine what due diligence needs to be performed in connection with the potential purchase of the stand-alone store location.

10. Verify whether the business has the appropriate information technology systems and network necessary for its operations.

    a. Back-up and disaster recovery

    b. Appropriate privacy, data security, and credit card policies

11. Determine if there are legal compliance issues raised by the operation of the business.

    a. Licenses and permits

    b. Compliance under environmental, health, and safety laws

    c. Compliance with the franchise agreement

    d. Compliance with local laws

    e. No default under material contracts

12. Verify whether the franchisor is in compliance with its obligations. Obtain a clear understanding of the relationship with the franchisor, including whether it is a good partner.

13. Consider whether the nature of the business raises any issues regarding environmental compliance.

IV. Business Valuation

1. Determine the value of the business.

   a. Understand what material assets are used in the operation of the business.

   b. Review how the assets are owned. If some of them are not owned outright, review the terms of any lease, license, or franchise.

   c. Determine if the assets are subject to any liens, encumbrances, or security interests.

   d. Consider whether there are any other issues affecting the value of the assets, including the condition of physical assets.

   e. If the assets include IP, consider what additional due diligence is required.

2. Evaluate the financial status of the business by reviewing:

   a. Financials, P&Ls, and revenue and expense statements for the LLC and each location

   b. Long- and short-term financing or other debt obligations

   c. Lease obligations

   d. Obligations created by contract or other agreements

   e. Outstanding financial obligations to members of the LLC

   f. Outstanding judgments, awards, or fines

   g. Pending or threatened audits, claims, lawsuits, or legal proceedings by any person, agency, or regulatory body

3. Consider any potential tax issues that must be addressed.

4. Review the terms of the franchise agreements.

   a. Financial and nonfinancial obligations to the franchisor

   b. Financial and nonfinancial rights of the franchisee

5. Evaluate the financial picture as set forth in the financial statements, books, and records of the business.

6. Determine the potential business risks related to the franchise.

   a. Competition, including from the disgruntled former partner

   b. Financial condition of the franchisor

   c. Historical and projected demand for franchisor's products or services

7. Evaluate the financial sense of the pending purchase of the stand-alone location.

8. Consider the potential financial risks arising from the upcoming expiration of one of the leases.

9. Consider the financial issues related to the expiration of the manager's contract.

V. Personnel

1. Review the organizational chart for the business, if any.

   a. Identify key personnel at the management level.

   b. Identify key owner/nonowner employees.

2. Determine whether there are owner-employees who serve a significant role in the business. Evaluate the likelihood of their continued participation in the business.

3. Review the employment terms of key personnel and understand the general employment picture regarding the staff.

   a. Financial

   b. Nonfinancial terms and benefits

4. Determine if there are any liabilities related to personnel.

   a. Pending claims and lawsuits

   b. Threatened claims and lawsuits

   c. Compliance with payroll and other obligations relating to employment

5. Determine if there is legal documentation relating to personnel. Verify:

   a. Whether the company requires and retains properly all documentation related to personnel.

   b. Legal status of all employees.

   c. Whether employees and members signed confidentiality, invention assignment, and noncompete agreements, as appropriate.

6. Understand the staffing picture and whether there is sufficient staffing given the fact that this is a restaurant business—an industry known for having employee retention issues.

7. Determine if the company has well-defined written policies and procedures regarding employees. If so, find out if these policies are followed/enforced.

8. Identify the retention issues related to the operations manager of the four franchise locations.

   a. Evaluate the issues resulting from the fact that the employee who manages all four stores is in the last year of her contract.

   b. Determine if the manager be retained on reasonable employment terms.

   c. If the manager cannot be retained, verify the existence and business sense of any back-up plan if the manager leaves.

Due Diligence Questionnaire for KMF Franchisee, LLC

Investor, Ellen Kay, is considering entering into an agreement concerning an investment in KMF Franchisee, LLC (the "Company"). In connection therewith, we request that the Company provide responses to the following questions and requests for information. For purposes of this questionnaire, references to the term "Company" includes KMF Franchisee, LLC, and all subsidiaries, affiliates, and divisions thereof.

If there are no documents or other information that are relevant to the particular due diligence request, indicate as such in response to the question.

If certain materials have already been provided or are unavailable or inapplicable, please indicate so in your response to this request. Please note that our due diligence investigation is ongoing and we will submit supplemental due diligence requests as necessary.

In certain instances, this questionnaire pertains only to matters that exceed certain material thresholds. In this respect, for the purposes of this questionnaire, the word "material" shall be understood to include all information regarding agreements, rights, and/or obligations that represent a value of

$50.00 or more or that are in some other way of considerable importance for the Company's business and/or activities.

The word "including" as used herein means including without limitation, unless noted.

I. Corporate Organization

1. Provide all documents related to the formation of the LLC, including with limitation, the articles of organization and operating agreement (and all amendments thereof).

2. Provide all corporate record books, including minutes of meetings of members, managing members or directors, and committees thereof.

3. List all officers, managers, and directors of the LLC.

4. List

   a. All jurisdictions where the LLC, its subsidiaries, and its affiliates (the "Company" or "Companies") is incorporated or qualified to do business.

   b. The address of the chief executive office; any other jurisdiction and the address where the Company owns, stores, leases, or licenses properties or assets; has employees, agents, or customers; or keeps books and records related to the Company.

5. Provide all certificates of authority, existence, or good standing, and tax status certificates of each Company for its respective jurisdictions.

6. Provide a list of all assumed names, division names, or other names under which any of the Companies is conducting or has conducted business.

7. Has the Company changed its identity or corporate structure? If so, indicate the nature of such change; give the names of each company that was incorporated, merged, or consolidated with or acquired by the Company; and provide the address of each place of business thereof prior to such incorporation, merger, consolidation, or acquisition.

8. Provide a list of any corporations, partnerships, LLCs, joint ventures, or other entities in which any of the Companies has an interest or is affiliated, along with a description of the interest or affiliation.

II. Corporate Ownership Structure

1. List the number of authorized and outstanding membership interests/units of each class of ownership interests in the Company.

2. List the names of each member of the LLC, and number and class or type of membership interest held.

3. List the holders of any options, warrants, rights, subscriptions to acquire, or securities granting right to acquire, exercisable for, or convertible into, membership interests in the LLC; the terms of such right to acquire, exercise, or convert (and all agreements relating thereto); and the number of membership interests/units issuable in connection therewith. Provide all documents relating to such rights to acquire interests in the LLC.

4. Are there any employee options, bonus, or other similar plans? If so, provide all documents relating to such plans.

5. Provide all membership agreements, investor rights agreements, buy–sell agreements, redemption agreements, revocable and irrevocable proxies, voting agreements, and similar agreements with or among the members of any of the Company.

6. Provide documents related to the buyout of Mishy, including any purchase agreement and loans made in connection with the buyout.

III. Financing Obligations

1. Has the company borrowed or committed to borrow any money? Provide all promissory notes, commercial paper, loan or credit agreements, indentures, and other agreements or instruments related to borrowing of money or a commitment to borrow money involving the Company.

2. Provide all guarantees, repurchase obligations, surety contracts, and other arrangements whereby the credit of the Company is obligated for the indebtedness of a person.

3. Provide all documents purporting to create liens, mortgages, security agreements, pledges, charges or other encumbrances on the membership interests of the Company, or on any assets, real or personal property, of the Company or in favor of the Company.

4. Provide all letters of credit, financial surety bonds, or similar credit support devices outstanding and related reimbursement or indemnification agreements.

5. Provide all agreements pursuant to which the Company is or will be subject to any obligation to provide funds to or to make investments in any other person (in the form of a loan, capital contribution, or otherwise).

6. Provide all material correspondence with any creditor of the Company.

7. List any existing defaults under credit arrangements or financing obligations of the Company and any events that have occurred that, with the giving of notice or the passage of time, will become such a default.

8. Provide all notes payable to or notes receivable from any employee, manager, affiliate, agent, or member of the Company.

9. Has the Company entered in any other financing agreements relating directly or indirectly to the Company which have not been provided in response to Questions 1-9? If so, provide all such financing agreements.

10. Has the Company granted any security interests in its assets, property, or rights? Has it pledged any of its assets, property, or rights as collateral or security in connection with any obligation or for any other reason? Does there exist any encumbrance, lien, or security interest in the assets, property, or rights of the Company? If so, provide all documents and information relating thereto.

IV. Financial Information

1. Provide all monthly, quarterly, and annual financial statements and balance sheets for the past six years and the current year to date, and all supporting schedules to such financial statements.

2. Provide all quarterly projected income statements and cash flows for the next three years.

3. Provide a schedule of any contingent liabilities.

4. Detail any liabilities not reflected in the financial statements.

5. Detail all aged accounts receivables and payables as of each quarter for the past three years and for each quarter of the current year to date.

6. List all accrued expenses as of each year end for the past three years.

7. Set forth all net operating loss carry-forwards.

8. Provide all capital expenditure schedules (current and projected).

9. Provide all information concerning the number of customers, average purchase size/amount per transaction, and highest grossing products and highest margin products broken out by location of each store/restaurant and by season.

10. Provide all agreements and detail all arrangements with merchant processors and credit card companies.

11. Detail all monthly charge-backs and issued credits for the past 24 months.

12. Provide all business plans, market surveys, and reports, and any report or summary regarding the financial condition of the Company.

V. Tax Matters

1. Provide all federal, state, and local tax returns (for income, gross receipts, sales or use, property, employment, or other taxes) for the past six years.

2. Provide all federal, state, and local audit and revenue agents' reports, settlement documents, and correspondence related to the Company.

3. Provide all agreements that are in effect waiving statutes of limitations or extending time in connection with federal, state, and local tax matters.

4. Have there been any deficiency assessments filed against any of the Companies by federal, state, or local tax authorities, and has there been a resolution of such assessments? If there have been any assessments, provide all documents relating thereto.

5. Provide all copies of all documentation concerning any elections made under the Internal Revenue Code or other tax laws that could have a material effect on any of the Companies.

6. Other than for the current fiscal year, has the Company filed and made all payments in connection with federal, state and local tax returns? Other than for the current quarter, has the Company filed and made all payments in connection with all sales and use tax returns?

VI. Contracts, Agreements, and Commitments

1. List each Company's major suppliers and dollar volume of purchases from each for each fiscal year. (A "major supplier" means the top ten suppliers [by purchase volume]).

2. List any supplier for which practical alternative sources of supply are not available.

3. Provide all license, sublicense, royalty, and franchise agreements, including the franchise agreement with Rocky Robbins Ice Cream (the "Franchise") and all agreements, contracts, undertakings, and documents related to the Franchise.

4. Provide all distribution, agency, manufacturer, and similar contracts.

5. Provide all joint venture or partnership agreements.

6. Provide all management, services, and marketing agreements.

7. Provide all hold-harmless, indemnification, or similar agreements.

8. Provide all leases and the status of negotiations to renew any of the leases.

9. Provide all material agreements related to the sale or lease of the company's assets.

10. Provide all material warranty and service agreements.

11. Provide all any agreements out of the ordinary course of business to which the Company is a party or by which it or its properties are bound.

12. Provide all standard form agreements used by the Company.

13. Provide all brokers or finders agreements.

14. Provide all confidentiality and nondisclosure agreements binding the Company.

15. Provide all agreements related to any merger, acquisition, divestiture, consolidation, reorganization, spinoff, or disposition of assets, and any documentation related to any previous or proposed transaction.

16. Provide all agreements affected in any manner by a change in control of any of the Companies or that require consent of a third party to assign.

17. Provide all insurance agreements and policies held for the benefit of the Company (e.g., fire or casualty insurance, loss of business, key man) or its directors, officers, or employees.

18. List and provide copies of all agreements and arrangements between any of the Companies and any officer, manager, or member, or any of their respective families or affiliates currently existing.

19. Provide all agreements that prohibit or restrict the Company's ability to compete in any business anywhere in any geographic area, or the customers with which the Company may do business, or the prices the Company may charge for its services.

20. Provide all material correspondence related to any of the foregoing contracts, agreements or undertakings, including notices of default in the performance or observance of any term thereof.

VII. Intellectual Property and Technology

1. List all patents, trademarks, service marks, logos, copyrights, and licenses worldwide, including all issued, registered, or pending applications ("Intellectual Property"). Provide details regarding the status of all patents, trademarks, copyright issuances, registrations, or applications.

2. Provide all contracts and proposed contracts concerning Intellectual Property owned, used, or licensed by or licensed to the Company, including license and royalty agreements.

3. List all domain names owned or used by the Company and to whom they are registered.

4. List all technology and software owned, held for use by, or being developed by or for the Company.

5. List all material third-party computer software used by the Company or incorporated into any software or product of the Company; and open source, freeware, or other software with similar licensing or distribution models used by the Company or incorporated into any software or product of the Company.

6. List all trade secrets and other proprietary know-how or processes owned or held for use by the Company.

7. Provide all agreements and proposed agreements pursuant to which any Intellectual Property is assigned, sold, or otherwise transferred, or licensed by the Company to any party or subject to a covenant not to sue.

8. Provide all documents concerning any liens, pledges, or encumbrances against the Intellectual Property of the Company.

9. Are there any claims, causes of action, disputes, or threatened claims against the Company or brought or contemplated by the Company concerning the Intellectual Property or claims or threatened claims of infringement and the like. If so, set forth the details of all claims, causes of action or disputes, and all threatened claims or disputes.

10. List all technology and software owned, leased, or licensed to the Company and provide copies of any related agreements.

11. List all software programs and applications sold, distributed, or licensed by the Company to any third party.

12. Does the Company have and if so provide a description of procedural safeguards respecting the trade secrets/ confidential information and internal policy statements or manuals for procedures related to the trade secrets and confidential information.

VIII. Information Technology Systems and Networks

1. Provide copies of all agreements related to the provision of information technology, data, or Internet-related products or services to or by the Company.

2. Describe all computer systems, software packages, networks, and computer services ("Computer Systems") in use by the Company, by location.

3. Provide copies of all policies, procedures, and plans relating to the Company's Computer Systems.

4. Does the Company have, and if so describe, any backup and disaster recovery arrangements, facilities management, and ongoing support arrangements, including details of service levels and charges.

5. Describe and provide copies of all documents related to whether the Company has access, or rights of access, to the source code of material licensed software to ensure adequate maintenance and updating of that software.

6. Describe any Company procedures to monitor compliance with the terms of software licenses, including whether these procedures monitor the use of software by the Company to ensure that multiple copies of any software are not used in breach of the relevant license terms.

7. Describe and provide copies of the Company's web site security policies and procedures.

8. Confirm whether the Company owns all Intellectual Property in the design and content of its web sites.

9. Describe any insurance coverage for business losses related to the Company's Computer Systems.

10. Describe any material interruptions of the Company's Computer Systems during the past three years.

IX. Privacy and Data Security

1. Provide copies of all current and historical privacy and data security policies and practice manuals of the Company, including all privacy policies and procedures for the Company's use and disclosure of customer or personal information.

2. Provide copies of all policies, procedures and written information about security programs for compliance with data protection and privacy legislation.

3. Provide copies of all reports or audits (internal or external) that have been performed on the Company's information security program(s) or any other reports prepared by or for the Company concerning the implementation of information security program(s).

4. Provide copies of any other documentation and information regarding the Company's collection, use, storage, or disposal of customer or personal information (whether the Company's or a third party's).

5. Provide copies of all agreements that the Company has with any third parties that act as the Company's agents or contractors and receive customer or personal information subject to any statutory or regulatory data privacy or security requirements from or on behalf of the Company.

6. Provide details regarding any actual or potential data and information security breaches, unauthorized use or access of the Company's computer systems or data, or data and information security issues impacting the Company that have been identified during the past three years.

X. Real Property

1. List the real property owned by the Company, including size, location, and use of each parcel. Provide documents of title, title insurance, mortgages, deeds of trust, leases, and security agreements for these properties.

2. List all real property under contract for purchase by the Company. Provide any title report or title search in connection with any real property under contract to purchase.

3. Provide any appraisals or surveys of real property owned or being purchased by the Company.

4. Provide copies of all outstanding leases for real property to which the Company is either a lessor or lessee, including ground leases and subleases, estoppel certificates, and related subordination or nondisturbance agreements.

5. Provide any option or development agreements involving real property to which the Company is a party.

6. Provide all certificates of occupancy related to any real property owned or leased by the Company.

7. List all material encroachments, liens, easements, or other encumbrances on any real property owned or leased by the Company.

8. Provide any building, structural, engineering, and other inspection reports related to any property owned or leased by the Company.

XI. Personnel and Employment

1. Provide an organizational chart listing directors, officers, and key personnel, and their title and job responsibilities.

2. Provide all employment, consulting, or management agreements with any current or former (if any term thereof is still in effect) employee or consultant of any of the Companies.

3. Provide all confidentiality, nondisclosure, invention assignment, and noncompete agreements with any current or former director, officer, partner, employee, or consultant of the Company.

4. Provide all termination or release agreements with any current or former employee or consultant of the Company.

5. Provide descriptions (and plan documents, if any) of all significant fringe benefits, including holiday, vacation, personal leave, insurance policies, or plans (medical, disability, life, travel, accident, dental, vision, or other), deferred compensation, salary continuation, and severance plans of the Company.

6. Provide all plan documents related to any pension and retirement plans, including defined benefits plans, defined contribution plans, and simplified employee pension plans of the Company.

7. Provide descriptions of any other benefits offered or provided to employees on retirement or current retirees of the Company.

8. Does the company have, and if so, provide all documents relating to any bonus, profit sharing, stock option, stock bonus, phantom stock, stock appreciation rights, or other incentive plan of the Company.

9. Provide a description of material labor disputes, requests for arbitration and grievances, and union or labor organizational activities of the Company.

10. Provide a list of all officers, directors, management personnel, and any other employee or consultant of the Company earning more than $30,000, together with such person's total compensation and all contracts.

11. Provide a list of all current personnel (including directors, officers, employees, and consultants), setting forth function, years of service, and compensation (base, bonus, granted options, vested options, or other compensation rights).

12. Provide a list of the total number of employees by category, location, union/nonunion status, starting date, and current compensation.

13. Provide all employee manuals for each Company.

14. Provide all notices and election forms provided to qualified beneficiaries advising of Comprehensive Omnibus Budget Reconciliation Act (COBRA) coverage, initial notice advising participants of COBRA rights, documentation showing such notices have been provided, a list of individuals covered by COBRA and date eligibility will terminate, and a list of qualified beneficiaries who are eligible to elect COBRA but who have not yet done so and the date the COBRA election period will end.

15. Provide a description of all loans or advances to or from directors/managers, employees, or consultants of the Company, including the amount of such loan or advance, its purpose, repayment terms, and, if applicable, a copy of any promissory notes or agreements relating thereto.

16. Provide all filings with and material correspondence to or from the Department of Labor, the Internal Revenue Service, or any other government agency related to employment or labor issues.

17. Provide a description of any union organizations or membership drives that are threatened or pending or that have occurred.

18. Provide all Equal Employment Opportunity Commission (EEOC) compliance files and notices of violations under any laws related to EEOC or other employment-related or antidiscrimination laws.

19. Provide a description of worker compensation policies, procedures, and claims (pending or concluded).

20. Provide a detailed status of negotiations with the operations manager (Lara Melanie), and list any other key personnel positions that remain to be filled or eliminated.

21. Provide all material correspondence and documents related to the forgoing not otherwise provided hereunder.

XII. Litigation and Claims/Legal Compliance

1. Provide a list and summary of any insurance claims outstanding.

2. Provide a list and summary of all actual or threatened civil or criminal actions, litigation, proceedings, arbitrations, claims, or investigations by any person, entity, or third party, or government, administrative, or regulatory authority involving the Company during the past ten years.

3. In addition to question 2, detail and provide all documents concerning any criminal or civil, claims, causes of action, proceedings, litigations, or investigations involving any executive officers, directors, employees, and directors/managers (e.g., bankruptcy, criminal, securities, taxation, employment).

4. Provide all orders, injunctions, judgments, or decrees of any court or regulatory body applicable to any of the Companies or any of its properties or assets.

5. Provide a description of settlements of litigation, arbitration, and other criminal or civil proceedings and copies of settlement agreements, releases, and waivers related thereto.

6. Provide all documents and a description of any litigation or threatened litigation concerning any Intellectual Property owned or used by the Company.

7. Provide all documents and a description of any litigation, claims, or causes of action or threatened litigation, claims, or causes of action concerning environmental matters.

8. Provide all documents and a description of any litigation or threatened litigation against or by any employees or related to any employment matters.

9. Provide all copies of any notices, citations, reports, letters, or other communications from federal or state government agencies.

10. Provide a description of all bankruptcy proceedings in which any of the Companies is a creditor or otherwise interested.

11. Provide a description of any contingent liability of any of the Companies not referenced herein or in the financial statements provided hereunder.

12. Provide all government permits, licenses, and other approvals.

13. Provide a list of all material claims and proceedings that have been settled, stating the amounts claimed, the amounts ultimately paid, and any equitable relief.

14. Provide a list and summarize all suits, actions, claims, pending or that existed, during the past 10 years; any criminal actions, convictions, settlements, awards, judgments, fines, and the like pertaining to the Company, directors/managers, managers, and the shareholders/members.

15. Are there any claims, causes of action, litigation, proceedings arbitration or investigations pending or threatened against the Company or any of its assets not covered by questions 1-14 and, if so, provide a summary and documents relating thereto.

16. Has the company filed for or has involuntary petition filed against the Company, for bankruptcy or has there been an assignment for the benefit of creditors, dissolution, reorganization, appointment of a receiver or trustee, merger, or consolidation of the Company or its assets, and if so provide all documents relating thereto?

XIII. Environmental Matters

1. Provide a list of all real estate now or previously owned, operated, or leased by the Company, including a description of current and past uses thereof.

2. Provide a list of all hazardous substances used, generated, treated, stored, and/or disposed of by the Company.

3. Provide a list of (and copies of) all licenses and permits (including conditions) issued to the Company related to environmental or health code laws.

4. Provide a list of (and copies of) all pending or threatened claims, investigations, administrative proceedings, litigation, regulatory actions, arbitrations, mediations, judgments, settlements, and demands for remedial actions or for compensation alleging noncompliance with or violation of environmental laws, health code, or permit condition, or seeking relief under any environmental law or health code.

5. Provide a description of any contingent liability arising from or out of any environmental matter or health code violation.

6. Provide any environmental reports, including Phase 1 and Phase 2 assessments in connection with any real property owned or to be purchased by the Company.

I hereby certify on behalf of the Company that the information and documents provided in response to this Due Diligence Questionnaire are true and correct to best of my knowledge. I hereby further confirm that there is no other information and there are no other documents that could be relevant to a decision of the Investor to enter into and complete the intended transaction.

By: _____

Name/Title:

Date:

KMF Franchisee, LCC Personal Questionaire

The following questionnaire is to be provided by all directors, managing members, and members of KMF Franchisee, LLC.

1. Have you ever been found or pleaded guilty (including a plea of nolo contendere) to a felony or misdemeanor, or has there been any criminal investigation against you during the past five years? If so, describe.

2. Have you ever filed for bankruptcy?

3. Are there any lawsuits pending against you or your spouse, or have you or your spouse received any notice of a potential lawsuit? If so describe.

4. Have you ever been the subject of a criminal or civil proceeding or investigation by any government, regulatory, or administrative agency or body (including the Securities Exchange Commission)? If so, describe.

5. Do you have any tax liabilities other than those related to the current tax year? Have you been audited during the past six years? If so, describe.

6. Do you have any material disputes with potential liability in excess of $10,000? If so, describe.

7. List all companies in which you or your spouse hold equity of 5% or more.

8. Are you currently bound by a personal guarantee of a third party's obligations? If so, describe. Yes ____ No ____

9. Are you currently bound by a noncompete or nonsolicitation agreement? If so, describe. Yes ____ No ____

10. Will you agree to a personal background check regarding issues such as any pending criminal indictments or investigations, any civil lawsuits, bankruptcy filings, and the like, as well as agree to a credit check? Yes ____ No ____

I hereby certify that the information and documents provided in response to this Personal Due Diligence Questionnaire are true and correct to best of my knowledge. I hereby further confirm that there is no other information and there are no other documents that could be relevant to a decision of the Investor to enter into and complete the intended transaction.

By: _____

Name:

Date:

Due Diligence Questionnaire for Overlook, Inc.

Lender is considering making a loan to Overlook, Inc. (the "Company"). In connection therewith, we request the Company provide responses to the following questions and requests for information. For purposes of this questionnaire, references to the term "Company" include Overlook, Inc., and all its subsidiaries, affiliates, and divisions thereof.

If there are no documents or other information that are relevant to the particular due diligence request, indicate as such in response to the question.

If certain materials have already been provided or are unavailable or inapplicable, please indicate so in your response to this request. Please note that our due diligence investigation is ongoing and we will submit supplemental due diligence requests as necessary.

In certain instances, this questionnaire pertains only to matters that exceed certain material thresholds. In this respect, for the purposes of this questionnaire, the word "material" shall be understood to include all information regarding agreements, rights, and/or obligations that represent a value of $50.00 or more or that are in some other way of considerable importance for the Company's business and/or activities.

The word "including" as used herein means including without limitation, unless noted.

I. General Corporate Background

1. What is the Company's exact corporate name as it appears in its certificate of incorporation? What is the jurisdiction of incorporation of the Company?

2. Provide copies of all documents related to the formation of the Company, including the certificate of incorporation, bylaws, shareholders' agreements, good standing certificates for any jurisdiction in which the Company operates, certificates of authorization to do business in any state or foreign jurisdiction, and any amendments thereto.

3. Provide all corporate records books (including minutes of meetings, resolutions, and consents of the board of directors and shareholders of the Company and committees thereof).

4. Is the consent of any person or entity required to approve the proposed transaction that is the subject of this due diligence investigation?

5. Has the Company ever changed its name? If so, state each name the Company has had.

6. Does the Company do business under any other name or assumed name? If so, state each such name and provide "doing business as" (d/b/a) certificates.

7. Does the Company use or has it used any trade names or trade styles? If so, list each of them.

8. Has the Company changed its identity or corporate structure? Changes in corporate structure include incorporation of a partnership or sole proprietorship, mergers, consolidations, and acquisitions. If any such change has taken place, indicate the nature of such change and give the names of each corporation or other entity that was incorporated, merged, or consolidated with or acquired by the Company in such a transaction (including each name under which each such corporation or entity has done business) and the address of each place of business of each such corporation or entity immediately prior to such incorporation, merger, consolidation, or acquisition and within four months prior to the date of this questionnaire.

9. State the complete address of the Company's chief executive office and the office where the books and records related to its accounts or contract rights are kept, if different from its chief executive office.

10. Has the Company's chief executive office or office where the Company keeps its books and records related to its accounts or contract rights been located at any other address? If so, specify each address.

11. State the complete address of each business, office, and location that the Company has currently and list all jurisdictions in which the Company is qualified to do business or otherwise operate in.

II. Financial Information

1. Provide all financial statements, income statements and balance sheets by quarter (including annual reports) for the past six years and the current year to date, and all supporting schedules to such financial statements.

2. Provide all federal, state, local income, sales, and other tax returns and filings for the past six year ends.

3. Provide all quarterly projected income statements and cash flows for the next three years, as well as cash flow projections, business plans, and budgets for the next three years.

4. Other than for the current fiscal year, has the Company filed and made all payments in connection with federal, state and local tax returns? Other than for the current quarter, has the Company filed and made all payments in connection with all sales and use tax returns?

5. Provide a list of material assets.

6. Provide a list of all accounts receivables, including a list and summary thereof; all purchase orders, contracts, and agreements related to such receivables; and any letters, claims, or other documents disputing any of the accounts receivables.

7. Provide a list of material liabilities, including contingent liabilities, leases, and indemnification agreements.

8. Has the Company granted any security interests in its assets, property, or rights? Has it pledged any of its assets, property, or rights as collateral or security in connection with any obligation or for any other reason? Does there exist any encumbrance, lien, or security interest in the assets, property, or rights of the Company? If so, provide all documents and information relating thereto.

9. Provide all agreements and information evidencing borrowings by the Company, whether secured or unsecured, documented or undocumented, including loans, lines of credit, promissory notes, letters of credit, and the like and (a) including any agreements granting a collateral or secured interest, liens, pledge, mortgages, deeds of trust, or encumbrances of any kind in or against any property, assets, intellectual property, and real estate; (b) all guarantees, suretyship, assignment of right to receivables, and pledge of assets; and (c) a list of all creditors and amounts owed.

10. Provide all documents concerning any liens, pledges, or encumbrances against the intellectual property of the Company.

11. Provide all documents related to any loans granted by the company, including, loans or other financing arrangements with any current or former directors, employees, officers, or shareholders.

12. Has the Company entered in any other financing agreements relating directly or indirectly to the Company which have not been provided in response to Questions 8-11? If so, provide all such financing agreements.

III. Litigation and Claims/Legal Compliance

1. List, summarize, and provide all documents concerning all actual or threatened civil or criminal litigation, proceedings, claims, causes of action, or investigations by any person, entity, or third party, or government, administrative, or regulatory authority involving the Company or any of its assets, including intellectual property, during the past ten years.

2. Summarize and provide all documents concerning any civil or criminal litigation, proceedings, claims, causes of action, or investigations by any person, or entity, or government, administrative, or regulatory authority involving any officers, directors, or employees during the past ten years.

3. If not provided in response to question 1 in this section, list, summarize, and provide all documents concerning all actual or threatened civil or criminal litigation, proceedings, claims, causes of action, or investigations by any person, entity, or third party, or government, administrative, or regulatory authority concerning environmental matters.

4. Provide all letters, notices, or other communications from any federal, state, or local tax authorities or agencies related to any assessments, audits, liens, claims, and waivers of statute of limitations.

5. Provide copies of any notices, citations, reports, letters, or other communications from federal, state, or foreign government agencies.

6. List and summarize all settlements, awards, judgments, fines, and the like related to the Company, any of its assets (including intellectual property), directors, officers, employees, and shareholders.

7. Provide documents, if any, related to any bankruptcy filings, assignment for the benefit of creditors, dissolution, reorganization, appointment of a receiver or trustee, merger, or consolidation of the Company.

IV. Insurance

1. Provide all insurance policies related to the Company, its business, and its assets.

2. Provide copies of all insurance agreements naming the Company as the insured party related to any directors, officers, employees, or shareholders (including any "key man" insurance policies).

3. Does the Company have any written plans, protocols, policies, or procedures related to disaster recovery or catastrophic events?

I hereby certify on behalf of the Company that the information and documents provided in response to this Due Diligence Questionnaire are true and correct to best of my knowledge. I hereby further confirm that there is no other information and there are no other documents that could be relevant to a decision of the Lender to enter into and complete the intended transaction.

By:_____

Name/Date:

Title:

Due Diligence Questionnaire for ABB, Inc.

Jack Enterprises, Inc. (the "Purchaser") is considering entering into an agreement to purchase certain assets of ABB, Inc. (the "Company"). In connection therewith, we request that the Company provide responses to the following questions and requests for information. For purposes of this Questionnaire, references to the term "Company" includes ABB, Inc., and all its subsidiaries, affiliates, and divisions thereof.

If there are no documents or other information that are relevant to the particular due diligence request, indicate as such in response to the question.

If certain materials have already been provided or are unavailable or inapplicable, please indicate so in your response to this request. Please note that our due diligence investigation is ongoing and we will submit supplemental due diligence requests as necessary.

In certain instances, this questionnaire pertains only to matters that exceed certain material thresholds. In this respect, for the purposes of this questionnaire, the word "material" shall be understood to include all information regarding agreements, rights, and/or obligations that represent a value of $50.00 or more or that are in some other way of considerable importance for the Company's business and/or activities.

The word "including" as used herein means including without limitation, unless noted.

I. Corporate Organization

1. What is the Company's exact corporate name as it appears in its certificate of incorporation? What is the jurisdiction of incorporation of the Company?

2. Provide copies of all documents related to the formation of the Company, including the certificate of incorporation, bylaws, shareholders' agreements, good standing certificates for any jurisdiction in which the Company operates, certificates of authorization to do business in any state or foreign jurisdiction, and any amendments thereto.

3. Provide all corporate records books (including minutes of meetings, resolutions, and consents of the board of directors and shareholders as of the Company and committees thereof).

4. Is the consent of any person or entity required to approve the proposed transaction that is the subject of this due diligence investigation?

5. Has the Company ever changed its name? If so, state each name the Company has had.

6. Does the Company do business under any other name or assumed name? If so, state each name and provide "doing business as" (d/b/a) certificates

7. Does the Company use or has it used any trade names or trade styles? If so, list each of them.

8. Has Company changed its identity or corporate structure in any way within the past four months? Changes in corporate structure include incorporation of a partnership or sole proprietorship, mergers, consolidations, and acquisitions. If any such change has taken place, indicate the nature of such change and give the names of each corporation or other entity that was incorporated, merged, or consolidated with, or acquired by, the Company in such a transaction (including each name under which each corporation or entity has done business) and the address of each place of business of each corporation or entity immediately prior to such incorporation, merger, consolidation, or acquisition and within four months prior to the date of this questionnaire.

9. State the complete address of the Company's chief executive office and the office where the books and records related to its accounts or contract rights are kept, if different from its chief executive office.

10. Has the Company's chief executive office or office where the Company keeps its books and records related to its accounts or contract rights been located at any other address? If so, specify each address.

II. Financial Matters

1. Provide all financial statements, income statements and balance sheets by quarter (including annual reports) for the past six years and the current year to date, and all supporting schedules to such financial statements.

2. Provide all information concerning the number of customers, average purchase size/amount per transaction, highest grossing products, and highest margin products.[1]

3. Provide all agreements and information evidencing borrowings by the Company, whether secured or unsecured, documented or undocumented, including loans, lines of credit, promissory notes, letters of credit, and the like and (a) including any agreements granting a collateral or secured interest, liens, pledge, mortgages, deeds of trust, or encumbrances of any kind in or against any property, assets, intellectual property, and real estate; (b) all guarantees, sureties, assignment of right to receivables, and pledge of assets; and (c) a list of all creditors and amounts owed.

4. Provide all documents concerning any liens, pledges, or encumbrances against or related to the Company's patents, trademarks, logos, copyrights, domain names (collectively, "Intellectual Property").

5. List any existing defaults under any financing obligations, including any loans, notes, or credit arrangements of the Company and any events that have occurred that, with the giving of notice or the passage of time, will become such a default.

---

[1]Because the transaction involves the purchase of assets (and not the entire business), questions II-1 and II-2 are not necessary if the purchaser has conducted a separate valuation of the assets.

6. Has the Company granted any security interests in its assets, property, or rights? Has it pledged any of its assets, property, or rights as collateral or security in connection with any obligation or for any other reason? Does there exist any encumbrance, lien, or security interest in the assets, property, or rights of the Company? If so, provide all documents and information relating thereto.

III. Tax Matters

1. Provide all federal, state, and local tax returns (for income, gross receipts, sales or use, property, employment, or other taxes) for the past six years.

2. Has there been any audit by any federal, state, or local tax authorities related to the Company? If so, provide details and status of each such audit.

3. Provide all deficiency assessments filed against the Company by federal, state, or local tax authorities and the resolution of such deficiency (if any).

4. Other than for the current fiscal year, has the Company filed and made all payments in connection with federal, state and local tax returns? Other than for the current quarter, has the Company filed and made all payments in connection with all sales and use tax returns?[2]

IV. Contracts, Agreements, and Commitments

1. Provide all license, sublicense, royalty, and other agreements related to the operation of the Company or to the use and operation of the assets of the Company.

2. Provide all joint venture, partnership, management, services, and marketing agreements.

3. Provide all agreements, contracts, and undertakings involving any retailers, including the following chain stores [insert names]. List all agreements with retailers which require consent as a condition of assignment of such agreement.

---

[2]In the context of an asset sale, the tax questions in this section not only aid in confirming the information in the company's financial statements, for which valuation of the assets remains an issue, but also they address whether there are any tax delinquencies that can result in liens or impose financial obligations on the purchaser under bulk sales laws.

4. Provide all material warranty and service agreements.

5. Provide all agreements out of the ordinary course of business to which the Company is a party or by which it or its assets are bound.

6. Provide all standard form agreements used by the Company in the sale of its products and services.

7. Provide all agreements that prohibit or restrict the Company's ability to compete in any business anywhere in any geographic area, or the customers with which the Company may do business or the prices the Company may charge for its services.

V. Intellectual Property and Technology

1. List all patents, trademarks, service marks, logos, copyrights, and licenses worldwide, including all issued, registered, or pending applications or other Intellectual Property. Provide details regarding the status of all patents, trademarks, copyright issuances, registrations, or applications.

2. Provide all contracts and proposed contracts concerning Intellectual Property owned, used, or licensed by or licensed to the Company, including license and royalty agreements.

3. List all domain names owned or used by the Company and to whom they are registered.

4. List all technology and computer software owned, held for use by, or being developed by or for the Company.

5. List all material third-party computer software used by the Company or incorporated into any software or product of the Company; and open-source software, freeware, or other software with similar licensing or distribution models used by the Company or incorporated into any software or product of the Company.

6. List all trade secrets and other proprietary know-how or processes owned or held for use by the Company.

7. Provide all agreements and proposed agreements pursuant to which any Intellectual Property is assigned, sold, or otherwise transferred, or licensed by the Company to any party or subject to a covenant not to sue.

8. Provide all documents concerning any liens, pledges, or encumbrances against the Intellectual Property of the Company.

9. Are there any claims, causes of actions, disputes, or threatened claims against the Company (including assertions by any former shareholder) or brought or contemplated by the Company concerning the Intellectual Property or claims or threatened claims of infringement and the like. If so, set forth the details of all claims, causes of action or disputes, and all threatened claims or disputes.

10. List all software programs and applications sold, distributed, or licensed by the Company.

11. Provide all technology contribution, technology assignment, and invention assignment agreements between the Company and any person or entity (including any current or former shareholder, employee, or consultant).

VI. Information Technology Systems and Networks

1. Describe and provide copies of all documents related to whether the Company has access, or rights of access, to the source code of material licensed software to ensure adequate maintenance and updating of that software.

2. Provide copies of the Company's web site security policies and procedures.

3. Confirm whether the Company owns all Intellectual Property in the design and content of its web sites.

4. Describe any material interruptions of the Company's web site, software applications, or other technology during the past three years.

VII. Privacy and Data Security

1. Provide all current and historical privacy and data security policies and practice manuals of the Company, including all privacy policies, procedures, and security programs for the Company's use and disclosure of customer or personal information and compliance with data protection and privacy legislation.

2. Provide all documentation and information regarding the Company's collection, use, storage, or disposal of customer or personal information (whether the Company's or a third party's).

3. Provide all agreements, undertakings, or policies that prohibit or may prohibit the assignment or transfer of customer lists, customer information, and customer e-mail accounts and information to the purchaser.

4. Provide all agreements the Company has with any third parties that act as the Company's agents or contractors and receive customer or personal information from or on behalf of the Company.

5. Provide all details regarding any actual or potential data and information security breaches, unauthorized use or access of the Company's computer systems or data, or data and information security issues impacting the Company identified during the past three years.

VIII. Litigation and Claims/Legal Compliance

1. Provide a list and summary of any insurance claims outstanding.

2. Provide a list and summary of all actual or threatened civil or criminal actions, litigation, proceedings, arbitrations, claims, or investigations by any person, entity, or third party, or government, administrative, or regulatory authority involving the Company during the past ten years.

3. Provide all orders, injunctions, judgments, or decrees of any court or regulatory body applicable to any of the Companies or any of its properties or assets.

4. Provide a description of settlements of litigation, arbitration, and other criminal or civil proceedings, and copies of settlement agreements, releases, and waivers related thereto.

5. Provide all documents and a description of any litigation or threatened litigation concerning any Intellectual Property owned or used by the Company.

6. Provide all documents and a description of any litigation, claims, or causes of action or threatened litigation, claims, or causes of action concerning environmental matters.

7. Provide all copies of any notices, citations, reports, letters, or other communications from federal or state government agencies.

8. Provide a description of all bankruptcy proceedings in which any of the Companies is a creditor or otherwise interested.

9. Provide a list of all material claims and proceedings that have been settled, stating the amounts claimed, the amounts ultimately paid, and any equitable relief.

10. Provide documents, if any, related to any bankruptcy filings, assignment for the benefit of creditors, dissolution, reorganization, appointment of a receiver or trustee, merger, or consolidation of the Company.

I hereby certify on behalf of the Company that the information and documents provided in response to this Due Diligence Questionnaire are true and correct to best of my knowledge. I hereby further confirm that there is no other information and there are no other documents that could be relevant to a decision of the Purchaser to enter into and complete the intended transaction.

By: _____

Name:

Title:

Date:

Index

Get the eBook for only $10!

Now you can take the weightless companion with you anywhere, anytime. Your purchase of this book entitles you to 3 electronic versions for only $10.

This Apress title will prove so indispensible that you'll want to carry it with you everywhere, which is why we are offering the eBook in 3 formats for only $10 if you have already purchased the print book.

Convenient and fully searchable, the PDF version enables you to easily find and copy code—or perform examples by quickly toggling between instructions and   applications. The MOBI format is ideal for your Kindle, while the ePUB can be utilized on a variety of mobile devices.

Go to www.apress.com/promo/tendollars to purchase your companion eBook.

Other Apress Business Titles You Will Find Useful

***Know and Grow the
Value of Your Business***
McDaniel
978-1-4302-4785-2

Metrics
Klubeck
978-1-4302-3726-6

The Street Smart MBA
Babitsky/Mangraviti
978-1-4302-4767-8

***Tax Strategies for the
Small Business Owner***
Fox
978-1-4302-4842-2

***Plan to Turn Your Company
Around in 90 Days***
Lack
978-1-4302-4668-8

Startup
Ready
978-1-4302-4218-5

***Venture Capitalists at
Work***
Shah/Shah
978-1-4302-3837-9

The Employer Bill of Rights
Hyman
978-1-4302-4551-3

***Compensating Your
Employees Fairly***
Thomas
978-1-4302-5040-1

Available at www.apress.com